Integrating Mission and Strategy
for Nonprofit Organizations

Integrating Mission and Strategy for Nonprofit Organizations

James A. Phills, Jr.

OXFORD
UNIVERSITY PRESS
2005

OXFORD
UNIVERSITY PRESS

Oxford University Press, Inc., publishes works that further
Oxford University's objective of excellence
in research, scholarship, and education.

Oxford   New York
Auckland   Cape Town   Dar es Salaam   Hong Kong   Karachi
Kuala Lumpur   Madrid   Melbourne   Mexico City   Nairobi
New Delhi   Shanghai   Taipei   Toronto

With offices in
Argentina   Austria   Brazil   Chile   Czech Republic   France   Greece
Guatemala   Hungary   Italy   Japan   Poland   Portugal   Singapore
South Korea   Switzerland   Thailand   Turkey   Ukraine   Vietnam

Library of Congress Cataloging-in-Publication Data
Phills, James A.
Integrating mission and strategy for nonprofit organizations / by James A. Phills, Jr.
p.   cm.
Includes bibliographical references and index.
ISBN-13 978-0-19-517128-0
ISBN 0-19-517128-4
1. Nonprofit organizations—Management.   I. Title.
HD62.6.P47 2005
658.4'012—dc22   2004021136

9 8 7 6 5 4 3 2

Printed in the United States of America
on acid-free paper

In memory of Wendi

Preface

Applying Knowledge from the World of Business to Nonprofits

In 2001, after many years of research and teaching concentrated almost entirely on business, I shifted the central focus of my academic activity to the creation of social rather than economic value when I became codirector of the Center for Social Innovation at Stanford Business School. While the personal and institutional factors that led to this shift are probably relatively uninteresting to most readers of this book, the fact of the shift is not. This is because it bespeaks the fundamental approach or perspective (or bias, if you will) that informs my approach to the leadership and management of nonprofit organizations: specifically, one that emphasizes the fundamental similarity of the challenges facing managers of organizations, whether they be for-profit, public, or nonprofit, and the relevance of ideas about mission, strategy, and execution across all three sectors. There are important differences, to be sure, but we have yet to bridge the divides between the sectors and take full advantage of the skills, knowledge, and practices that have transcended historical, legal, and intellectual boundaries, although this condition has been changing rapidly in recent years.

Essentially, though the number of nonprofit organizations, as well as the number of people working in them, whether paid or volunteer, has grown dramatically over the last twenty years, the leadership, management, and organizational capability of the sector has been neglected, in terms of both attention and investment. This is not to suggest that nonprofit executives are any less intelligent, talented, or capable than their private-sector brethren. In fact, Peter Drucker has suggested that nonprofits are on average better managed than most businesses.[1]

In my own experience I have been very impressed by the leaders of nonprofits who have attended outside executive education programs. However, that comment is meant to suggest that, until relatively recently, nonprofits have had limited access or exposure to the types of knowledge, tools, and practices taken for granted by business: strategy, leadership, business process design, entrepreneurship, and advanced information technology, to name a few.

But even when these ideas have been available either through board members, consultants, or professional development opportunities, penetration and adoption have been hampered by psychological barriers that have less to do with the validity, relevance, or utility of these ideas than with the social significance of their adoption. For example, many fields within the nonprofit sector have long viewed corporate America as an adversary, the embodiment of greed and self-interest, and as a major contributor to social ills such as inequality, rampant consumerism, and environmental degradation. Hence, ideas associated with the business world have been viewed with suspicion in the social sector. Moreover, until recently, academics in professional schools of business have shown relatively little interest in studying or applying their theories to nonprofits. Although some universities have created schools of public administration or nonprofit management, the resources available to these schools are generally dwarfed by those controlled by major business schools.

Finally, because of the very real differences between nonprofits and for-profits, there has been a very legitimate concern that tools and frameworks developed from the study of businesses cannot simply be transplanted to nonprofits. This is an important concern, one that must be taken seriously. Indeed, it is a point around which experts in nonprofit management disagree.[2] In part the answer is that it depends on both the specific nonprofit

1. P. F. Drucker, "What Business Can Learn from Nonprofits," *Harvard Business Review* 67, no. 4 (1989): 88–93.

2. Hansmann notes differences but accommodates these within the same general theory of ownership. Others, like Weisbrod, draw stark contrasts and highlight perils of understating or ignoring differences. Still others, like Oster, draw on business models but take great pains to draw contrasts and to adapt business frameworks. S. Oster, "Nonprofit Management: Is Managing Save the Children Any Different from Managing General Motors?" *Yale Management* 4

organization or industry and the domain of knowledge. So theories about tax accounting and capital markets are largely irrelevant. Theories of leadership and group behavior and business process design are characterized by few differences at the sector level. Strategy is probably somewhere in the middle. The implication is that one of the challenges in this book will be trying to tease out those features of nonprofits, social problems, or environments that necessitate adapting ideas or assumptions based on business models.

Dissolving Boundaries: A Phenomenon and a Philosophy

Over the last ten to fifteen years, the boundaries that once separated the for-profit and nonprofit sectors have begun to break down. Today, non-profits are more receptive than ever before to the ideas that help businesses to be more innovative, effective, and efficient. Indeed, faced with perennial budget constraints and constantly burgeoning needs, nonprofit leaders have been forced to seek out new and better ways of designing and managing their organizations.

At the same time, the entrepreneurial zeitgeist that fueled the economic boom of the 1990s created tremendous wealth among a relatively young group of entrepreneurs and investors. In part because they amassed their fortunes early in life, the members of this group have turned their attention from simply creating economic value to creating social value by working to improve their communities and joining the fight to address social problems. And, in doing so, they have sought to contribute more than just their money. They have sought to bring the values and practices of business to the social sector—as board members, philanthropists, and volunteers.[3] This influx of financial and human capital has begun to transform

(1992): 16–21; B. A. Weisbrod, "The Nonprofit Mission and Its Financing," in *To Profit or Not to Profit: The Commercial Transformation of the Nonprofit Sector*, edited by B. A. Weisbrod (New York: Cambridge University Press, 1998), 1–22; H. Hansmann, *The Ownership of Enterprise* (Cambridge, Mass.: Belknap Press).

3. Consider, for example, the philanthropic activity of entrepreneurs like Jeffery Skoll of eBay, Bill Gates of Microsoft, and Michael Dell of Dell Computer. M. Conlin et al., "The Top Givers: Today's Philanthropists Aren't Leaving the Good Works to Future Generations—They're Making Their Mark Now," *Business Week* (1 December 2003): 78.

the management paradigms of the nonprofit sector. In particular, there has been a tremendous surge of interest on the part of nonprofit executives in business perspectives on concepts such as strategy, leadership, performance measurement, return on investment, and innovation, as well as on values such as accountability, productivity, and performance. Not only are the nonprofits increasingly interested in—indeed, *hungry for*—these ideas, so are the foundations, philanthropists, government agencies, and others that fund them.

As leaders in the nonprofit and social sector have begun looking to the business world for more innovative and sustainable approaches to social problems, their attention has focused on solutions that improve upon traditional governmental and philanthropic approaches. Pushed by declining government funding and support, and inspired and intrigued by the role of managerial and entrepreneurial skills in producing economic growth and prosperity in the private sector, nonprofit leaders have come to believe that these skills and knowledge can be adapted to address the challenges of organizations focused on education, the environment, health care, affordable housing, community development, social services, and the arts.

In addition, a growing number of businesses, from major corporations to entrepreneurial start-ups, have become concerned with (and scrutinized for) the social impact of their economic activities. As a result, many have undertaken new activities and reconfigured old activities to reduce the negative, or increase the positive, social impact of their operations. This trend, as well as the underlying concern, exceeds simple conceptions of social responsibility to encompass more proactive aspirations about the private sector's potential to make substantial contributions to the quality of life in the communities in which they operate.

In part, the perspective represented in this book is predicated on a philosophy of dissolving boundaries between the for-profit sector and the nonprofit and public sectors.[4] First and foremost, this effort involves facilitating the exchange of ideas, values, and talent between sectors and areas of endeavor. It includes recent interest in increasing the sense of accountability and the emphasis on performance—which are both key areas of

---

4. Although the focus is more on nonprofit organizations, I apply the ideas to many areas in which nonprofit and public organizations coexist with private-sector firms (e.g., health care and education). As I will argue in the next section, the legal form of an organization is less important than its social purpose.

focus in for-profit organizations—in the nonprofit and public sectors. But exchange implies that the flow goes both ways—and indeed it has, as is illustrated by concern with increasing the sense of responsibility and the awareness of social impact in the private sector.[5] Nonprofits that are willing and able to learn from the best ideas and practices of the world of business have tremendous potential to increase the social value they create.[6] Similarly, though the topic is not the focus of this book, there is much that the corporate world can learn from the social sector.[7]

Dissolving boundaries also encompasses the effort to enable dialogue between different professional fields and academic disciplines. This dialogue is in the service of integration: the effort to develop knowledge about complex social problems, which, because of their fundamental nature, do not respect the artificial boundaries that have arisen within academic institutions and professions. For example, reforming urban schools to make them more effective and equitable clearly requires an understanding of education. But, as many educational leaders have discovered, the political dynamics and fiscal implications of public policy, the motivational impact of incentive systems and labor markets, and the social structure of communities mean that effective action also requires at least a tacit understanding of economics, political science, psychology, and sociology, as well.

Dissolving boundaries also involves enabling the dialogue between scholars who have been engaged in basic disciplinary research and those who have been involved in more problem-driven applied research. This dialogue is in the service of improving the implementation of knowledge generated through traditional disciplinary inquiry. Far too often, basic research is ignored, even when it is potentially relevant to our understanding and management of real problems. And, just as often, our models and frameworks for thinking about such problems are not informed by the rigorous and systematic research that tends to be focused on narrower, but important, parts of practical problems.

---

5. J. D. Margolis and J. P. Walsh, "Misery Loves Companies: Rethinking Social Initiatives by Business," *Administrative Science Quarterly* 48 (June 2003): 268–305.

6. See B. Bradley et al., "The Nonprofit Sector's $100 Billion Opportunity," *Harvard Business Review* 81, no. 5 (2003): 94–103.

7. R. M. Kanter, "From Spare Change to Real Change: The Social Sector as Beta Site for Business Innovation," *Harvard Business Review* 77, no. 3 (1999): 122–32; Drucker, "What Business Can Learn."

Objectives

One of my overarching aspirations in writing this book is to contribute to a larger effort to cultivate and nurture the leadership, management, and organizational capability of the nonprofit sector. The logic linking this goal to the outline and focus of this book is the following:

- The work of addressing society's most critical social needs and problems is done primarily through social-sector institutions.
- Our collective progress in addressing these problems and needs is directly related to the effectiveness of these organizations.
- As in the private sector, the leadership, management, and organizational capability of these institutions (in particular, the building blocks of direction, motivation, and design) shapes and determines their performance.
- These challenges are fundamentally similar (though not identical) for nonprofits and businesses, because both are complex formal organizations that exist in environments characterized by some degree of competition.
- By drawing on the considerable knowledge that exists in the world of management, and then applying (and, where necessary, adapting) this knowledge to the nonprofit sector, we can provide those who lead, manage, govern, and fund nonprofits with knowledge, skills, and insights that will allow them to help their organizations become more innovative, efficient, and effective.
- As a result, these organizations, and the sector as a whole, should be able to attract additional resources and funding.
- These resources will be allocated to the areas of greatest benefit (within, as well as across, organizations).
- Ultimately, this effort will lead to greater progress in addressing important social needs and problems.

Proceeding from this logic, I set out with three specific objectives in mind:

1. To draw on a core body of general management knowledge about strategy and organization, knowledge that has been developed primarily from the study of business organizations, and to show how this knowledge can be applied and adapted to help nonprofit leaders deal with the challenges they face; and, importantly, to do

so in a way that does not patronize these leaders by diluting or oversimplifying the business frameworks;[8]

2. To integrate and apply this knowledge in an action-oriented framework that combines rigorous strategic analysis with a disciplined, compelling approach to mission, and links both to the practical challenges of execution and change;

3. To provide a shared language and a discipline that can serve as the basis for more productive discussions between the individuals who lead nonprofits, the business executives who serve on their boards, and the grant-makers and government officials who support their organizations and programs.

The last objective is critical, because too often nonprofit leaders and board members complain that they cannot seem to gain the expected benefits of the expertise of their supporters, funders, and volunteers from the business sector. My own experience as a board member and consultant to nonprofits suggests that this is often the result of an inability to speak the same language and draw on a common understating of key concepts (such as competition, strategy, and mission).

This book draws on a core body of general management knowledge that is deeply rooted in practice, as well as grounded in academic research, but is primarily based on the study and observations of private-sector firms. In applying these ideas to nonprofits, we need, I believe, to do so in a way that does not water down or trivialize the ideas and concepts. Ultimately, I hope that *Integrating Mission and Strategy for Nonprofit Organizations* provides a unique perspective and represents a valuable contribution to the field of nonprofit management, and, more important, that it will become a useful reference for nonprofit leaders in all kinds of organizations, as well as for those who work closely with them.

Acknowledgments

The original ideas and frameworks (as well as the adaptations of others' work) presented in this book are based on over seven years of experience

---

8. A key feature of this knowledge is that it is grounded in rigorous empirical research and theory drawing on basic social science disciplines (e.g., economics, psychology, sociology, and political science).

teaching executive programs on strategy, mission, and execution for non-profit leaders. In this endeavor, I have worked closely with my friend and colleague, Joel Podolny, and the content of this book reflects his contribution as much as my own. He has also been an invaluable source of support and feedback as I have worked on this project. Initially, we taught this material in a program sponsored by National Arts Stabilization, called Strategic Leadership for a Changing Environment, during which we benefited enormously from the feedback and encouragement of Ed Martenson. Chip Heath, who has joined me in teaching these programs over the last four years, has also contributed insights and refinements. More recently, we have incorporated these ideas into the Executive Program for Nonprofit Leaders offered at Stanford University's Graduate School of Business, as well as into a Master's of Business Administration elective on strategic leadership of nonprofits. The students and participants in all of these contexts have contributed to the refinement and clarification of this material through their avid, critical, and practical discussion of the ideas.

In addition, I have benefited enormously from helpful comments on earlier drafts of this manuscript by a number of other friends and colleagues, including Jeff Bradach, Roger Martin, and Sharon Oster. Elaine Goldberg and Paul Mattish provided invaluable assistance with copyediting and proofreading. I am deeply indebted to Peter Economy, who functioned as an agent, a muse, an editor, and the project manager for this book.

Finally, I am grateful for the generous funding for research and writing of this book that was provided by the Center for Social Innovation at Stanford Business School.

Contents

Integrating Mission and Strategy
for Nonprofit Organizations

Introduction

The Role of Mission and Strategy in Enhancing the Performance of Nonprofit Organizations

The endurance of organization depends upon the quality of leadership . . . that capacity of leaders by which, reflecting attitudes, ideals, hopes, derived largely from without themselves, they are compelled to bind the wills of men to the accomplishment of purposes beyond their immediate ends, beyond their times.
—Chester Barnard, *The Functions of the Executive*

The Role of Nonprofits in Addressing Social Needs and Problems

The range of social problems and needs faced by societies around the world is vast, and growing more complex and more pressing every day. But, while the issues faced by industrialized democracies differ markedly from those faced by developing countries, every country must provide basic education, health care, and social services to its citizens. Every society is humanized and enriched by artistic and cultural endeavor. Citizens in every nation have a right to clean water, air, and soil. And every country—no matter how wealthy—has disenfranchised poor who are often hungry, sick, or otherwise unproductive, and simply resigned to the inevitability of their plight. Moreover, the emergence of global problems such as climate change, international conflict, terrorism, and AIDS affects all nations while continuing to up the ante for all those who choose to address these problems.

Although governments play an important role in addressing such issues, in many countries the vanguard in confronting these needs and problems increasingly consists of nonprofit and social-purpose organizations—the so-called civil society or voluntary sector. Not surprisingly, the nonprofit sector is booming, engaging *millions* of employees and volunteers, and taking in *billions* of dollars a year in revenues. The *Nonprofit Times* reports that the top 100 nonprofits alone accounted for more than $45 billion in revenues in fiscal year 2003.[1] But there has also been tremendous growth in the number of nonprofit/tax-exempt organizations in the United States, which went from about 1.26 million in 1989 to just over 1.58 million in 1999, an increase of 25 percent. More striking is the 67 percent increase in the number of 501(c)(3) organizations (public charities and private foundations), from 464,000 to 774,000 over the same period.[2] Between 1970 and 2000, nonprofits' share of gross domestic product (GDP) went from 3.1 percent to 4.2 percent. During this time, government spending as a percentage of GDP declined from 13.9 percent to 10.8 percent.[3] In 1999, independent-sector organizations—including 501(c)(3), 501(c)(4), and religious congregations—reported revenues of more than $1.03 trillion, and held assets of more than $1.65 trillion.[4]

But, despite the magnitude of resources in the hands of nonprofits, there is still a pervasive sense that we have made limited progress in solving our most pressing social problems and addressing fundamental needs. Indeed, in many areas, these problems and needs have intensified, even as the growing number of nonprofit and public organizations have struggled to address them. These ever-increasing demands seem to continually outstrip our capacity to meet them.

This begs the obvious question: how can we advance our collective efforts to improve society? There are clearly many ways to do so, including more money, better public policy, and more advanced technology to name but a few. My perspective, however, focuses on an organizational approach: strengthening the nonprofits that are central to social progress. The premise is that if we can enhance the leadership, management, and organizational capacity of the sector, then the other factors will follow.

The Importance of Leadership, Management, and Organizational Capability

In recent years, the philanthropic community, scholars, and nonprofit leaders have come to believe that social-sector organizations not only can but *must* become more effective, efficient, and innovative to meet today's great challenges. And, though there are certainly many different ways to improve the effectiveness of any organization, an essential path to building stronger organizations is developing the capability of those who lead and manage these institutions (as well as those who fund and govern them).

The capability of nonprofit executives is not the only lever for improving the effectiveness of the sector; public policy, sufficient resources, cooperation between nonprofits and the public and private sectors, and public awareness and support are also key. But these determinants are, in part, a function of the skills and knowledge of those who guide the actions of our nonprofit organizations.

Public policy changes when advocacy is effective. Resources flow to organizations that show demonstrable progress in solving problems. Partnerships become appealing to governments and corporations when they see an opportunity for positive impact. Public understanding of and concern about particular social needs and problems grow to the extent that the sector is able to communicate and educate the masses. Thus, the capability of nonprofit leaders is a critical determinant of the health, prosperity, and effectiveness of the sector. Moreover, these leaders' skills and knowledge determine their ability to guide and manage their organizations effectively.

But why, then, have leadership development, management training, and capacity building been neglected for so long in the nonprofit sector?

The focus of many organizations is on pressing problems and urgent needs. There is tremendous pressure within nonprofit organizations—from both internal (board members, executives, workers, and volunteers) and external (clients, community activists, donors, government, and media) sources—to apply as much of their scarce resources as possible to activities that directly accomplish their mission. Therefore, resources tend to be targeted to direct service rather than to building organizational capacity or professional development. Indeed, the argument for general operating support is a relatively recent innovation in philanthropy.[5]

Fortunately, concern with capacity building is growing. For example, consider the emergence of Grantmakers for Effective Organizations, a network of funders committed to building effective nonprofit organizations.[6] Or look at the recent explosion of nonprofit management education programs. In 1990, just 17 American universities offered graduate degree programs with a concentration (three or more courses) in nonprofit management. By 1997, this number had grown to 86. Moreover, more than 180 colleges and universities today offer at least one or more courses in nonprofit management.[7] One estimate puts the number of nonprofit training centers founded within the United States during the ten years from 1990 to 1999 in the hundreds.[8]

Despite these trends, the rate at which the body of knowledge about management and organization—knowledge developed primarily from the study of business organizations—has penetrated the social sector has been relatively glacial. The question arises, why?

There are a number of reasons at the heart of the answer to this question. Because of the nature of the work that many organizations in the social sector do—fighting for those who have been marginalized by society, fighting for equality and opportunity, and protecting the environment—the interests of business, with a singular focus on profits, were in the past viewed as antithetical to their own. Indeed, the decade of the 1980s, with rampant takeovers, mergers and acquisitions, sharply rising executive compensation, and conspicuous consumption, was viewed— perhaps rightly—as evidence of the ascent and glorification of the most unabashed and greedy type of self-interest.

Thus, there was a feeling on the part of many nonprofit leaders that business was the enemy and that to adopt any of the enemy's practices not only would bring with it the contamination of undesirable values, but, moreover, would be traitorous. In addition, there was a sense that nonprofits were fundamentally *different* from businesses. They were mission driven; they were concerned with progress, not profits. Fortunately, these attitudes are changing: the social sector has become increasingly receptive to ideas and tools from the world of business. A number of factors have contributed to this evolution.

One factor—competition—has played a significant role. As noted, the number of nonprofits has grown dramatically over the last decade, far more than revenues have. This means that more organizations are chasing a large but limited pool of money. This condition is the essence of competition, and it is a point well worth stressing, because nonprofit leaders often bristle at the use of the word *competition*. They say, "We are not competitive. We are collaborative." But, though collaboration is the norm in many fields, in the economic world of strategy, competition is not an attitude: it is a fact of life. Competition arises from the fact that there are not enough resources for every organization to do everything that it would like to do in pursuit of its mission. It arises from the fact that funders and clients of nonprofits make trade-offs and choose among alternative providers. Thus, the assertion that nonprofits have a collaborative orientation may very well be accurate, but this orientation does not change the reality of competition for scarce resources.

A number of factors have contributed to nonprofits' receptivity to business ideas and values, including the growing commitment of professional grant-makers to more rigorous measurement and evaluation of impact, scarcity of resources, growing complexity of critical social problems, and frustration over our limited progress in addressing such problems. This shift has been accelerated by the emergence of a new generation of philanthropists. These are young, energetic entrepreneurs who have acquired tremendous wealth in the so-called new economy, who want to support the social causes they believe in, but who want to contribute their business acumen and entrepreneurial zeal, as well as their money. Their underlying assumption has been that these talents can help to dramatically improve the effectiveness of the nonprofit organizations they support.

Leadership Matters: The Path to Impact

Much as venture capitalists respond to impressions and assessments of an entrepreneur's leadership capability when they decide whether to fund a start-up, and much as institutional investors consider the competence of senior managers when they make their investment decisions, funders in the social sector have increasingly come to operate on the belief that the skills and knowledge of nonprofit leaders matter.

If we accept the premise that the quality of management and leadership matters, the question then becomes, how do we facilitate the development of management acumen and leadership capability in the sector? Just as in the private sector, knowledge and skill, I believe, are essential. Specifically, sector leaders require substantive frameworks for thinking about social needs or problems (educational reform, climate change, economic development, etc.), but they also need frameworks for understanding, managing, and building effective organizations.

It is organizational frameworks that have been traditionally neglected in the social sector. Despite the recent proliferation of nonprofit management assistance centers, degree programs, and consulting firms, nonprofit leaders typically receive less training and professional development than their counterparts in the private sector. To the extent that opportunities for continuing education arise, these tend to be in the technical (program) domain rather than in the managerial realm.

The corporate analogy is that high-tech firms clearly need an understanding of technology and engineering to design and produce competitive products. But few would dispute the claim that they also require knowledge about organizational design, general management, and entrepreneurial processes if they are to succeed as a firm over the long haul. Fortunately for them, there is an abundance of books, educational programs, and consultants to help them acquire and implement such knowledge. Although nonprofit managers are not yet so fortunate, this book aims to close the gap.

Dealing with Sectoral Differences

The notion of dissolving boundaries does not mean that we should ignore differences between nonprofits and for-profits (or worse yet, assume none exist). Along many dimensions, there are significant and consistent differences between nonprofits as a group and for-profits as a group.[9] Perhaps the most significant is the defining feature of nonprofit form, the nondistribution constraint. Highlighted by Henry Hansmann, this is the legal requirement that precludes nonprofits from distributing surplus profits to managers or investors.[10] In this sense, the nonprofit has no "owners," an institutional design feature that is intended to ensure that nonprofit organizations serve the public good. Closely related to this feature are a number of other characteristics: the primacy of nonfinancial measures of performance, such as mission, limited availability of resources, lower compensation of staff and managers, and the absence of direct incentives for increasing productivity. Sharon Oster draws attention to another key feature that stems from the nature of the markets in which nonprofits tend to arise: the need to raise money to subsidize the provision of goods and services.[11]

Despite the existence of these very real generic differences, this book adopts a perspective that focuses not on sector-level differences but on organizational-level variation. Let me illustrate. Looking at any two nonprofit organizations in different industries with different histories, we would expect to see significant differences in strategy, culture, organizational design and, ultimately, the specific nature of the effective managerial practice. This view implies that the differences between two nonprofit organizations in different industries might be larger than the differences between either of the nonprofits and a comparable private-sector organization, or between the nonprofit and private sectors in general. For example, a performing-arts organization is likely to have very different economics and competitive dynamics from a hospital or community clinic, functioning much more like a for-profit Broadway theater than like a nonprofit hospital. Similarly, a venture philanthropist will be more like a venture capitalist than like an environmental advocacy nonprofit.

Although these are extreme examples, the point here is that it is important to avoid broad generalizations about the differences between the nonprofits and businesses that mask or ignore fundamental similarities with respect to the central management and leadership challenges. A more useful approach is to specify the characteristics of a particular organization—the tasks, environment, or problems—that have implications for how to apply a given framework. Although these characteristics may correlate with for-profit versus nonprofit status at a sector level, there will be many instances in which they do not; hence, it is important to be able to identify the relevant characteristics of a particular situation that create the need to modify or adapt a conceptual framework.

For example, one salient characteristic of many nonprofit organizations is that they raise money from one group in order to provide services to another group. In effect, the users or clients of the organization do not pay for the services they receive. Rather, these services are paid for by a funder or by the government on their behalf. This leads to a decoupling of the source of an organization's revenue and the recipient, or beneficiary, of its products or services (in contrast to the traditional commercial situation, in which the buyer and user are the same). Decoupling is important from the point of view of strategy because it alters, and introduces additional complexity into, the relationship between an organization and its customers. Dealing with this complexity is at the core of some efforts to adapt traditional models of strategy to the nonprofit sector.[12]

Although this complexity does characterize many nonprofits, there are others for which the bulk of their revenue comes in the form of income from their customers (e.g., many performing-arts organizations and some social service organizations). More to the point, however, consider two for-profit industries that are also characterized by this decoupling of customer and payor: many players in the newspaper and broadcasting industries receive the bulk of their revenue from advertising. These revenues are based on the quality of service (or appeal) that the company provides to a third group of individuals: readers or viewers. Thus, like nonprofit grant-makers, advertisers base payment for and evaluation of an organization on a product that is delivered to a third party.

Another example of this similarity is the health insurance industry. In the traditional model of third-party payor, an insurance company pays for medical services provided to a third party (the patient). Although the patient might in some circumstances pay the insurance company for his or her coverage, these payments are more likely to come from an employer. These relationships have implications for thinking about basic strategic issues of competition, buyer preferences, and customer segmentation. As with publishing and broadcasting, we again see that the source of the complexity introduced into our strategic analysis is not whether the organization or industry is nonprofit or for-profit, but rather the nature of the relationship between the buyer and the user or beneficiary of the organization's output. The lesson here is that it is important to identify the features of individual organizations that influence the applicability of a particular conceptual framework. The relevant features may or may not be a function of the organization's legal status (i.e., nonprofit, public, or private).

The Role of Concepts and Frameworks

Frameworks versus Best Practices

The approach advanced in this book stresses the value of using conceptual frameworks. It provides a basis for reasoning about organizational effectiveness, as opposed to approaches that rely on the enumeration and emulation of "best practices." Although best practices are appealing because they are relatively simple to use (and may be appropriate for some tasks), the knowledge embedded in frameworks reflects a deeper understanding of the way the world works.

Frameworks recognize the value of disciplined thinking about the causal structure of management problems. They provide a way to organize experience, inform the exercise of judgment, and deal systematically with complexity and uncertainty. Frameworks allow managers to make decisions based on systematic reasoning and fact-based inferences, as opposed to making superstitious or random choices, blindly imitating the actions of others, or even relying on lists of the seven, ten, or twelve universal steps for solving any problem.

Application Adaptation and Extension of Existing Frameworks

One of the central issues involved in the development of management theory that is of relevance and value to the social sector is this question: to what extent should or can knowledge developed primarily from the study of businesses be applied directly to the social sector?

Some might argue that businesses are simply complex organizations and that such theories should be directly applicable to organizations in the social sector.[13] Others might argue that the difference between being mission driven and being profit driven is so fundamental that theory or frameworks based on the study of businesses are unlikely to have relevance or validity in the nonprofit sector. The truth is more complicated than either argument suggests. Some business-based management frameworks can be meaningfully applied to nonprofit organizations, whereas others cannot, at least not without substantial modification.

There are two important points to consider when one thinks about this question. The first is that the applicability of knowledge about any particular field of management depends on the field in question. So, for example, in the area of operations management and business process design, many of the principles of capacity planning and management are directly applicable to nonprofit organizations. The analyses and mathematics, as well as the principles, can be translated directly from one sector to the other, helping nonprofit managers to improve productivity.

In the area of governance, however, the fundamental characteristic of nonprofit organizations—the nondistribution requirement—alters the nature of the role of directors of a nonprofit from maximizing shareholder value to something much more elusive. In addition, the complexity created by the common practice of confounding the governance role with fund-raising alters the role of board members in the nonprofit sector. Moreover, the multidimensional nature of the notion of performance, or the absence of what Jensen calls the "unified objective function," complicates and alters the task of governance.[14] So, although in business process design a large percentage of the frameworks and analytical tools from the world of business may be applicable, in the area of governance a much smaller fraction of the existing knowledge may be directly transferable.

Other areas, such as strategy, organization design, and human resource management, tend to be somewhere in the middle. The argument and frameworks presented in this book suggest that a significant portion of the work in strategic management and leadership can be translated directly to the nonprofit sector. Moreover, with some minor modifications, even more ideas can be adapted to provide considerable value and utility to nonprofit managers.

Drawing on ideas and frameworks that have been developed in the corporate world is not meant to suggest that nonprofits should be run exactly like for-profits: indeed, there are good reasons to think they should not. But consistent with the ethos of dissolving boundaries, I believe that the ideas of strategy, industry analysis, competition, and implementation of change that have largely been developed in the business world can inform the thinking of nonprofit leaders and help them to improve the effectiveness of their organizations.

Generation of New Frameworks

Despite the growing interest in business frameworks, there has been very little systematic research examining the validity or utility of these ideas and tools in the world of nonprofits. Moreover, many of the unique management and organizational problems of the nonprofit sector have been virtually excluded from the mainstream of general management by prominent faculty in traditional business schools, with only a handful of exceptions.[15] This exclusion creates both a need and an opportunity for an integrative and boundaryless approach to applying the cutting edge of management and leadership theory to the challenges of the nonprofit sector.

Fundamental Building Blocks of Organizational Effectiveness: Direction, Motivation, and Design

Virtually all observers recognize that some organizations are more effective than others, raising the following question: what is it that makes one organization thrive, while a similar organization in the same competitive space wilts and dies? There appear to be certain fundamental ingredients that effective organizations share. These building blocks correspond to the three key leadership functions originally described in the classic writing of Chester Barnard: direction, which is "to formulate and define the purpose, objectives, and ends of the organization"; motivation, which is "to promote the securing of essential efforts"; and design, which is "to provide the system of communication."[16] These three building blocks have been echoed and elaborated by a host of contemporary management scholars and practitioners.[17] Despite different emphases, the vast majority identify functions that fall within the scope of Barnard's original model.

Direction

Direction is often articulated in terms of strategy and mission. There are a number of ways of framing and talking about direction, but all deal with basic questions: Why do we exist? What do we do and why? What are our deepest aspirations? Where are we headed? How will we prosper in the marketplace? Descriptions of the role of the general manager or chief executive officer highlight shaping the organization's strategic direction, mission, or vision as the primary task. In contrast to the rest of the organization, which is seen as focused primarily on executing this strategic direction, the leader's key function is setting, monitoring, and (when necessary) changing the fundamental direction.

Motivation

One of the hallmarks of an effective organization is coordinated action. For such action to occur, the interests and motivations of individuals must be aligned with those of the collective. One of the key requirements for getting work done, therefore, is motivating or inducing people to exert effort in the service of the organization's goals. In the for-profit sector, the dominant motivational focus is economic. Firms reward people for behaving in a desired manner through compensation, whether in the form of salary, stock options, or bonuses, thereby creating the conditions necessary for high levels of motivation.[18]

In the nonprofit sector, norms and resource limitations preclude using financial exchanges as the primary basis for motivating individuals. In fact, legal statutes that define what it means to be a nonprofit prohibit the use of any form of equity or profit sharing as part of the exchange with staff. It is therefore necessary to find ways to articulate a direction, build an organization, design jobs, and provide incentives that not only transcend economic rewards but are effective forms of motivation, as well.

The other key characteristic of the sector is that most nonprofits engage in fund-raising—raising money from outside contributors or donors to subsidize the work that the organization does for its clients, whether those individuals are less able to pay for themselves, or whether its work is done for the general societal good, as with environmental organizations. So the challenge for the nonprofit leader includes motivating external stakeholders and supporters, as well as people within the organization. Here again the mission becomes central.

Design

Design, in Barnard's words, is the "system of communication" within an organization. But this encompasses more than just the telephone system or the bulletin board; it includes the social mechanisms and structures through which the parts of the organization interact with one another to produce coordinated action. This broader view is more explicit in contemporary perspectives on general management that shift from the term *design* to the more elaborate notion of *architecture*.[19] At the root of this notion is a more sophisticated view of organizational design, one that has expanded to encompass not just the boxes, but also the formal and informal mechanisms that allow people to work together, whether they be cross-functional teams, information technology, intranets, voice mail, or communication devices. These are the technical, physical, and social mechanisms that enable coordination across the individuals in a large, formal organization.

Frameworks and Fulfilling the Building Blocks

Simply knowing the three building blocks of effective organizations is not enough. Leaders need knowledge and skills that allow them to analyze their organization and its particular situation and then generate, evaluate, monitor, and modify choices about direction, motivation, and design. Is the direction a good one? Is motivation adequate and sustainable? Is it eliciting behavior consistent with the direction? Is the design supportive of the direction and motivation? Are all of the elements of the design consistent with one another? In an increasingly dynamic world, all of these questions must be evaluated on an ongoing basis to ensure continued effectiveness.

Specific guidance with respect to the fundamental decisions associated with the task of implementing these building blocks requires a knowledge that is sufficiently robust and flexible to work in a wide variety of settings. It must also be able to deal with the complexity of the real world and the overload of information and data that bombards leaders. This type of knowledge typically takes the form of a *framework*. In contrast to precise and narrow models or theories, frameworks organize information and tell one what to pay attention to and what to ignore. They provide a set of principles and categories that allow one to reduce the complexity of and draw inferences about the world, and to design effective action.

This book outlines just such a framework for fulfilling the functions of direction, motivation, and design by drawing on and integrating existing management theories that are relevant to each of the three building blocks: mission, strategy, and execution. Chapters 2, 3, and 4 will outline each component in detail and show how, together, they provide the knowledge necessary for fulfilling the challenges of direction, motivation, and design.

The Funnel

Effective leadership starts with the organization's mission, is made viable by the organization's strategy, and is implemented through the choices about how to perform key activities, how to allocate scarce resources, and what policies to put in place to guide decision making. This process can be illustrated with a funnel that is broad at the top and narrows toward the bottom (see figure I.1).

Mission, Strategy, Execution

An organization's direction begins with *mission*—the top of the funnel. Because mission captures the essence of what an organization does and why—its raison d'être, it is at the core of its aspirations, and hence direction. In addition, mission has a primacy in the nonprofit sector, because it also serves as a source of inspiration by defining the significance and importance of the organization's work. In addition to being the initial source of direction, mission serves as a source of inspiration by defining the significance and importance of the organization's work. In this sense, mission is the psychological and emotional logic that provides the energy that drives the organization. Thus, it also serves the motivation function by inducing people both inside and outside the organization to invest their

Figure I.1. The funnel.

resources, their time, their energies, and their passions in the service of the direction embedded in the mission.

As clear and as compelling as a mission may be, its purpose is chiefly to guide and inspire. Missions are typically framed at levels so broad that they cannot provide sufficient detail or focus for an organization to make concrete choices about how to execute its mission. Consider the mission of Innermotion, a Florida dance company for survivors of childhood and sexual abuse: "to eradicate childhood sexual abuse through healing and education." This mission can inspire, it can tell us what direction we are going in, but it is not precise enough to tell us how the organization should be designed, how specific activities should be performed, where resources should be allocated, or what policies should prevail.

It is also the case that the mission, because it is produced and evaluated in accordance with a framework that is fundamentally psychological in nature, is not likely to be useful for evaluating an organization's economic viability. It may well be that we can all agree we are excited about making an attempt to eradicate childhood sexual abuse, but that is not sufficient to tell us whether we are going to be able to get enough money to do what we need to do to achieve that goal.

What the mission cannot and should not be expected to do is provide the basis for ensuring the economic viability of the organization. Economic viability stems from the ability of an organization to secure from the environment the resources it needs to create its products and deliver its services. This is where strategy—the next step in the funnel—comes in.

Strategy is the economic logic of an organization. It is the body of knowledge directly concerned with the success and failure of organizations. On the most basic level, this is manifested as survival: do they live or die? In the competitive and unforgiving markets in which for-profits exist, life and death are routine occurrences. In the not-for-profit sector, market forces and social investors have historically been more forgiving, and death may not be as quick to come to underperforming organizations. However, this pattern appears to be changing, as the high-profile failures of a number of nonprofits in recent years testify.

Above and beyond survival, strategy is most concerned with performance. For a for-profit organization, performance is typically defined in terms of profitability or economic returns to its owners. For the nonprofit (as well as for some for-profits), performance is defined more broadly,[20] typically in terms of achieving the mission. Regardless of the specific conception of performance, the role of strategy is to help managers understand, predict, and control the long-term prosperity of their organizations and industries.[21]

Strategy is more specific than mission in terms of the parameters that it places around what an organization does, for whom it does it, and how it goes about doing it. Indeed, many stress that strategy is fundamentally about *choice*.[22] Strategy should also be evaluated with criteria that are different from those used to evaluate mission. For this reason alone, it is important to maintain clarity about the function of mission and the function of strategy. The fact that strategy is important and has its own unique role to play in defining the direction and design of a nonprofit does not mean that mission should be subservient to strategy. Perhaps one of the defining features of a nonprofit is that the mission should take priority over the economic concerns that are the province of strategy.

But mission cannot, and should not, serve as the basis for evaluating or ensuring a nonprofit's economic viability. Similarly, strategy should not be put to the test of being exciting or inspiring. The benefit of being clear about the mission, as well as the strategy, is that it allows each to be evaluated in accordance with appropriate criteria drawn from frameworks developed precisely to ensure that each of these two important features of any organization can be formulated effectively.

Although strategy is inherently more bounded and specific than mission, it must still be translated into action through the large number of concrete choices that are made in every organization on a day-to-day basis. This translation is what is often referred to as *implementation*. I, however, prefer and will use the term *execution*, because its behavioral focus connotes action and links it more directly to *outcomes* and *performance*. Implementation, by contrast, has grown to focus on *processes*, such as strategic planning, and *structures*, or organizational design in the classic sense (i.e., formal reporting relationships and boxes on an organization chart).[23]

There are three primary categories of choices that embody the execution of strategy: *activities, resource allocation decisions,* and *policies*. In the strategy literature, different theorists emphasize one over the others.[24] However, depending on the context, it may be more useful to the practitioner to think in terms of the particular type of choice. Moreover, to ensure the integration and coherence of the choices that, in aggregate, reflect and produce the implementation of strategy, it is also helpful to be explicit about the relationship among these three types of choices.

Overview of the Book

Chapter 1 introduces the idea of mission and, in particular, the different functions of a mission—what it should do for an organization—as well as its inherent limitations. The importance of mission for an organization's success cannot be overemphasized. According to Frances Hesselbein, legendary former leader of the Girl Scouts, "Mission is the star we steer by. Everything begins with mission, everything flows from mission."[25]

Chapter 2 considers the purpose and importance of strategy. Just as organizations need mission to provide an overarching direction, they need strategy to determine exactly how they will pursue and accomplish their mission: what resources will be devoted to the effort, how much, by whom, and when. I will examine exactly what strategy is (and is not) and explore the application of frameworks from the for-profit world to nonprofit organizations.

Chapter 3 introduces industry structure as a framework for analyzing an organization's competitive environment. More specifically, I will illustrate how industry analysis provides a systematic way of identifying the key external challenges that must be addressed in the development and evaluation of strategy. This chapter will also explore some of the more complicated and often counterintuitive issues in the application of industry analysis to the nonprofit sector.

Chapter 4 delves into the nature of execution: translating mission and strategy into action through recurring choices. These choices include the allocation of resources, the activities that employees are directed to undertake, and the policies that they will follow during the course of their work. In addition, this chapter will look at how to reduce and balance the natural tension between mission and strategy, a tension that often arises because strategy deals with the reality of resource constraints and competition, whereas mission deals with values and aspirations.

Chapter 5 delves into two more advanced issues of strategy related to designing and managing the interdependence associated with intra- and interorganizational relationships. Specifically, these include developing corporate strategy in a multibusiness, multiprogram organization, establishing and maintaining alliances and partnerships within and across industry-sector boundaries, and creating large-scale collective action at the industry level.

Chapter 6 looks at the role of leadership in formulating and then executing the mission and strategy of a nonprofit organization. In particular, I will relate these tasks to the functional approach to leadership and the basic functions of direction, motivation, and design.

Chapter 7 considers the challenge of strategic change, whether internally or externally driven. In particular, I introduce a metaframework that identifies three specific types of knowledge necessary for leading the process of intelligent strategic adaptation: a theory of organizational performance, a theory of change, and a theory of intervention.

Finally, chapter 8 highlights a host of recurring themes and challenges encountered by nonprofit leaders as they strive to use the mission, strategy, and execution frameworks to diagnose and improve the performance of their own organizations. These include the process of developing mission and strategy, key analytical and organizational pitfalls, and tips for avoiding or dealing with these and other constraints.

1

Mission

The Psychological and Emotional Logic

Mission is perhaps *the* defining feature of a nonprofit organization. Non-profit organizations are distinguished from private-sector organizations in that their goal is "something other than to provide a profit for its owners," which is generally understood to be a social mission. In the United States, the purpose embedded in this mission is central to the 501(c)(3) legal designation that grants nonprofits their tax-exempt status.[1] But, at the same time, mission is one of the most elusive constructs in the arena of nonprofit management. The term is often used to describe an organization's purpose, aspirations, output, and strategy, to name but a few possibilities. Despite the consensus about the importance of mission, there is actually little agreement about what it really is, what it is supposed to do, and how it should be evaluated. In order to gain some purchase on the notion of mission, we may think about what mission is not and what it should not be expected to do for an organization, as well as what mission is and what it should be expected to do.

What Mission Is Not and What It Should Not Be Expected to Do

Mission is not a *strategy*, nor is it a strategic plan. Yet, even in the for-profit world, the terms *mission* and *vision* are often used interchangeably with *strategy*. This reflects the confusion and imprecision surrounding the notion of strategy (a problem in its own right).[2] As I will discuss in the next chapter, strategy is an economic logic. It serves functions that are economic in nature and that must satisfy economic criteria to be considered effective. Although mission statements may contain elements of a strategy, they are typically broader and more abstract than effective strategy statements.[3]

And, though it is often viewed as being the nonprofit analogue of *profit*, mission is actually not a very good substitute. It lacks the key features of profit (or, more generally, economic value), such as being quantifiable, comparable, distributable, and exchangeable.[4] First, profit is measurable (although accounting decisions influence it). Whether the measure is in dollars, pounds, or yen, we can attach a definite number to a firm's profitability. This allows us to discriminate between differing levels of performance and changes in performance. Second, the profits of different organizations can be compared to one another. Although ambiguity results from quality of earnings and source, and likely future earnings, we can fairly compare the quarterly profits of IBM to General Motors and Microsoft. Third, profits can be divided and distributed to owners (or to other stakeholders, for that matter). Fourth, shares or portions of profit can be exchanged among individuals who should be indifferent between a dollar of profit from one company and a dollar of profit from another. Although mission defines the social value that is created by an organization, this is a fundamentally different type of value, because it lacks these key features of economic value. Hence, mission cannot fulfill for nonprofits the function that profit serves for businesses.[5]

Similarly, mission should not be expected to fulfill other functions. It cannot, for example, explain, predict, or ensure an organization's financial viability. Although it can contribute to a nonprofit's ability to raise money, the mechanism through which this happens needs to be made explicit and should be built into the strategy. Indeed, it is common for key elements of an organization's mission to appear in its strategy; however, the implications of these mission elements must then be tested in the context of the economic logic and criteria used to evaluate strategy. By itself, mission should not be expected to provide a clear guide to the allocation of resources or the configuration of activities or policies in a nonprofit. It does not—and should not be expected to—provide a detailed plan for achieving an organization's goals. All of these functions are the province of strategy.

Finally, unlike strategy, an organization's mission need not be unique. Because mission serves psychological and emotional functions, competition, which is the core of strategy, is irrelevant. In fact, one might expect nonprofits working in the same field to have similar missions. But, as we will see in the next chapter, they should have different strategies.

What Mission Is and What It Should Be Expected to Do

So what, then, is mission? Mission is the psychological and emotional logic that drives an organization. It is why people get up in the morning and go to work in a nonprofit; it is why donors support nonprofits (even though they get a tax deduction): because they are motivated to do so by the mission. Mission is the fuel that provides the psychological energy that motivates and inspires people to contribute their time, their energy, and their money to the organization. Mission is the source of passion; it is what people care most deeply about. It is what causes them to forgo the financial rewards of higher-paying private-sector jobs.

Mission does all of this by defining the *social value* that the organization creates. The key feature of social value—whether it is spiritual, moral, societal, aesthetic, intellectual, or environmental—is that it transcends economic value. Thus, it is inextricably linked to fundamental human values, which are the basis for intrinsic worth or importance.

To understand why mission is so important to nonprofits, we may draw a contrast with the for-profit sector. In a traditional business organization, the primary goal is clear: to create value and, particularly, to make a profit for its owners. Although businesses create products and provide services that meet the needs of customers—and, to be fair, in many instances the needs of society—the fundamental reason they exist is to create economic value. Although this goal may seem to be of questionable moral and social value to some, many years of generally accepted economic thought contend that, when firms maximize the economic value they create, then social welfare is also maximized.[6]

While there are many differences between nonprofits and for-profit businesses, the most fundamental feature is the nondistribution constraint.[7] This is the provision that prevents a nonprofit from having *owners* in the traditional sense, or from distributing its surplus profits to those who have invested in it or who manage it. Since distribution of value (profit) is central to the incentives that allow a business to function, an organizational form that lacks these incentives has to rely on another motivational mechanism. For nonprofits this is mission.

First and foremost, the reason for the existence of mission in a nonprofit must be focused on something other than the creation of economic value. Hence, the centrality of a purpose—whether it be creating opportunities for teenage mothers to attend (and graduate from) high school, bringing innovative dance theater programs to a community, or working to protect endangered ecosystems.

The Contribution of Mission to the Economic Logic

Mission provides the meaning and psychological value that substitutes for economic (monetary) value. It is part of, and also lubricates, the exchanges among stakeholders. Staff members work not just for the monetary compensation paid by a social-purpose organization, but because of its mission. Consider research by Cornell University economist Robert Frank, which demonstrates people must be paid a "moral reservation premium" to work for organizations that are perceived to be less socially responsible. In a survey of graduating Cornell seniors, Frank found that the majority of those surveyed would prefer to work as an advertising copywriter for the American Cancer Society rather than as an advertising copywriter for Camel cigarettes. Not only that, but these same respondents reported that Camel cigarettes would have to pay them a salary premium of 50 percent over the same job at the American Cancer Society. Similarly, Frank found that, when given the choice between working as an accountant for a large art museum and working in the same position for a large petrochemical company, survey respondents wanted a salary premium of 17 percent to work for the large petrochemical company.[8] Work in a similar vein by Anne Preston shows a wage differential of about 20 percent but indicates further that this is not a function of differences in education or skills, industry, or job characteristics.[9] These results reinforce the view that lower wages represent a trading of monetary compensation for the ability to contribute to the creation of social value.

Donors to nonprofits contribute not for financial return, but for the satisfaction and pleasure of aiding the creation of social good. Clients often patronize or use the organization's services not just because of the positive attributes of a particular service or product, but because they believe in and support the mission. People—staff, donors, and others—are drawn to nonprofits because they feel an affinity for what the organization does and for the individuals, groups, or causes that the organization supports. Mission is the expression of what an organization is all about, and the more compelling it is, the more highly motivated will be those who read it to help the organization achieve its goals any way they can.

Although this general principle is a start, to move toward a more precise definition of mission, we must first understand its functions, what it is supposed to do for an organization. When one asks a group of nonprofit leaders what they expect from their missions, there are a host of answers:

- It should guide the choice of activities.
- It should inspire and motivate stakeholders and staff.
- It should appeal to donors.
- It should provide a basis for evaluating the organization.
- It should provide an overarching guide to the organization's direction.
- It should justify and explain the organization's reason for being.
- It should guide the conduct of organization members—not just what they do, but also how they do it and why they do it.
- It should provide boundaries on the range of strategies that will be considered acceptable.
- It should inform and shape the culture and influence the selection and retention of staff and board members.
- It should inform and guide the noneconomic decisions and choices, especially those with moral implications.

Even though we could no doubt identify a host of other expectations, this list is sufficiently daunting: this is a lot to expect from something that is typically expected to be short and simple.

Fortunately, though perhaps also ironically, Jim Collins and Jerry Porras's research on the topic of mission from the world of business sheds light on this phenomenon.[10] In particular, their work suggests that, in order to fulfill these many and varied functions, the overarching construct of mission must be much more complex and multifaceted than its definition in common usage, which is typically viewed as *purpose*, or raison d'être. Mission must also encompass three other elements: *core values*, *primary goals*, and *vision*. Each of these four elements plays an essential role in the ability of the overall package (i.e., mission) to fulfill the many functions we identified.

The first two elements, purpose and core values, are the enduring ones. They ensure continuity and stability, and allow an organization to be guided by its past. The second two, primary goals and vision, are oriented toward the future, and they embody an organization's aspirations. Below, I review Collins and Porras's description of each of these components and how they are manifested in the corporate sector. I then draw on examples and applications from the nonprofit sector that illustrate the way in which the fundamental social purpose of nonprofit organization can make this framework even more powerful than it is in the world of business.

Mission in the Private Sector

Interestingly, despite the dominance of economic perspectives on the role of business, many leaders have advocated framing the corporation's purpose in terms of objectives that go beyond the simple creation of wealth. Long before the idea of corporate social responsibility gained prominence in business school curricula, leaders such as General Robert Wood Johnson of Johnson & Johnson argued that business should contribute to the greater good: "Institutions, both public and private, exist because people want them, believe in them, or at least are willing to tolerate them. The day is past when business is a private matter—if it ever really was. In a business society, every act of business has social consequences and may arouse public interest. Every time business hires, builds, sells, or buys, it is acting for the people as well as for itself, and it must be prepared to accept full responsibility for its acts."[11] David Packard of Hewlett-Packard concurred: "I think many people assume, wrongly, that a company exists simply to make money. While this is an important result of a company's existence, we have to go deeper and find the real reasons for our being."[12] Over the last thirty years, management scholars have echoed this view and, more recently, provided evidence of the positive impact of mission on corporate performance.[13] While multiple mechanisms are involved, such as motivation, focus, and trust, mission appears to contribute to this improved performance.

At the same time, just as in the nonprofit sector, there has been considerable confusion about the meaning of mission in the business arena.[14] Collins and Porras's work has probably been among the most influential attempts to add precision and comprehensiveness to the idea of mission. So drawing on this work to identify the various elements of mission that are necessary to fulfill the various functions, or expectations, for nonprofits seems to make sense.

Still, the initial puzzle remains: how and why did mission become a popular concept with leaders of for-profit organizations? My own suspicion is that mission is one tool that business executives learned from nonprofits. Perhaps some corporate manager serving on a board somewhere a long time ago recognized the motivational power of articulating a compelling mission and applied it to defining the significance of his business.

Whatever their source may have been, culture, values, and mission became fashionable in the 1980s with the popularity of business best-sellers such as *In Search of Excellence* and *The Fifth Discipline*. In fact, Peter Senge tells a story about going to interview the CEO of an insurance company about his company's mission. Initially dubious about the prospects of hearing anything inspiring, Senge was impressed by the CEO, who talked about his view of the importance of his company's work. Said the CEO, "We exist because life is unfair. Our mission is to protect and insulate people from the vagaries of life's unfairness." This mission makes insurance seem inspiring and important—not the typical view outsiders have of the industry.[15]

If a compelling mission can have such a dramatic impact in the for-profit sector, imagine what a compelling mission can do for Save the Children or the Nature Conservancy.

A Framework for Understanding and Analyzing Mission

In their research, Collins and Porras examined the psychological and emotional logic of eighteen visionary companies and a group of comparison companies (a quasi control group). The results showed that that companies with meaningful and deeply shared and understood psychological and emotional logic outperformed matched peers by a factor of more than 6 to 1, and the market by 15 to 1, over a period of sixty years.[16] Their book, *Built to Last*, became a best-seller, not only because it demonstrated the economic value of mission for the business world, but also because of the intrinsic appeal of infusing even mundane endeavors like insurance with meaning and significance.

Unfortunately, there are no directly comparable studies of the relationship between mission and performance in the nonprofit sector. In part, this is no doubt related to the elusive nature of performance in this context, but it also reflects the confusion about the meaning of mission, as well as the tendency to conflate mission and strategy. Hence, a major part of the utility of Collins and Porras's work is the conceptual clarity that it provides in understanding the essential elements of an effective psychological and emotional logic.[17]

With mission as the overarching concept, let us take a closer look at the four components identified by Collins and Porras.

Core Values

Core values are the "essential and enduring tenets. . . . timeless guiding principles that require no external justification."[18] These are, first and foremost, *values*: abstract concepts (e.g., principles, qualities, or conditions) that are considered inherently good, meaningful, or valuable—such as freedom, justice, or equality. People in an organization care deeply about these values and would sooner go out of business than violate them. Attaching *core* to *values* denotes values that are held uncompromisingly. Core values are limited in number, typically no more than four or five.

In the nonprofit sector, consider the example of New York City's "conductorless" Orpheus Chamber Orchestra, which has core values of democracy and participation. Unlike many other orchestras, it has shared and rotating leadership roles. Important decisions are made by consensus and, even if there were some advantage to be gained by a more hierarchical or autocratic management style, Orpheus would never even entertain the possibility. Double-bass player and founding member Don Palma's words echo the experience and sentiments of many in the orchestra:

> I took a year off from Orpheus at the very beginning and went to the Los Angeles Philharmonic. I just hated it. I didn't like to be told what to do all the time, being treated like my only value was just to sit there and be a good soldier. I felt powerless to affect things, particularly when they weren't going well. I felt frustrated, and there was nothing I could seem to do to help make things better. Orpheus keeps me involved. I have some measure of participation in the direction the music is going to take. I think that's why a lot of us have stayed involved for so long.[19]

The American Red Cross considers community service to be one of its core values (according to American Red Cross statistics, in 2002, Red Cross chapter Community Services provided almost 22 million services to individuals, including home-delivered meals, food pantries, rides to medical appointments, homeless shelters, transitional housing, caregiver education support groups, friendly visitors, and even more).[20] Howard University in Washington, D.C., has published a list of core values, stating, for example, that "this University must engender and nurture an environment that celebrates African-American culture in all its diversity."[21]

Core values must be reflected in what people actually do rather than what they say. In fact, part of the function of these values is to guide people's behavior and decision making. The values establish a moral line or boundary that must never be crossed or violated. They also help in the selection and retention of members of the organization. People who do not share the core values are less likely to want to join or support the organization—provided, of course, that these core values are clear and explicit.

For core values to be effective in unifying the organization and guiding behavior, there can be only a limited number of them—typically not more than five—with the understanding that not every single thing that an organization and its stakeholders care about is necessarily going to be a core value. For example, wholesomeness and imagination are core values for the Walt Disney Company, but customer service is not. Even though in some aspects of the firm's operations it may value and deliver good customer service, it is not a central and inviolable value.

This does not mean that other values are not important or do not influence behavior and decision making. It just means that they are not defining characteristics of the organization's identity. They may be "instrumental" values, or values that are followed because they provide some benefit to the organization—for example, quality or innovation. If they ceased to provide a benefit, they would be abandoned. Core values would not. This is what makes them core.

Rather than being invented or established, core values are discovered through a process of reflection and careful observation of history. To determine whether a particular value is truly a core value, Porras offers a few simple tests: Has it guided the organization since its inception? Will it still be guiding the organization in a hundred years? Are there examples of the organization's making a choice based on the value and being punished for doing so?[22]

Purpose

While core values are an organization's timeless guiding principles, purpose is an organization's enduring reason for being. It is the closest thing to what most organizations will typically call their mission. Purpose provides meaning and significance to the work of the organization. It establishes direction for an organization at a level that should inspire and motivate stakeholders—what legendary nonprofit leader Frances Hesselbein called "the star we steer by." The navigational analogy is illuminating here, because purpose is never really fully achieved. As with the star, we never reach purpose (which is unlike goals), even though it is the direction in which we journey.

Purpose is also not the work we do or the output we produce. It is why we do what we do in a deep, psychological way. Collins and Porras use the example of consulting firm McKinsey and Company. McKinsey's purpose is not to do management consulting (something that they certainly do); McKinsey's purpose is *why* do they do management consulting. They note that by continuing to ask "why do you do what you do?" we eventually (after perhaps three or four or five times asking) arrive at the true purpose, which, in the case of McKinsey, is "to help leading corporations and governments be more successful." Similarly, the purpose of mortgage lender Fannie Mae is not just to provide loans to prospective home owners; Fannie Mae's true purpose is to "continually democratiz[e] home-ownership."[23]

In both of these examples, the purpose is something that will always be strived for, but never completely attained. McKinsey will always seek to help organizations be more successful, but the organization will never be able to make every organization successful. Similarly, Fannie Mae will always seek to democratize home ownership, but the organization will never be able to ensure that every citizen qualifies to buy a home. As we have seen in the "test" recommended, an organization's purpose should last for one hundred years. If it cannot, then we have not yet stripped away enough layers of the organization: the question "why?" needs to be asked until we get down to the very essence of why the organization does what it does.

In the context of for-profits, we noted earlier that, from an economic point of view, the purpose of a corporation is widely accepted to be maximizing shareholder wealth. In the strategic and operational context, this definition is adequate because it provides focus and a criterion for evaluating trade-offs. But, from a psychological and emotional perspective, it is woefully inadequate. As Collins and Porras note, it is unlikely to get most people's "juices flowing."[24]

Of course, in the nonprofit setting, it should be easier to articulate a compelling purpose. And yet, even here, we often find relatively uninspiring statements of activities and programs. For example, "We provide shelter for the homeless," or "We provide scholarships to allow disadvantaged students the chance to go to college." Purpose must go beyond this level of articulation if it is to serve the motivational function. It must answer the *why* question.

So why does the organization provide scholarships to allow minority students the chance to go to college? Because they would not otherwise be able to go. So why is that fact important? Well, because they are unable to go only because of financial constraints, and that is unfair. We believe equality of opportunity and the social good in terms of contribution to society is enhanced by nurturing potential, and by avoiding the costs of stifling mobility and destroying hope. The organization's purpose therefore is to overcome the barriers that prevent disadvantaged minority students from having the access and opportunity to pursue higher education and realize their full potential. When stated this way, for most people (or at least the kind we hope will work for and support this organization), the importance of this purpose is self-evident. Moreover, it is much more inspiring than a simple description of what the organization does. This is the challenge of discovering purpose and building a mission that fulfills its promise and potential to harness the energy and passions of staff, volunteers, clients, and donors.

Another approach to articulating the true purpose of an organization proposed by Collins and Porras is to try to answer the following question: "What would the world lose if this organization did not exist?" For an environmental organization, the answer might be entire ecosystems or species of living things, or because of global warming, a habitat capable of supporting human existence in a hundred years. These are responses that will get people's attention.

The key tests of purpose are two: Is it enduring (i.e., can it last for a generation or more)? And, second, does it energize and inspire the key stakeholders? Typically, leaders of nonprofits that I have worked with can quickly—but not automatically—get to a statement of purpose that meets these tests, largely because the sense of purpose is often so deeply embedded within their psyche that it cannot be accessed easily. The questioning of a naïve outsider, "Gee, why do you do that? Is that really important? To whom? Why? Why should I care about this?" can lead in the space of ten minutes to a much more powerful statement of purpose than what is usually found in the annual report or strategic planning document of most organizations.

Primary Goal

The third key component of an organization's mission is its primary goal. This is not just any old goal, but it is a special type of goal, one that "applies to the entire organization and requires 10 to 30 years of effort to complete."[25] This mission-level goal provides focus, attention, and structure to the efforts of an organization's members, and it is also a more immediate source of motivation than purpose (like the motivation of seeing the finish line in a sprint versus that feeling of the accomplishment and satisfaction that motivates one to train for a marathon).

While the energy provided by purpose lies in the meaning and significance, the motivation of the primary goal is satisfaction and accomplishment. Indeed, a large body of research has demonstrated that goals are powerful sources of motivation for both individuals and organizations.[26] Two key features of motivating goals are that (1) they must be challenging but attainable, and (2) they should be sufficiently concrete that you know when you have achieved them.

A classic example of this type of goal cited by Collins and Porras is President John F. Kennedy's 1961 target of putting a man on the moon and bringing him back safely by the end of the decade. That was the primary, or mission-level, goal; it was clear, challenging, and inspiring. It is instructive to note that this primary goal can be broken down into a host of subgoals. For example, to accomplish the moon mission, NASA's engineers had to figure out how to design and build a rocket powerful enough to propel tons of metal into orbit and beyond, and they had to precisely calculate the trajectory and timing of the spacecraft by the orbits of the moon and the earth. Although each of these subgoals was important (and may have even been primary for subunits within the organization), the overarching goal, the one that goes into the mission, is the primary one. Tests for goals include the following: Does the prospect of achieving the goal get people excited? Is it sufficiently difficult but still attainable? (A good rule of thumb is that we should say, "We think we can do that but don't yet know exactly how.") Is it sufficiently concrete and tangible that we know when it has been accomplished? This is what I like to refer to as the "Veuve Clicquot test": will you know when to open the champagne?

Vision

Vision is the "vibrant, engaging, and specific description of what it will be like to achieve the [primary goal]."[27] It is rich, textured, and vivid; it need not be short, pithy, or focused. This is where the poetry and the music should emerge. The test of a good vision is simply, does it paint a picture that is sufficiently real and vivid, by which people can see, taste, and feel the future? Does it evoke the experience of achieving the primary goal in their imagination? As we turn to examples of real-life missions, we will see that the best visions do this in ways that are extraordinarily powerful.

Business Example: Apple Computer

Let us consider an integrated example so we can see how the pieces fit together. Apple Computer has been considered a colorful, entrepreneurial, and innovative Silicon Valley firm since the late 1970s. Especially in its early years, it was a firm characterized by idealism and an antiestablishment ethos. Perhaps more than any company that I have used as a case study with MBA students, Apple evokes the most powerful feelings—almost to the point where it is difficult to have a reasoned discussion of the firm's strategy and performance with students; there are always a few who are devoted Mac users. Arguably, the psychological and emotional logic of Apple has driven much of its product success and customer loyalty and devotion.

The 1984 shareholders meeting at which cofounder Steve Jobs unveiled the original Macintosh to a standing ovation provides a wonderful window onto the values, purpose, goal, and vision of the company. The event resembled a revival meeting much more than it did a typical shareholders gathering.

Core Values

From the opening musical interlude, an upbeat, reworded version of the Irene Cara song "What a Feeling" from the movie *Flashdance*, to the famous 1984 commercial, and from John Sculley's earnest introduction to the playful but taunting (of IBM) speech by Jobs, the values of the young Apple company were transparent:

- *Freedom of choice*: Introducing the famous 1984 commercial, Jobs says, "Apple is perceived to be the only hope to offer IBM a run for its money. Dealers . . . now fear an IBM-dominated and controlled future. They are increasingly turning back to Apple as the only force that can ensure their future freedom."
- *Accessibility*: In hyping the new Macintosh product, Jobs notes: "We

are introducing it at a mainstream price point of $2,495, with its radical ease of use (point and click, menus, cut and paste)."

- *Being different*: In his introduction, John Sculley declares, "Being the best is more important than being the biggest. We must be bold enough to be importantly different."
- *Innovation*: Sculley also asserts, "We intend to be the leader in innovation." In describing the dramatic advances of the Macintosh, Jobs stresses its technical superiority with respect to microprocessor speed, random access memory (RAM) capacity, hard drive storage, and display resolution, among other features. He proudly promotes its compact size, commenting, "It fits in a box that is one-third the size and weight of an IBM PC."[28]

It is important to note that one can identify these core values not by looking at the annual report or by reading a plaque mounted on the wall at the company's executive offices. Instead, one can identify Apple's core values in the symbols, tone, and language that permeated the entire event. Although one could no doubt find evidence of other possible core values from additional data, these four pass the tests that should be applied to core values and illustrate the nature of this element of mission.

Purpose

The enduring raison d'être is less obvious, but embedded in the opening video were images of everyday people using computers in a variety of ways that appeared to make them more productive, happier, and more creative. The impression left with viewers was clear: "We are Apple, leading the way to a brighter day." A reasonable characterization of the purpose might be, "to enrich people's lives by bring insanely great personal computing products to everyday users."

Primary Goals

The clear enemy in the event was the "eight-hundred-pound gorilla," IBM. At that time, IBM's PC had usurped the Apple II as the top-selling personal computer. Backed by its huge sales and distribution network, and strong presence in corporate America, the behemoth appeared poised to dominate the industry. Jobs's speech referred to Big Blue in the following way: "It is now 1984 . . . IBM wants it all and is aiming its guns on its last obstacle to industry control—Apple. Will Big Blue dominate the entire computer industry? The entire information age? Was George Orwell right?" Then the 1984 commercial appeared on a large screen: Orwellian images of hundreds of mesmerized men in prison garb and with shaved heads marching into a large auditorium, watching a despotic-looking authority figure preaching obedience. Flashes of a young, athletic woman sprinting away from jackbooted police in riot gear then appeared. In the final segment, she charged into the auditorium and hurled a large sledgehammer into the on-screen image of the authority figure, shattering his control over the audience. Then, in full screen with voice-over, the narrator announced, "On January 24th, Apple Computer will introduce Macintosh. And you will see why 1984 won't be like *1984*."[29]

The message is clear: Apple's crusade was to save the world from the hegemony of IBM's threatened authoritarian dominance of the Information Age, preventing the apocalyptic tyranny predicted by George Orwell. Apple's primary goal was to compete successfully with IBM by liberating the computer from the computer professional and putting it in the hands of everyday people. This goal was made concrete by Jobs's assertion: "What we want to do now is to build great personal computers and bring them to tens of millions of people," a powerful aspiration that one reporter at the time described as "transforming the computer from a geek's expensive toy into a household appliance."[30]

Vision

What does the world look like in which Apple achieves its primary goal? Although it has no official vision statement, vision is reflected in the imagery and language of 1984. From the commercial, to the demonstration of the new Macintosh, in which the computer talks playfully and jokes about the size and weight of IBM PCs and displays images of graphics, art, and other creative products, a vision emerges. At least to me, the world in which Apple has achieved its primary goal is one where regular people—adults and children—are playing, working, and learning with Apple computers on their desks. Apple's technology is making these people more productive, happy, and empowered. They can open the box and start using the Mac without ever having to open a manual. There are handy peripherals and accessories that expand the capabilities of the personal computer and work seamlessly and flawlessly. Apple is the icon of "cool," as well as the vanguard, the cutting edge, of personal computing technology. IBM is humbled.

Mission and Change

The Collins and Porras framework reflects the basic assumption that core values and purpose are enduring and do not change, whereas primary goals and vision will change over long periods of time as the goals are attained. So what does this mean in the case of Apple?

Looking at the firm in 2005, we see basic values and purpose have remained the same, but the specific goal of beating IBM evolved as the dominance of Big Blue in the PC industry waned in the 1990s. In fact, the enemy became Microsoft. The objective was still to provide an alternative, but this time in operating system rather than hardware. Indeed, as Apple's survival was threatened and Microsoft came under attack from the U.S. Justice Department's antitrust suit, Apple forged an alliance with Microsoft—much to the dismay, at the time, of the faithful. Bill Gates was booed at the annual Apple Users conference, where Jobs announced the alliance. Even its original adversary, IBM, has today become a close partner of Apple, jointly producing the new-generation G5 microprocessor that Apple views as critical to competing against the Windows-Intel standard.

Nonprofit Example: City Year

The framework works just as well for a nonprofit as it does for a for-profit organization. Consider the example of City Year, a Boston-based nonprofit that provides community service, leadership development, and civic engagement to a diverse group of young people from seventeen to twenty-four years of age. (See chapter 2 for a detailed discussion of City Year.)

City Year was founded on the belief that one person can make a real difference in the world around him or her. But, according to CEO and cofounder Alan Khazei, City Year is not just a think tank; it is an "action tank"—an organization that strives to turn its ideas into reality: "An 'action tank' is both a program and a 'think tank'—constantly combining theory and practice to advance new policy ideas, make programmatic breakthroughs, and bring about major changes in society. City Year is . . . working to advance and improve the concept and delivery of voluntary national service so that one day, giving a year of service will become a common expectation—and a real opportunity—for millions of young Americans."[31]

This aspiration is very important to the organization—to those who run it and those who work within it, and to the community it serves and the people and organizations that donate money to fund its programs. While City Year has made great progress (as evidenced by the one thousand young leaders who will complete more than 1.7 million hours of service under its programs this year alone), it hopes to motivate stakeholders to achieve even more. According to City Year's official mission statement, "An 'action tank' for national service, City Year seeks to demonstrate, improve, and promote the concept of national service as a means of building a stronger democracy. City Year unites a diverse group of young people, ages 17 to 24, for a year of full-time, rigorous community service, leadership development, and civic engagement. City Year's vision is that one day, the most commonly asked question of an 18-year-old will be: 'Where are you going to do your service year?'"[32]

Let us apply the framework to City Year, to see how the four basic components allow the organization to fulfill its core functions.

Core Values

What values do City Year's stakeholders—its employees and volunteers, its program participants, its customers, its donors—care most deeply about, the values that they would sooner go out of business over than violate? In the case of City Year, there appear to be three:

- *Unity and equality—appreciation of diversity and tolerance*: "The community we strive for is inclusive of all peoples. Regardless of race, class or lifestyle, all people are first seen as individuals with their own unique set of life experiences that have shaped their worldviews. A beloved community is one in which all people hold a vital and valued place in a collective effort to achieve goals for the common good."
- *Citizenship and civic responsibility*: "City Year unites a diverse group of 17- to 24-year-old young people for a year of full-time, rigorous community service, leadership development, and civic engagement. On Opening Day, corps members pledge their dedication before an audience of friends, family, corporate executives, service leaders, and civic officials."

- *Idealism and community*: "At cyzygy, City Year's Annual Convention of Idealism, the entire City Year community comes together to celebrate the power of national service and convene City Year's National Service Policy Forum, a discussion of the future of the national service movement that brings together corporate and civic leaders, social entrepreneurs, policy experts, foundation program officers, and other champions."[33]

While City Year formally published a list of its core values, they are readily apparent in the beliefs of those who founded the organization; in the actions of those who run the organization and participate in its programs; and in the faces, hearts, and minds of those who are touched by its people. City Year may be many things to many people, but, above all else, the organization is defined by these core values.

Purpose

As you will recall from our earlier discussion, an organization's purpose is its enduring reason for being. It is something that is never completely fulfilled, so it is not simply the organization's short- or long-term goals. Not only that, but the organization's purpose is not simply a description of its output or customers. In the case of City Year, the organization's purpose—its enduring reason for being—is "to demonstrate, improve, and promote the concept of national service as a means of building a stronger democracy."[34] The organization will always strive toward this end, yet it will never be finished. It will make progress and achieve milestones, but there will always be a need to strengthen democracy through service.

Primary Goals

In 1991 City Year had two primary goals: getting youth service onto the national agenda and expanding City Year to other cities beyond Boston.[35] The expansion goal was articulated concretely as having eight to ten sites up and running by 1995. The organization would know whether it had achieved this goal, but, though founders knew what national service meant, what it would look like was still somewhat unclear. Ultimately, City Year's success and promotion of national service contributed to two key events that met this goal. First, the organization was named a "demonstration project for national service" by President George H. W. Bush in June 1992, receiving $7.2 million in federal support. Second, in November 1992, President-Elect Bill Clinton identified national service as one of his top priorities. And in 1993, based in part on the City Year model, AmeriCorps, a network of national service programs, was established.

Vision

City Year's formal statement of vision is very simple: "City Year's vision is that one day, the most commonly asked question of an eighteen-year-old will be: 'Where are you going to do your service year?'" It tracks the goal of establishing national service very closely, but it does not include the rich texture that is apparent in other descriptions of the organization's aspirations. Consider the following statement, which could be viewed as elements of the vision: Young people in City Year will be "a powerful resource for addressing our nation's most pressing issues," and "one day service will be a common expectation—and a real opportunity—for citizens all around the world."[36] In other words, by bringing diverse groups of young people together to serve with, and learn from and about, one another, national service could be the next step in the civil rights movement: "The Civil Rights Movement ended discrimination within the law, but not in the hearts and minds of citizens. By uniting diverse Americans to work side by side for a common purpose, national service [can] show that there is more that unites us than divides us."[37]

Nonprofit Example: The American Repertory Theatre

The Boston-based American Repertory Theatre (ART) is considered by many to be one of the most innovative, thought-provoking, and engaging theaters in the country, if not in the world. *Time* magazine named the ART "one of the three best theatres in the country."[38] Founded in 1980 by Robert Brustein and Robert Orchard (both recruited from Yale University's School of Drama), the ART has won an impressive array of awards, including a Tony, a Pulitzer, a Jujamcyn, and more during its twenty-five-year history.

At its core the ART is about developing theater as an art form by fostering innovation and by nurturing and supporting promising artists. It is instructive to look at the ART's mission through the lens of the four components.[39]

Core Values

As already discussed, an organization's core values are the abstract concepts that are considered inherently good, meaningful, or valuable—in the words of Collins and Porras, "essential and enduring tenets . . . timeless guiding principles that require no external justification."[40] The values that are core to the ART can readily be inferred from the aspirations articulated by its leaders:

- "The American Repertory Theatre was founded as a nonprofit organization to give it the freedom to pursue truly innovative and experimental theatre, without the artistic constraints that the constant pursuit of a commercial agenda would necessitate. Experience proves without doubt that we need alternatives to the commercial model to give the public access to important works of art. Moreover, if we relied only on the marketplace, young untested talent and new forms of expression would suffer."[41]
- "You cannot have fine theatre without establishing an institution where actors can enjoy dignity derived from the quality of their work, where playwrights can develop plays without commercial pressure, where directors are free to experiment with new ways to penetrate text, where audiences can follow a company's artistic progress instead of tasting individual hits with no continuity of purpose."[42]

Embedded in these and other statements is a commitment to the values of innovation and experimentation, dignity and respect for artists, and institutional stability and continuity.

Purpose

Recall that the purpose of an organization is not *what* it does, or what it produces or sells. Purpose is *why* it does what it does—its enduring reason for being. Again, we can find the elements of the ART's purpose in Brustein's explanations of why it exists:

- "[We are] a theatre that has as its goal not profits and deals but artistic fulfillment, not the advancement of careers but of talent. [We are] a springboard not for opportunism but of spiritual development and growth."[43]
- "We came into being as an institution in order to extend hospitality to artists."[44]
- "We're not simply a producing organization, we're also a training organization."[45]
- "I think the [national foundations] recognized that we were serious, that we were uncompromising, that we don't make too many concessions to popular taste, that we are devoted to trying to improve the quality of theatre art in the country."[46]

Integrating these elements, a reasonable summary of the ART's purpose is: "To advance the state-of-the-art of theater by creating an artistic environment that nurtures and support artists and focuses on work that is uniquely theatrical."

Primary Goals

While every organization has a variety of goals, an organization's primary goals are special: they provide focus, attention, and structure to the members of the organization. In the case of the ART, it is difficult to identify the primary goal. There are aspirations, to be sure, but these are mainly at the more abstract and enduring level of purpose.

Perhaps if one were to go back to the founding of the ART in 1980, the goal at that point might be described as follows: "to establish the theater as the preeminent regional nonprofit theater in the country and the undisputed leader in the generation of new work and new artists." This goal is more concrete and achievable. Although we might not agree on when the ART accomplished this goal, by the 1990s, a string of awards and critical acclaim—along with the theater's dominance of the funding scene as reflected in grants from the National Endowment for the Arts and other arts grant-makers—are testament to its preeminence.

The challenge is, having accomplished this initial goal, what is to be the ART's new goal? Unfortunately, the answer is unclear, and, though there are goals in terms of growth and fund-raising, these types of goals are not the primary goals of mission. They are means to an end. The end, at least to the outside observer, is not readily apparent.

Vision

Given the original ART goal of becoming the preeminent regional non-profit theater in the country and the undisputed leader in the generation of new work and new artists, we find an abundance of rich and textured descriptions of the ART's vision of a world in which artistic director Robert Brustein sees "A theatre allied to the collective ideal, associated with training, organic in nature, continuous in operation, permanent in status. It is theatre that connects itself to the soul, mind, and emotions of the audience, to the public and private life of the polity . . . It is a theatre of danger, dreams, surprise, adventure, a theatre of the unexpected and the unknown."[47] Consistent with the focus on developing artists and presenting the "unexpected and unknown," the company presents a varied repertoire that includes new plays, progressive productions of classical texts, and collaborations between artists from many disciplines.

The ART's vision also includes a very tangible image of the theater's impact on the audience. Brustein asserts, "I want the audience to carry the play home with them and I want it to invade their dreams. I want it to change their consciousness in some way, or, more likely, their unconscious."[48]

Using the Framework to Evaluate Mission

There are two steps involved in the process of using the framework to evaluate an organization's mission: First, determine whether or not the mission contains each of the four essential components: core values, purpose, goals, and vision. If not, revisit the mission, and articulate or develop the deficient component. Second, evaluate all components to ensure that they meet the criteria necessary for them to fulfill the overarching functions of the mission.

Although it may be fairly obvious when a mission is missing one or more of the essential components, deciding whether or not the mission satisfies the necessary criteria—and whether it is internally consistent—can be a more difficult proposition. Say, for example, that a performing-arts organization has a core value of *accessibility*, manifested as a commitment to doing work that can be appreciated by and appeals to a broad segment of the population. But, at the same time, the organization has a primary goal of establishing itself as a "world class" organization with respect to artistic excellence. In this case, in the value of accessibility may be in conflict with the goal of being recognized as "world class," if the latter is defined by the field in ways that will push the organization toward more esoteric and arcane types of artistic work.

Another issue arises when funders or other influential stakeholders want to see particular elements in the mission statement—elements that may have no place being there. For example, nonprofits often say funders want to see "fiscal responsibility" or a commitment to an "operating surplus" as core values. These should never be in the mission, because then they can become ends in and of themselves. If generating a surplus were really fundamentally important in a deep moral sense, then an organization would not choose to be a nonprofit in the first place. It would be an investment bank. This is not to say that nonprofits cannot have financial goals. They can, and they should, but financial goals should not be part of the mission of the organization, because the economic logic and the psychological logic then become confused.

But what if a funder, implicitly or explicitly, insists? Imagine, for example, how the promise of a million-dollar contribution can affect the actions of the managers of a cash-strapped nonprofit. The pressures on a nonprofit organization hungry for financial support can be high indeed, and an organization's management may go out of its way to bend and twist (and sometimes break) the organization's mission to fit the desires of the funder.

My own suggestion is to have a public mission statement that reflects and addresses external demands, but to also have an internal mission statement that reflects and guides the people who actually run the organization and do its work. This way, there is greater clarity about what is really important and sacred. And that should not be financial. Again, it is not that these financial concerns are not important. They are. It is just that they should not have primacy in the context of the psychological logic of mission.

Using the Framework to Discover Your Organization's Mission

The process of articulating an organization's mission is more like discovery than like invention. For any established organization, there was some original source of energy or spark of inspiration that led to its founding.

Most organizations are initially created in the heat of passion—by people who truly believe that they are creating something that will achieve great things, solve difficult problems, or provide people with innovative products and services that will improve their lives. If you can find your way to the source of that energy, inspiration, and passion, then you will discover the mission.

Similarly, in the entrepreneurial context of creating a new organization, there is a seminal psychological and emotional logic, an energy or passion that motivates and inspires the entrepreneur. This energy and passion is the fuel that fires the organization's flame, and inspires its stakeholders, from funders to clients, to employees, to volunteers, to board members, to the community at large. The challenge, then, is to discover and articulate the mission.

Operationally, this entails examining and reflecting on each of the four components that comprise a mission (core values, purpose, goals, and vision) to identify what is really core, what is most important, what is most central to the identity of the organization. Generally, the most effective way to bring this about is to engage the people who are (or often were) central to the founding of the organization. Depending on the situation, it can also involve key staff members, clients, and board members. But discovering an organization's mission is not something that should necessarily be a democratic or participative process. Not only does a group that is too broad and too large risk diluting the energy and passion, but also it can lead to the organizational equivalent of a camel—that is, a mission that is nothing more than a horse designed by a committee.

Let us consider how to use the framework to discover and refine the four components of mission.

Core Values

When considering the core values of an organization, management's job is to identify what comprises the defining characteristics of the organization, and what tenets its members would sooner slit their wrists for than violate. Ideally, to get to the values that are truly at the heart of what an organization does, the list of core values must be narrowed down to four or five. More than that diffuses their importance and makes it likely that there will end up being values that are not truly core in nature. Figuring out which are core involves asking what the organization and those within it feel most deeply about—the values that are absolute and inviolable.

Sometimes, multiple values can readily be integrated under a higher-order value. For example, some organizations in the nonprofit sector will decide that affordability is a core value, and that being multilingual or embracing diversity are also important core values. But if they are pushed hard enough and asked why is it important to embrace diversity or why is it important to be affordable, it becomes apparent that both of these values are subsumed under the higher-order values of equality or justice. Moreover, specific practices such as ensuring broad-based access to the organization's services or affirmative action in recruiting senior staff members can be understood in terms of a single core value, providing greater simplicity and clarity to the mission.

There is a process of working through the meaning of these values by asking questions: What would it look like to make a decision that would be consistent with these values? What kind of decision would we not make because it would violate these values, and how can we reframe, redefine, or reconceptualize one or more values in order to integrate them?

Keep in mind that some desires cannot be integrated and should not be core values. When working with a group or team that has been tasked with the development of an organization's mission, you can keep core values manageable by telling the group that there can be only a limited number of such values. People will offer core value number 1, core value number 2, 3, 4, and 5, but, when someone wants to add core value number 6, I simply explain that, since there can be only five, one that is already on the list will have to be removed before a new one can be added. This process always sparks debate and discussion—a very healthy part of the process of discovering an organization's core values.

Purpose

Discovering an organization's purpose involves understanding at a very deep level why the organization exists. This is more than just what the organization does. It is why it does what it does. Consider the example of Innermotion, a survivor dance company that provides its clients—survivors of child and sexual abuse—with opportunities to perform in workshops as dance therapy. The casual observer might think that the purpose of the organization is to conduct workshops and to do performances. Actually, however, these are *not* the purpose of the organization; they are just activities that it conducts. To find out the true purpose of the organization, management needs to ask, "Why?"—and it needs to ask more than once.

Someone who asks why might receive the following response: "Well, we do it because survivors want us to do it." And, if then asked, "Why do they want us to do it?" the response might be, "They want us to do it because they're in pain." Finally, to push to the heart of why the organization does what it does, the specific question eventually arises: "What does doing this for them have to do with their pain?" The answer—the true purpose of the organization—is, "We exist to heal survivors from the trauma of sexual abuse." And, in this particular case, the organization actually has a dual mission: it is not just healing, but is also eradication, based on the belief that healing is central to breaking the cycle of abuse. Innermotion exists to prevent future abuse by healing potential perpetrators.

By going through this process of attempting to articulate the organization's purpose, making it more specific and then seeing if it would prevent you from taking actions that naturally fall within your organization's purpose, you describe the purpose by alternately narrowing and broadening it until it is just right. And, as people articulate the mission, it can continue to be tested by asking questions such as, "Do you get excited about this?" and "Is the importance of this aspiration self-evident?"

Goals

An organization can have all sorts of goals to accomplish all sorts of things, including financial targets, project milestones, program initiation and completion, and many more. But what goals are most important to an organization, and which ones are critical components of the organization's mission? Using the framework to discover an organization's most important goals leads to questions like the following: Where should this organization be five years from now, and what would be a real milestone in accomplishing that purpose or taking the organization in that direction? Do these goals really apply to the entire organization, or just to some subset of the organization? Are these goals really achievable (and, if not, what goals would be more realistic)?

But how can you know if a goal is really achievable or not? Let us say that you have a goal of writing a book that is going to be the best-selling *New York Times* fiction book ever. That is well and good, but what is the likelihood that you are actually going to be able to achieve this goal?

Unless you can write like Stephen King or John Grisham, I would guess that the probabilities are not very much in your favor. Indeed, given the difficulty that even well-known authors have achieving such an accomplishment, your chances of attaining this particular goal are likely to be quite low. Unrealistic goals are not particularly inspiring to people in an organization, because everybody knows that they probably will not be achieved. And if they know the goals probably will not be achieved, they will not even bother trying.

Goals that will be a part of an organization's mission should have at least a fifty-fifty chance of being achievable. People should say, "I think we can do that, but I don't quite know how we are going to yet." The most effective goals stretch individuals, and they make those individuals push hard to achieve them, but they are attainable. They are also concrete and often measurable. Without a level of specificity that allows people to know when they have achieved the goal, it is impossible to hold them accountable, and accountability is critical to the power of goals.

Vision

Vision comes from the answer to the question, what does the world look like in which we have achieved our primary goal? Far from the discipline needed to get at core values, vision is the place to be inclusive, expansive, enthusiastic, poetic, and passionate. Vision has to be compellingly rich, evocative. It does not have to be concise. It has to bring the organization members and key stakeholders in touch with the world they are striving to create and help them to believe that their effort and commitment can turn the possibility into reality. Says Robert Greenleaf in his essay "The Leadership Crisis," "The test of greatness of a dream is that it has the energy to lift people out of their moribund ways to a level of being and relating from which the future can be faced with more hope than most of us can summon today."[49]

One of my favorite examples of a great vision—and its relationship to the other elements of mission—comes from Dean & Deluca, the well-known New York specialty foods retailer. A number of years ago, I worked with top managers at the firm to help them reflect on and develop their mission. Their core values included a "passion for food of incomparable quality and taste" and the belief that "fine food should be enjoyed in its most authentic and original manner." They articulated the goal of being the "preeminent purveyor of fine food and related merchandise in the world." As we talked about what this would look like, the following vision emerged from the animated discussion:

> When people talk about fine food, Dean & Deluca will be mentioned in the same breath. The food and wine critics will write about Dean & Deluca and recognize our unique position as opinion leaders and the vanguard of emerging trends within the food culture. Our stores will be international food emporiums unlike any other stores in the world. Upon entering a Dean & Deluca market, the customer will be drawn in by the enticing aromas and vibrant colors of food, which is abundantly merchandised and elegantly displayed. Music will celebrate their arrival, and customers will be treated like guests in our home, with all the hospitality, friendliness, and generosity that implies. And like patrons entering a theatre, they will be entertained and engaged in the sensuality, romance, and magic that define Dean & Deluca.[50]

This image weaves a rich tapestry that was both retrospective and prospective. It was based on capturing the essence of the Dean & Deluca experience at existing stores, and it was also used by managers to define the experience of new stores as the company expanded to new locations around the country.

In the next chapter, we will closely examine the concept of strategy: what it is (and what it is not), and what it can do for the nonprofit organization. We will explore a framework for developing, articulating, and evaluating strategy, and learn how to apply it in practice.

2

Strategy

The Economic Logic

The Function and Importance of Strategy

Why does strategy matter? Strategy matters because it is the domain of knowledge that is fundamentally concerned with trying to understand, explain, and influence the success or failure of organizations. On the most basic level, this is survival (whether they live or die). On a broader level, this is performance. For private-sector organizations, the definition of performance is relatively simple: it is profitability or return on capital—in effect, the ability to create and capture economic value.[1]

Retrospectively, strategy is an *explanation for*, and, prospectively, is a *plan for*, attaining superior economic performance in an industry: surviving longer and achieving higher returns or profits than other organizations providing similar products or services. Thus, within the world of business, the motivation underlying the creation of strategy is a desire to outperform the market. As we shall see, strategy is also fundamentally about *choice*—a commitment to undertake one set of actions rather than another, for choice in the face of trade-offs is the basis for delivering unique sources of value that lead to above-average performance.[2]

The Function of Strategy in Nonprofit Organizations

In the case of a nonprofit organization, by definition, performance cannot be defined solely, or even primarily, in financial terms. Rather, it must be measured in terms of the social or environmental value that the organization creates—hopefully as specified by its mission. But strategy, I have argued, is essentially an economic logic, one explicitly tied to profitability and competition, leading some to question its relevance to nonprofits. Indeed, strategy and its basic premises are often viewed with suspicion by nonprofit leaders who, focusing on the primacy of their social (versus economic) purpose, tend to eschew the idea of competition to emphasize instead a cooperative stance toward other organizations in their industry.

Even though this initial reaction is understandable, given its business and military origins, strategy is not only relevant to nonprofits but also indispensable, for two reasons. First, though not the ultimate desideratum, financial outcomes and economic viability are essential to an organization's survival, whether it be a for-profit or a nonprofit. Every organization needs money to pay salaries, rent, utilities, and the other costs of its operations. Without money, an organization will die. Moreover, the ability of an organization to secure financial resources directly influences its capacity to undertake the activities necessary for it to fulfill its mission. Ask any group of nonprofit leaders what their greatest challenges and concerns are, and, reliably, the most common response is, "securing adequate funding." Second, competition is not a stance or an attitude. It is a function of scarcity of resources, especially money, and as such is a fact of life. To the extent that a nonprofit does not have *all* of the resources that it needs or wants to pursue its mission, then it is in competition with other organizations. Strategy makes mission possible.

Thus, the economic logic of strategy is just as important to nonprofits as it is to business. It is more useful, however, (and perhaps philosophically more acceptable) for nonprofits to reframe profitability simply as a form of *prosperity*—the abundance or sufficiency of resources for the organization's work and pursuit of goals. Prosperity gives an organization what Robert Burgelman and Andy Grove refer to as "control over its destiny."[3] This is why strategy matters for nonprofit organizations.

As a point of contrast, an organization that lacks prosperity has considerably less control over its destiny, because the desperate pursuit of money limits its ability to be selective in accepting funding for programs or activities that are consistent with its mission. The inevitable result is "mission creep," the blurring of an organization's mission over time as it seeks to take on activities outside the scope of its core competencies. For example, as government funding dried up in the 1980s and 1990s, many arts organizations expanded into education or youth programs to secure funding. Although we may value youth education at a societal level, the problem at the organizational level is that such programs pull attention away from the nonprofit's core activities, and often require more resources than anticipated. Ultimately, this dynamic erodes the organization's competitiveness, as well as its ability to fulfill its mission. Even when nonprofits are able to resist the temptation to pursue funding opportunistically, the simple lack of resources can strangle their ability to invest in or sustain the organizational capacity necessary to be effective. Hence, for nonprofits, the notion of prosperity provides a useful analogue to profit in the private sector.[4]

Returning to the simplest manifestation of performance, survival, the outcome of economic failure is no different for a nonprofit than for a business. There was a time when the death of a nonprofit was rare. In fact, the prospect of imminent death has served as a great rallying cry for many major fund-raising appeals. But, more recently, in areas from performing arts to social services, outright failures are becoming more common.

Consider the demise of the Oakland Symphony. Founded in Oakland, California, in 1933, the Oakland Symphony had a distinguished history of artistic achievements until—to the surprise of many fans of the venerable organization—facing a deficit of almost $750,000 (more than twenty-seven times larger than forecast) on a budget of just over $2.5 million, it declared bankruptcy in August 1986. Unable to reach an agreement for wage and contract concessions with the musicians union, it subsequently filed for liquidation on September 12, 1986. The explanation of the failure is a complicated one, detailed in a report, *Autopsy of an Orchestra*, prepared for funders of the symphony.[5] However, two key factors stand out: unrealistic growth expectations and blurring of the artistic missions and strategy: "While quality of the artistic product did not contribute significantly to the symphony's downfall, quantity of product did. The number of concerts increased far beyond the public's demonstrated ability to absorb them, and packaging and repackaging of the concerts into a confusing array of series served to cloud the orchestra's artistic purpose and identity."[6]

The facts illustrate the magnitude of this problem. Beginning in 1970, under the leadership of a new music director, the symphony expanded its concerts dramatically, going from thirty-five performances in the 1973–1974 season to seventy-three planned for the 1986–1987 season. Closely related to this expansion of quantity was a diffusion of content that increased the competition between Oakland and its major rival across the bay: "The Oakland Symphony lost its programming niche and its distinct artistic mission after the departure of [music director] Gerhard Samuel in 1971. Under [his successor], the shift away from the contemporary music focus of the Samuel years to a more standard programming of traditional symphonic classics blurred the distinction between the Oakland Symphony and the San Francisco Symphony."[7]

Clearly, there are deeper explanations and contributing factors—poor labor relations, a costly facility renovation, and deteriorating demographics and economic conditions, to name but a few—but the fact remains that the Oakland Symphony posted a string of deficits in nine out of its last ten years of existence. This is the very essence of a lack of prosperity. Could the strategy framework presented in this chapter have helped save the Oakland Symphony? Maybe, maybe not, but it certainly provides a compelling explanation of the economic decline that led to its failure.[8]

In an increasingly competitive environment, survival is a very real concern for many nonprofits, and strategy is a key determinant of prosperity (or lack thereof) and, hence, survival. Thus, even for nonprofits, strategy has relevance, even though, or perhaps because, its primary concern is economic. So, if we accept the importance and relevance of strategy, the next step is to understand what it is and whence it came.

Historical Roots of Strategy

The notion of strategy has a very long and rich tradition that extended centuries before it ever entered the lexicon of business and, indeed, before management even became a field of endeavor. Classic conceptions of strategy emerged from a military context, and in recent years seminal works such as Sun Tzu's *The Art of War* and Carl Von Clausewitz's *On War* have resurfaced to influence the thinking of strategic management scholars.[9] These early notions of strategy stress its essence as a plan distinct from tactics.

In the *Oxford English Dictionary* (OED), *strategy* is defined as follows: "The art of projecting and directing the larger military movements and operations of a campaign. Usually distinguished from tactics, which is the art of handling forces in battle or in the immediate presence of the enemy." A second, more general, definition in the OED focuses on "circumstances of competition or conflict" and strategy as a "plan for successful action based on the rationality and interdependence of the moves of the opposing participants."[10]

As nations industrialized, business became a new arena where competition flourished. Drawing on military conceptions of high-level plans, the field of strategic management sought to develop more specific descriptions of the features of "plans" that were relatively likely to lead to actual success in business. Early formalizations highlighted the role of strategy as the tool of the general manager and the mechanism of integration of functional policies in the firm. Andrews, for example, framed strategy in terms of the "pattern of goals, policies and actions that define the way an organization positions itself in its environment."[11] Another pioneer, Igor Ansoff, observed, "Business firms whose behavior is totally unplanned and unguided do not survive for very long, except in monopolistic or subsidizing environments. Strategic behavior of firms which do survive is guided and managed, however well or poorly."[12]

Although a complete history of strategy is beyond the scope of this chapter, it is important to note that major advances in the conception of strategy are associated with the entry of microeconomic theory into the field. This is where the present conception has its roots.[13] And this is also where—in part to avoid the confusion with popular usage of the term *strategy* as any plan for reaching a goal—the modifiers *business*, *competitive*, and *corporate* were linked to the term strategy in order to denote the specific usage of *strategy* in the context of business and market competition. Throughout this text, we will use the term *strategy* to refer to this domain.

Confusion about the Meaning of *Strategy*

Unfortunately, there is a tremendous amount of confusion and imprecision in the use of the term *strategy*, and this confusion exists just as much in the private sector as it does in the nonprofit sector. Despite required courses in strategy at virtually every top MBA program, a number of the faculty who have written the textbooks for and teach these courses have lamented the legions of professional managers who do not understand the meaning of *strategy*, much less its application.[14] An example from my own experience illustrates this confusion.

A number of years ago, I consulted with members of the strategic planning department of a *Fortune* 500 firm to help them articulate their group's role in supporting the firm. As part of this process, I interviewed a number of senior general managers of this well-respected and profitable firm. But, when I asked them about their strategy, not a single manager could articulate anything remotely resembling a competitive strategy. One executive asked if I meant "company strategy." After I replied, "Yes," he responded that the company had no strategy at the firm level because they were a "product-driven firm." I then asked for an example of a product strategy, to which he replied, "It depends what you want to do with every single product and what you are trying to accomplish. But the strategy, there is no strategy for a product; there are goals and objectives for the product, and then strategy is to help you achieve what you want to do on the goals. And definitely, there are several strategies for every single product." Somewhat nonplussed, I kept probing and asked for an example of such strategies, to which he replied, "Let's say you want to have a product where you want to position it [for a specific use] in a particular segment. And then you will use strategies to say, in order to reach this, we need to focus more on [consumer] education, so we build a strategy that involves [consumer] education, or about [distribution channel] communication, depending on what you want to do."

The problem was that this manager (and in fact the company) lacked a fundamental understanding of strategy—what it really was and how it might impact the organization. Moreover, when we began to actually do an analysis of the company's strategy for a major part of its business, using the framework presented in this chapter, the executives realized by the end of the discussion that they, in fact, had no strategy at all, and that the business was likely in very serious trouble. Fortunately, the firm was in an industry that was structurally attractive, or fairly profitable even for the average incumbent.

No doubt, those of us who do research on and teach about strategy are implicated in this confusion. Even a cursory scan of management journals illustrates the proliferation of alternative conceptions of *strategy*, including strategy as *hustle, decision making, stretch,* and *revolution,* to name but a few.[15]

The point here is that, even in the private sector, the understanding of strategy is highly imperfect. Why is this important to nonprofits? It is important because nonprofit leaders routinely get advice about strategy from board members and funders who come from the business sector. These men and women are presumed to know what they are talking about when they promote strategy or other common business ideas—whether or not they really do. The fact is that there are varied understandings of strategy among individuals, and nonprofit leaders can receive inconsistent advice from different businesspeople. And, even if the advice they receive is consistent, it may very well be flawed because it is based on an inaccurate or incomplete model of strategy. To add insult to injury, we have not even considered whether or not the businesspeople advising nonprofit leaders are able to translate their model of strategy to the nonprofit sector. Quite often, they cannot.

What Strategy Is Not and What Strategy Should Not Be Expected to Do

Before we consider exactly what strategy is, as well as its implications for managing the nonprofit organization, it is instructive to briefly consider what strategy is *not*. Sometimes people mistake various artifacts or statements for a strategy. These include formal planning documents (such as five-year plans, long-term objectives, and business plans); public statements about the company's strategy by the CEO and other senior executives; financial or growth objectives (such as earnings per share, or market share); and popular slogans (such as "We focus on the customer" or "Quality is our strategy").

Despite widespread beliefs to the contrary, none of these is necessarily a strategy, because strategy is defined by a pattern of concrete choices and actions. Hence, a strategic or long-range plan or speech by the CEO may be consistent with or may inform the actual strategy, but it is not itself an actual strategy. Similarly, despite the reverence with which pundits cite the now famous "strategy" often associated with Jack Welch during his tenure at General Electric—be number 1 or number 2 in every business or get out— being number 1 or 2 is not a strategy: it is the result of a strategy.

Focusing on customers or quality are generally good things to do, but, since ignoring customers or quality are not exactly viable alternative "strategies," neither of these ideals makes choices, or provides much direction or assistance for making operational decisions. The problem with these slogans is that they are platitudes that may make people feel virtuous but which do not provide enough specificity to tell an organization how it is really going to achieve superior prosperity.

So what exactly is strategy? We now turn our attention to answering this question.

The Functions of Strategy

The next section develops a precise definition of what strategy is, but first it is instructive to outline what strategy should be expected to do for an organization. Given the fundamental relationship between strategy and performance, the primary goals of a strategy are (1) to provide a way of understanding (diagnosing) organizational performance, and (2) to provide a coherent and actionable plan through which an organization can achieve superior performance. Again, in the corporate context, superior performance means outperforming competitors with respect to long-run profitability. In a nonprofit context, it means increasing long-run prosperity, along with a greater likelihood of survival. Any such plan must be based—implicitly or explicitly—on a theory about the determinants of performance and how to shape or manipulate those determinants in order to produce higher levels of performance.

To lead to superior performance, strategy must reflect an accurate understanding of the environment and the dynamics of competition. Similarly, it must reflect accurate assumptions about the relationship between organizational actions and performance, given the context. And, to become reality, it has to be translated into concrete choices. Strategy must provide a guide for decision making and action; otherwise it is no more than a "marketing slogan that will not withstand competition."[16]

Even a robust strategy predicated on valid assumptions and an accurate picture of the environment will not lead to better performance unless it is implemented. Implementation has, within the field of strategic management, attracted its own abundance of attention and research. Rather than detail this literature here, I summarize the essential features of it by noting the following: organizations consist of hundreds, thousands, and even hundreds of thousands of individuals. The collective effort and decisions of these individuals must be focused and coordinated on a consistent basis for the organization's plan to come to fruition. For the strategy to accomplish this objective, it must be clear, broadly understood, and widely accepted within the organization. Only then can the strategy provide a guide for actions on a day-to-day basis that will lead to the achievement of competitive advantage.

In the realm of business, it is generally accepted that there are two broad classes of determinants of firm performance: the nature of the industry in which a firm competes, and the characteristics of the firm itself. More specifically, industrial economists have studied the structure of industries and the competitiveness of the firm, and found that industry accounts for approximately 20 percent of the variability in firm performance.[17] Though a wide range of industry variables have been studied, the most commonly accepted integrative framework is Porter's five forces framework. We will discuss the structural analysis of industries in the next chapter, but for now it is sufficient to note that strategy must also deal with the challenges posed by an organization's competitive environment. In the present chapter, we focus on the firm level, where the most central concept has been competitive advantage.[18] Competitive advantage is evidenced by above-average profitability (i.e., performance) and is central to business or competitive strategy. *Competitive strategy* refers to how a firm competes in an industry, particularly how it positions itself relative to competitors. Throughout this text, when I use the term *strategy*, I am talking about *competitive strategy*.

In chapter 5, we will also explore a second type of strategy, *corporate strategy*, which "refers to the overarching strategy of the multi-business enterprise, including the range of businesses in which it participates and how it manages interrelationships among those units."[19] But, for the most part, we are going to focus on competitive strategy, because, even though nonprofits are increasingly competing across multiple activities and businesses, corporate strategy is above all founded on sound competitive strategy.

The Definition and Elements of Strategy

On a descriptive level, strategy is a pattern of intentions and actions that defines how an organization competes in an industry. It is the economic logic that governs performance—specifically, financial outcomes of profitability and prosperity. Strategy reflects the implicit or explicit assumptions and rationale of an organization's approach to competing in a marketplace. Normatively, a good strategy must be *complete* (meaning fully developed and specified to guide operational choices—*execution*—which will be defined in detail in chapter 4) and *robust* (meaning that it will produce the expected levels of performance, all other things being equal).

A complete strategy contains three elements: scope, competitive advantage, and logic.[20] *Scope* is the range of products and services the firm will offer, the customers and markets where it will offer them, and the types of activities it will undertake. *Competitive advantage* is the basis on which the firm will win against competitors in the marketplace, and *logic* is the explanation of how it will achieve a competitive advantage. Although there are occasionally other components included, or labels used, in definitions of *strategy*, these three central elements appear consistently throughout the mainstream strategic management literature.[21] In the sections that follow, we shall take a close look at each of these elements.

Scope

Scope describes where an organization will compete. It specifies who the customers are, what products or services are offered, and what activities the organization performs. Scope can be defined along a number of different dimensions:

- *Segment*, including product varieties and customer groups
- *Geography*, or areas, regions, or countries in which a firm competes in a coordinated fashion
- *Industry*, or related businesses in which the firm competes in a coordinated fashion
- *Vertical scope*, or activities typically performed in house or by independent suppliers

Although scope gives the "who, what, when, and where" of an organization's strategy, it does not tell *why* the organization's customers would prefer it over other organizations providing the same or similar products or services. This is the role of competitive advantage.

Competitive Advantage

Competitive advantage resides in the unique sources of value that the organization offers its customers. It explains why an identifiable group of customers (defined by the organization's scope) will prefer its products or services to those offered by other organizations. Although there are many different specific advantages, like performance, durability, and selection, Michael Porter, in his seminal work on strategy, identifies two generic types of competitive advantage: *cost leadership*, which involves providing equivalent benefits to a customer at a lower price, and *differentiation*, which involves providing unique benefits to a customer that justify a higher price. Both create value because the price paid by customers, by definition, must exceed the cost of delivering the product or services. These generic forms of competitive advantage, in turn, lead to greater profitability and prosperity.[22]

Cost Leadership. Perhaps one of the most cited examples of a cost-based competitive advantage is Wal-Mart. Indeed, it is also a dramatic example of the magnitude of the economic value that can be created and captured through sustainable competitive advantage. When Sam Walton died thirty years after opening the first Wal-Mart in Rogers, Arkansas, in 1962, the company had delivered over two decades an average of 35 percent annual sales growth and 33 percent return on equity. In 2003 Wal-Mart was the largest corporation in the world, with 20 million customers a day, annual sales of $245 billion, and profits of $8 billion.[23] Why are so many people attracted to Wal-Mart? It is simple: Wal-Mart has a reputation for consistently offering the lowest possible prices on a wide array of products, from groceries, to clothing, to household goods, to CDs and DVDs, and much, much more.

A publicized event illustrates Wal-Mart's appeal poignantly. The day after Thanksgiving 2003, a Florida woman was trampled by a mob of fellow shoppers at Wal-Mart while she was trying to purchase a DVD player on sale. Traditionally the biggest shopping day of the year, November 29 was a record sales day for Wal-Mart, with the company generating $1.52 billion nationally.[24] Reflecting on the event a week later, a *New York Times* columnist commented: "When a Florida woman claimed to have been trampled in a holiday mob of Wal-Mart shoppers trying to get DVD players for $29.87, people across America were shocked—not at man's inhumanity to man, but by the price."[25] It is hard to imagine a more fitting setting for this story, had it been scripted as part of a movie. By definition, sustained profitability and low prices imply a low-cost advantage.

The billion-dollar question in the case of Wal-Mart is, how is it able to achieve such low costs? First, because of its large size, Wal-Mart is able to take advantage of huge economies of scale. For example, the retailer's aggressive negotiation of prices and terms with its suppliers (manufacturers) lowers the costs of goods sold. It can extract low prices because, in many cases, Wal-Mart is a supplier's largest customer (23 percent of Clorox sales, for example, are made through Wal-Mart, as well as 20 percent of Revlon's, 20 percent of R. J. Reynolds Tobacco's, and 17 percent of Procter & Gamble's).[26] In addition, Wal-Mart's distribution network is quite possibly the most efficient of any retailer's in the United States. The company uses a hub-and-spoke model built around multiple distribution centers. As a result, Wal-Mart is able to devote only 10 percent of the total square footage of its stores to storing inventory, as opposed to an industry average of 25 percent. This leads to very fast product turnover, enabling Wal-Mart to sell 70 percent of its merchandise before the company pays for it. Finally, Wal-Mart pioneered the use of automation to track purchases and inventory, linking up directly with more than 3,600 vendors to place orders, track inventory, make forecasts, and transfer funds through sophisticated electronic data interchange (EDI) programs. The use of EDI makes all of these functions happen much more quickly than they could using the old-fashioned paper-based systems, while dramatically reducing errors, transaction costs, paperwork, and archiving needs.

Although there are other factors that contribute to the company's competitive advantage (such as positional advantage as related to the historical strategic choice of locating stores in small rural communities), the appeal to consumers lies in Wal-Mart's ability to use its low-cost position to offer value through low prices in the form of programs like "Every Day Low Price," "Rollback," and "Special Buy."

Differentiation. There are a variety of ways of achieving cost leadership by being the lower-cost provider (*cost advantage*), and there are even more ways of being differentiated from the competition (*differentiation advantage*). It is important to note that differentiation does not mean just being different: it means being different in ways that are *valued* by customers and that at least some subset of them within your scope are willing to pay a premium price for, a price that exceeds the cost of creating the differences.

Consider the example of British Airways. Between 1980 and 1990, the airline underwent a dramatic change that *Business Week* celebrated as a transformation from "bloody awful to bloody awesome."[27] In 1981 and 1982, the company suffered losses of £240 million. By 1991 its profit was close to £167 million and growing by 337 percent to £728 million in 1996—this during a period when the highly competitive global airline industry was losing billions of dollars.[28] In addition, this formerly government-owned airline completed a successful privatization, jumped to first place in customer service, and won four airline-of-the-year awards.[29] The key to understanding British Airways' successful transformation is its competitive advantage based on differentiation.

British Airways introduced a singular focus on customer service, especially in the market for premium transatlantic air travel, in business and first class. But what did this mean? Aside from how customers were treated by employees, it involved the installation of industry-leading amenities in business and first class. The airline was one of the first to have seats that reclined fully into beds, allowing passengers to lie down and sleep. Each passenger had his or her own private video player where the passenger could select from ten different movies, and meals were offered from a gourmet four-star menu. Further, British Airways had special departure and arrival logistics, including a passenger lounge stocked with complimentary cocktails, sandwiches, and hors d'oeuvres. Upon arrival at London's Heathrow Airport, customers were ushered to a special customs and immigration lounge where the formalities were handled expeditiously and comfortably for the airline's coveted business travelers.

British Airways' chairman, Sir Colin Marshall, described the airline's choices:

> We also designed a whole new service—our Sleeper Service—for First Class customers flying long routes: They can eat a real dinner in the lounge before boarding and change into "sleeper suits" (pajamas) on the plane. Upon arriving in Britain, they can use our arrivals lounges, which are a major innovation. They're places where our First Class and Club World customers can get messages left overnight while they were in the air; have breakfast; read a newspaper; shower; get a manicure, haircut, or shave; have clothes pressed; and then catch a taxi or subway or train into town. We maintain full arrival-lounge facilities at Heathrow and Gatwick. . . . Our main arrivals lounges at the London airports are used by an average of around 200 customers each day. They unquestionably played a significant part in boosting our premium business by 9% during our last fiscal year, which ended March 31. The Sleeper Service has been similarly well received. Since its introduction in February 1995, First Class bookings between New York and London, for instance, have increased by as much as 25%. To varying extents, competitors are copying these initiatives, but British Airways enjoys the halo effect that comes from being first.[30]

Through these and other practices, British Airways was able to create a product that was truly differentiated—unique in ways that customers valued and for which they were willing to pay a premium.

All of these extras were costly, but the key to differentiation is getting a price that more than offsets the cost. During the mid-1990s, a regular advance-purchase coach fare from New York to London was in the $200–$300 range, business class was close to $5,000, and first class $9,000–$10,000. British Airways led the market for these classes of service and, more important, devoted a larger proportion of the space in its aircraft to these premium classes of service than most of its major competitors. The result: industry-leading profitability.

Sources of Competitive Advantage. As there are two generic *types* of competitive advantage—cost leadership and differentiation—there are two generic *sources* of competitive advantage: capability and position. *Capability* is the ability to solve problems involved in the production of high-quality or low-cost goods and services (or those that are both high quality and low cost). Such capability within an organization is generally very broadly based and a part of the organization's fabric, and it reflects the existence of skills and knowledge that allow the organization to reliably perform key activities better, faster, or more cheaply than competitors. A good example is Apple Computer's capability for innovative design that integrates ease of use with sophisticated technical functionality. Another commonly cited example is Disney's capability in the area of animation.

An essential aspect of a capability is that it is not dependent upon single, or small groups of, individuals; instead, it has been institutionalized in the organization's routines and structures. At the organizational level, the loss of one person, or even a group of people, will not change the organization's capability. For example, if the Memorial Sloan-Kettering Cancer Center were to lose one or even a few top physicians, it would still maintain its world-renowned capability in the diagnosis and treatment of diseases.

Also, because capabilities reflect know-how that is often tacit and widely distributed, they tend to be difficult for competitors to imitate and, hence, are more likely to be sustainable over time. On the individual level, think of a surgeon's skills and knowledge, which cannot easily be copied by someone off the street, even if he or she were able to observe what the surgeon did very closely and in great detail. Indeed, the inherent difficulty of transferring such capabilities intentionally, even to other specialists in the profession, is reflected in the long and elaborate apprenticeship and training methods of the medical field.

Position stems from the external relationship of the organization to its buyers, suppliers, or competitors. For example, organizations that have situated themselves as a unique intermediary between a buyer and a product have this source of competitive advantage. Consider a general store in a harbor that is located right at the dock. It may have the same goods as other stores located inland but, because it is geographically located where customers will have easier access to the store, it has the advantage of convenience and accessibility. Customers who care will pay a premium not to have to leave their boats and travel inland to other stores with lower prices.

Position in a network of relationships (rather than physical position) can also lead to competitive advantage. For example, having access to distribution or exclusive customer relationships has this effect. Consider a petrochemical firm that has captive retail channels in a region or country. This can confer a cost advantage (based on economies of scale in distribution logistics) or differentiation advantage (based on brand advertising and reputation or accessibility) for its retail fuel products. Although there are other factors that can serve as the basis for a positional advantage, the important point to note about this source of competitive advantage is that it is more closely tied to the attributes of the firm relative to its position in an industry, and less closely tied to features or attributes of its products or services in the way that capability-based advantages tend to be.

Distinguishing between Competitive Advantage and Its Sources. Competitive advantage is the unique value created for buyers who are willing to pay for it, framed in terms that remain close to the language of the customer. It is often confused, however, with *sources* of competitive advantage, the antecedents that enable the organization to create that value in the first place. Competitive advantage can have multiple sources: design capability, production processes, workers' diligence, proprietary technology, and much more. All contribute and are essential, but all are *sources* of competitive advantage—what Porter calls *drivers*—not the competitive advantage itself.[31]

Why is this important? Because when something a company does no longer creates value—and this can happen as industries change over time—it becomes a waste of resources. Identifying historical *sources* of competitive advantage as the competitive advantage *itself* contributes to the problem of means becoming ends in themselves. This in turn creates the potential for precious organizational resources to be wasted. Consider organizations that continue to invest in manufacturing technology, even when it no longer contributes to the company's ability to deliver something that customers value (i.e., products that arrive faster, perform better, or cost less than the competition). Or consider organizations that sink significant sums of money into quality-improvement efforts, even when buyers no longer value the incremental durability of the company's products.

The distinction here is that some of what customers value—either as a result of a capability (what an organization does well), or possibly as the result of a competitive position—are not in and of themselves competitive advantages. Rather, they are *antecedents* that allow the organization to create or deliver a product or service that is valued by a buyer. As much as it is important to understand the antecedent and how it relates to the competitive advantage, it should not be confused with the competitive advantage itself. For example, one might list Wal-Mart's large scale as a competitive advantage, but it would more correctly be classified as a source or antecedent of a cost advantage—resulting from the economies of scale—that allows the company to sell products at lower prices or obtain bigger margins at comparable prices. It is not the scale itself that is the competitive advantage, but the relative value (combination of price and quality in comparison to available alternatives).

A useful test for identifying the real competitive advantage is to ask, "Is there a customer we can identify that cares about X per se?" In the case of "large scale," the answer is probably "No," and hence it is a source rather than competitive advantage. Similarly, if one were to ask a Wal-Mart customer in a small town in rural Arkansas why she chooses to shop at the store, the customer is not likely to cite its locations in small underserved rural markets like her own town. Instead she will more likely talk about the fact that it is cheaper and has a better selection than her local options, and that it is more convenient than the stores in the big city that may be hours away.

Wal-Mart's competitive advantage, the reason that it is more attractive (cheaper and more convenient), is in part because of its geographic locations—and the fact that it "got there first"—but, again, these are the antecedents rather than the competitive advantage itself. The lesson here is that it is helpful analytically to understand where in the causal sequence the elements that create value actually lie. Is it at the end of the causal chain (i.e., in something that is identified by customers as valuable), or is it something that is logically prior but that enables the organization to infuse its product or service with attributes valued by customers? To arrive at the answer to this question, we need to first unbundle the causal chain that produces the ultimate sources of competitive advantage.

Finally, in thinking about the relationship between generic advantages of cost and differentiation, and capabilities and positions, one must keep in mind that cost and differentiation are broad *types* of competitive advantage, whereas capabilities and positions are *sources* of competitive advantage. The fundamental difference is one of where they lie in the chain of causality.

Actual versus Intended Competitive Advantage. In talking about competitive advantage—particularly when managers are analyzing their own organization —there may be a discrepancy between what people *want* their competitive advantage to be, and what the current competitive advantage really *is*. Because we want strategy to provide a guide to the future, as well as an understanding of the past and present, it can be helpful to draw an explicit distinction between an organization's *intended* and its *actual* competitive advantage.

Let us say, for example, that we are leading an organization that currently has a competitive advantage because of our superior customer service, but we would also like to achieve a competitive advantage based on some specific dimensions of product quality. The question then becomes, "What is the new or expanded logic that will allow us to achieve an intended competitive advantage based on quality?"

The answer to this question will probably reflect resource allocation decisions and policies different from those that are currently being implemented to create and sustain a customer-service-based competitive advantage. Being clear about the intended versus the actual competitive advantage is the first step to achieving it, but the organization also needs to account for implication of choices that are necessary to build a new source of competitive advantage. For example, can the firm increase quality and maintain service levels? Are there trade-offs? If so, how will these be made?

Real versus Imagined Competitive Advantage. Another point to note about competitive advantage is that the senior managers of an organization will often generate a much longer list of competitive advantages than a competitor or a knowledgeable customer. This happens because of a manager's tendency to focus on the effort or investment he or she makes to create advantages, as well as the strengths and competencies of the organization. These are all salient to the person trying to build them, but customers focus on what they value, and competitors focus on what customers value and their own choices about how to satisfy customers. Not everything that is unique about an organization is (or is a source of) competitive advantage. Indeed, not everything an organization does well translates into competitive advantage. For something to be a competitive advantage, it has to both be something that an organization does better than its competitors, *and* be something that matters to an identifiable customer who will pay for it.

To determine which is which when we are presented with the typical self-generated list of competitive advantages for a particular organization, we need to ask this question: "To whom does this matter?" For any perceived advantage to pass the test, there should be an identifiable group of buyers who for each such "competitive advantage" will say, "One of the reasons I choose this organization over its competitors is because of attribute X," where attribute X is one of the competitive advantages listed.

Logic

Finally, *logic* answers the question, "Why will the strategy work?" To do this it must make explicit the causal assumptions about the relationships between the organization's choices and behavior, the consequences of this behavior, and the interaction between these consequences and the world in which the firm operates (i.e., the environment). To be compelling, the logic must describe these choices at a very concrete level.[32] Moreover, the logic should be transparent enough that an independent observer could judge for himself or herself whether the strategy is likely to work given the state of the world.[33]

Thinking through logic involves unpacking the relationships between the key operational choices (i.e., execution), and competitive advantage. How will the organization be designed and managed so as to create a competitive advantage, which will produce the resources necessary to sustain and grow the organization? The generic structure of logic is captured in figure 2.1:

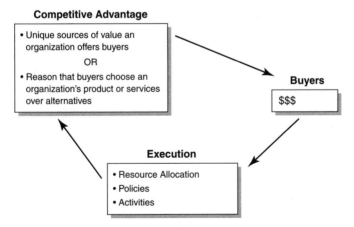

Figure 2.1. Generic logic.

Over time, this circle becomes a virtuous one in which the competitive advantage is strengthened through learning, establishing a reputation, and continued investment of a portion of the resources generated by the competitive advantage in the organizational capabilities and the competitive position that sustain and enhance it.

City Year, discussed in chapter 1, is a Boston-based youth program that provides opportunities for a diverse group of young people—from seventeen to twenty-four years old—to participate in a "year of full-time, rigorous community service, leadership development, and civic engagement." The organization seeks to "demonstrate, improve, and promote the concept of national service as a means for building a stronger democracy."[34] The central program for accomplishing these goals is the City Year National Youth Corps, a ten-month program in which participants engage in a variety of community-service activities, including serving as mentors, helping to run after-school programs, and leading children in other City Year programs. City Year places a significant emphasis on responsible citizenship and embracing diversity.

In this section, I will use City Year as an example for exploring the nature of logic, the explanation for why a strategy will work—including the key assumptions about cause-and-effect relationships, as well as the nature of key actors (buyers, competitors, suppliers, and others). One of the compelling features of City Year is that, from a strategic point of view, its competitive advantage is relatively clear. The young people who participate in the program, their parents, public officials who embrace the program, and corporate leaders who fund the program uniformly praise its positive impact on participants, as well as on communities and donors.

In the early 1990s, City Year provided a youth development and educational experience (through community service, to be more specific) for youth from seventeen to twenty-one years old in the greater Boston area.[35] Depending on how one defines the industry (e.g., education, youth development, community service), City Year was faced with a host of competitors and substitutes. To prosper in this environment, the organization needed a competitive advantage. As City Year evolved, this advantage turned out to be its unique and profound transformative impact on the youth in its program and the communities it served. Just as important was City Year's ability to engage corporate funders in ways that were much more meaningful than the typical volunteer or philanthropic activity, ways that directly tapped into their passion and idealism, and that also turned out to be transformative.

Given the abundance of public attention, scrutiny, press coverage, and introspection focused on City Year, it is relatively easy to identify City Year's strategy in hindsight. However, imagine looking at City Year in 1992 and thinking prospectively about how it would (and whether it could) succeed in achieving its goals of expanding across the country and serving as a model of national service. It may well have contemplated, "Do we really believe that it can? Why should City Year expect to be able to secure the funding that it needs to do this?" These are the questions that logic needs to address.

In order to articulate City Year's logic, we next need to understand how the organization produces its transformative impact on youth, community, and funders. Specifically, as a result of their year of service, Corps members gain confidence, experience a strong sense of community and esprit de corps, develop valuable skills, and mature as citizens. The program also has a positive impact on communities: whether by way of renewed hope and optimism in beleaguered elementary schools, or the tangible changes in cleaning up neglected community spaces. In communities where City Year's young people volunteer, the people in these neighborhoods recognize and experience the positive impact. Finally, the corporations that fund the program, as well as their employees, report feeling a direct sense of connection to the positive impact on the youth, as well as on the communities in which they serve. They experience a sense of satisfaction and engagement that comes from having an intimate connection with City Year, its staff, the young Corps members, and, most important, the community service activities fundamental to what the organization stands for.

So how does the logic work? First of all, there is the buyer—actually, two important categories of buyers: the "clients," or youth, who sign up for the City Year program, and the corporations and public officials that fund them. Who these buyers are is defined by City Year's scope. In this particular case, the scope is broad, including all youth aged seventeen to twenty-four and, at least initially, all businesses and private-sector organizations. What are the needs of these two constituencies that City Year manages to satisfy in ways that are unique? The needs of the youth are personal growth and development; the needs of the funders are to contribute to the positive impact on local youth, as well as the sense of satisfaction derived from being involved with an effort that is experienced as meaningful and socially beneficial.

The next question is, "How does City Year create this competitive advantage?" Or, "What is it about the way City Year is organized and managed that produces the transformative effects on youth, communities, and funders?" The organization does this through a set of resource allocation decisions and policies and activities that allow it to have a positive impact on the youth, the funders, and the communities. Resource allocation decisions include an extensive investment in training and education, and extensive recruiting (in particular, a very sophisticated and tailored approach to recruiting Corps members that takes into account the differing needs and concerns of youth from different backgrounds—for example, inner-city, at-risk youth as opposed to affluent, suburban, college-bound kids). There are smaller, but nevertheless important, resource allocation decisions, such as investment in uniforms and socialization of the Corps' members in community building, as well as public relations and active promotion of City Year and its cause.

There is also a set of policies and activities that contribute to the competitive advantage: for example, promoting staff members from within the organization from the ranks of Corps members, and an uncompromising commitment to maintain the diversity of the Corps—despite often quite significant public pressures to narrow the focus to at-risk youth. In addition, there are policies and activities that support the engagement of corporate sponsors. For example, City Year founders claim that, when raising money, they ensured the goal "was never to just get a check."[36] The Corps also has a very explicit reliance on rituals, myths, stories, and routines (like daily calisthenics) that convey and inculcate the values and purpose of the organization. Finally, there are policies in place to promote innovation and experimentation at the project level and to capture and formalize this learning and disseminate it throughout the organization.

This combination of resource allocation decisions and policies contributes to the creation of a unique culture essential to City Year's ability to impact youth in the way it does, because of its strength and capacity for disseminating and enforcing values among Corps members. These decisions and activities also contribute to broadening and building City Year's reputation for having a significant impact in the community. This means that, even if someone in the business community had no direct experience with City Year, he or she would be very likely, given City Year's visibility in Boston, to know of the program's reputation.

So, above and beyond activities designed to actually produce positive impact in the community, City Year undertakes and invests in activities designed to cultivate its reputation by making sure that everyone knows about this impact. Perhaps the classic example of this stress on reputation occurred in 1991, when it engaged the attention of the national news media, including CNN and NBC, and, ultimately, the interest of then presidential candidate Bill Clinton.

It is also helpful in understanding the process that creates the competitive advantage to focus on some intermediate outcome, such as quality of service provided to its community partners (organizations for whom City Year performs its service projects). This focus is essential because of the meaningful impact that the service must have if it is to serve as a source of pride and accomplishment for Corps members, as well as ensure a steady stream of opportunities for service projects. In addition, City Year's competitive advantage derives in part from its strong culture, which is essential to its unique ability to shape the attitudes and behavior of a diverse group of young Corps members.

In sum, there are a host of operational choices that City Year makes on an ongoing basis in order to ensure it is able to execute its strategy and, in particular, to create and sustain its competitive advantage. These include specific activities, policies, and resource allocation decisions that can be grouped into broad categories of culture building (e.g., calisthenics and uniforms), organization building (recruiting and training Corps and staff), reputation building (public relations and lobbying), funder engagement (service projects for corporate donors), and service delivery (selecting and monitoring projects for community partners). These are all necessary to ensure the quality of City Year's service projects, its transformative impact on youth, and its unique impact on funders, as seen in figure 2.2.

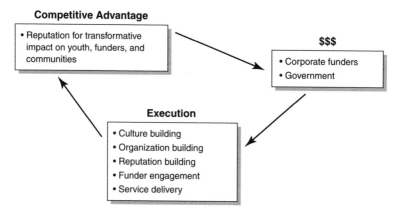

Figure 2.2. City Year: basic logic.

Although still somewhat abstract, the logic is more compelling than a simple description of City Year's competitive advantage, because it allows us to unpack the complex array of activities it performs that transform youth, communities, and its supporters. In return for this demonstrable impact, buyers continue to support City Year: youth seek to participate in the program in unprecedented numbers, demand far exceeds the number of slots available, and the funders in Boston have contributed at levels that have allowed the program to expand far beyond its humble beginnings, raising its profile to the national level. This funding is in turn invested in key activities that reinforce the very competitive advantage that begat those resources. This is the essence and purpose of logic.

Although we turn in the next chapter to understanding and analyzing the environment in which strategies are created, in chapter 4 I will elaborate on the concept of logic and provide more concrete examples of the choices involved in execution.

3

Industry Analysis

As we discussed in the previous chapter, there are two basic types of influences on organizational performance: (1) firm and business-unit-level determinants (i.e., strategy and competitive position) and (2) environmental determinants.[1] In the business world, the major locus of attention with respect to the environment has been industry characteristics.[2] The emphasis on industry characteristics stems in part from the theoretical orientation of classical industrial economics (or industrial organization) toward market or industry structures.[3] It also stems in part from the empirical observations that there are enduring and significant differences in the average profitability of different industries and that about 20 percent of the variance in firm profitability is explained by the industry in which a particular business competes.[4] Given the effects of industry on financial performance, analysis of such is obviously important for businesses, because it can inform choices about entering new industries and exiting from existing ones. In addition, it provides a way of understanding how the conduct of firms can influence industry structure, for better or worse.

Nonprofits, however, often do not make dispassionate choices about whether to enter or exit according to the attractiveness of industry structure. Rather, these choices stem from the identification of a social need or a sense of organizational identity. We establish a theater not because it is an attractive industry—in fact, it is one of the least structurally attractive industries one can imagine—but because we are theater artists: actors, directors, playwrights, and so forth. We form an environmental advocacy organization not because there is money to be made, but because there is a need that we exist to fill.

So, if choices about entry and exit are generally determined by mission, why is industry analysis important for nonprofits? It is important because an effective strategy cannot be developed without a clear sense of an organization's competitive environment and dynamics. Just as the industry environment in which steel companies do business is very different from the environment in which pharmaceutical firms do their business, so, too, is the environment in which a symphony orchestra works quite different from the environment in which a homeless shelter does its work. Industry analysis provides a framework for creating a comprehensive map of this context. Beyond this general role, there are at least four specific goals of industry analysis:

- To assess the overall level of prosperity the environment will support, the intensity and basis of competition, and key leverage points for strategy
- To anticipate and predict the impact of changes in the structure of the industry due to gradual evolution or dramatic shifts or dislocations, in order to design appropriate strategic responses
- To identify strategic choices and actions that, undertaken proactively, can improve the structure of the industry and hence the overall level of prosperity it can support (collaboration is key to such efforts, as we will discuss in chapter 5)
- To inform entry and exit decisions—where alternative providers ("competitors") exist and mission provides the latitude to *choose* whether or not to participate in a given industry

In sum, there is significant variation among industries in which nonprofits operate—in terms of prosperity and competition—and, just as with for-profits, this context can have dramatic effects on the success and failure of the nonprofits that inhabit it.

More important, when the provision of services is subsidized or supported by donors, the analysis becomes significantly more complex as compared to most for-profit industries, where the buyer and customer are one and the same. In such situations, strategy must take into account competition on two related but distinct fronts: clients or beneficiaries (such as at-risk youth) and donors (foundations, government, individuals). Often competition on the donor side is both broader and more diffuse because it occurs across all nonprofit arenas (e.g., education vies with the environment for dollars among some subsets of potential funders).

Given this added complexity, a systematic means of analyzing the environment is even more important for nonprofits. But in order to introduce the framework for conducting industry analysis in a way that is relatively easy to understand, I begin with an extensive description and explication of the ideas in the for-profit setting and deal later with the ways the framework can be adapted for use in the nonprofit setting.

Industry Structure and Performance

In extreme cases, the structure of an industry can have a dramatic impact on the profitability of organizations that comprise it. Consider the classic comparison of a highly attractive (profitable) versus a highly unattractive (unprofitable) industry: pharmaceuticals versus steel. Over the period from 1978 to 1996, the average rate of return on equity for steel was 10 percent less than the cost of that capital, while the rate of return for pharmaceuticals was 15 percent more than its cost of equity capital.[5] Explanations for these persistent differences emphasize the role of industry structure as "an underlying set of economic and technical characteristics" that determine the nature of competition between the industry players and other relevant actors (such as suppliers and buyers) and, ultimately, industry profitability.[6]

Examples of the types of characteristics studied by industrial economists include "the number and size distribution of sellers and buyers, . . . the extent and character of product differentiation, . . . and certain parameters of demand (elasticity, growth rate)."[7] From a practical point of view, a host of other dimensions might attract a manager's attention, such as competitors, prices, technologies, capacity, and variation among customers. How, then, is a manager to decide which aspects of her industry are most important from the perspective of her firm? How is she to make sense of this dizzying array of concerns, much less develop strategy for dealing with the challenges posed by the industry? To complicate matters further, consider the fact that industries are constantly changing—sometimes slowly, even imperceptibly, and sometimes dramatically, with discontinuities that can completely transform the competitive environment almost overnight.

Given the inherent difficulties in understanding industries (just as we saw with respect to strategy), a conceptual framework is essential for intelligent and effective managerial decision making. A framework for analyzing industries must provide a guide to determining which of hundreds of factors deserve attention, as well as a basis for explaining, predicting, and controlling industry-level influences on performance. The sections that follow will introduce a framework for analyzing industry structure and thinking through the implications for strategy.

What Is a Framework for Industry Analysis Supposed to Do?

In most organizations, discussions of strategy inevitably contain some assessment of the way the world is or will be, and the implications of this world for what the organization's leaders should or should not do. Indeed, representations of the environment are central to strategy, whether described as "threats" and "opportunities," "scenarios," or "landscapes."[8] At the same time, discussions of the environment can be confusing and controversial. Leaders of an organization may have divergent views about fundamental questions such as, "What is important?" "How is the environment changing?" and "What impact will it have on us?"

To be useful, a framework for industry analysis should do a number of things. First, it should ensure that no important features of the environment are overlooked in the assessment. It should also help to organize and interpret the huge number of facts and the many individual pieces of data about a given industry. It should facilitate the process of drawing inferences about the beneficence and likely pattern of industry evolution. Both of these are key inputs to the goals and plans embedded in strategy. And, finally, it should serve to guide discussions about the state of the world.

The dominant approaches to understanding industry-level phenomena are based on analyzing the key structural features of an industry. Analyzing the structure of an industry is a systematic way of identifying the key challenges, threats, and opportunities in the environment. It provides an understanding of the constraints that the environment places on the ability of an organization to secure scarce resources (particularly money) from the world around it. The analysis of industry structure does not tell an organization what it should do, and it does not provide an equation that can predict firm performance or industry profitability. Instead, an industry analysis facilitates the process of identifying the key characteristics of the environment in which an organization competes. This understanding can then inform the formulation and evaluation of strategy.

Entry and Exit Decision

Given our observation about the differences in the attractiveness of industry environments, one of the most critical times to conduct an industry analysis is when an individual entrepreneur or company is considering entering an industry. This is one point at which the analysis can influence decisions about whether or not to enter into an area of activity. So the ability to recognize that starting a steel company is probably a bad idea, given a lower return in steel than in most other industries (all else being equal), makes this intellectual exercise an especially valuable one.

The second point at which industry analysis can also influence the decision about whether to participate in a particular business is when a firm is considering whether to exit from an industry, by either shutting down or selling its operations. So there are times when fortune smiles on you and someone comes along and offers to buy your steel company for a "good" price (of course this happens only if he or she has not already done an accurate analysis of the industry's structure and factored it into the offering price). Understanding the inherently unattractive structure of your industry should prompt you to quickly accept the offer, "to take the money and run" (or, better yet, put it somewhere where it is more likely to generate a higher return).

Developing Strategy for Existing Operations

Despite the importance of industry analysis for entry and exit decisions, in most cases, managers are most often thinking about how to develop a strategy in a situation in which they are already participating in an industry. Thus, the most common challenge is not deciding whether to enter or exit an industry but, rather, how to thrive in particular industry. Even when the industry is a given, understanding the dynamics and structure of the industry is essential to strategy. At a minimum, in order to be effective, strategy has to deal with the problems posed by the industry. And, in the ideal world, strategy can even be designed to reshape industry structure in ways that make it more attractive.

A Framework for Analyzing Industry Structure: Porter's Five Forces

Michael Porter's 1980 book *Competitive Strategy* is perhaps the most influential strategy text of the last twenty-five years. Although Porter's ideas about the firm-level determinants of performance (e.g., strategy, positioning, and competitive advantage) are important, his most significant contribution is the integration of theory from industrial economics with insights from applied case-based work in the field of strategic management, resulting in "the five forces," a conceptualization of the key features of industry structure that determine the nature and intensity of competition and, ultimately, its profitability.

The five forces framework highlighted the fact that competitors are not the only actors whose behavior affects a firm's profitability; other players can also siphon off the value created by firms in an industry. These other players include firms offering *substitute* products or services, *potential entrants* to the industry (new competitors), *buyers* (or customers), and *suppliers*. Porter's five forces correspond to the threat posed by each of these groups to the industry's profitability:

- Rivalry among existing firms
- Threat of substitute products or services
- Threat of new entrants
- Bargaining power of buyers
- Bargaining power of suppliers

Each of these forces represents, in essence, a source of pressure on the profitability of an industry. It is important to understand not only who these actors are and how much pressure they exert on industry profitability, but also how that pressure changes as a function of gradual trends or dramatic shifts in the industry structure. In figure 3.1, I present a slightly modified version of Porter's five forces framework, and I follow it with a practical guide to applying this framework in the context of the nonprofit sector.

Competitors in the For-Profit Context

The first step in conducting an industry analysis is typically listing the major competitors. These are the organizations that provide some form of the product or service according to the definition of the industry.[9] There may be one, a few, hundreds, or even thousands of competitors in an industry. For example, in the long-distance telecommunications industry, before deregulation, we would list AT&T and that would be it. In the industry for personal computer operating system software, we would list Microsoft and Apple, and maybe Linux. In the automotive industry, the list would

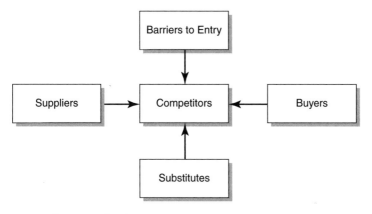

Figure 3.1. Elements of industry structure.

be less than about a dozen, including General Motors, Ford, Daimler-Chrysler, Toyota, Honda, Nissan, BMW, and a few others. For the restaurant industry in New York City, the list would be virtually endless.

In fact, the number of competitors is one of the key structural features of an industry. Typically, the more there are, the greater the level of competition. This can vary from one firm (i.e., a monopoly, such as AT&T before divestiture) to perfect competition when there is a large homogenous group of incumbents. Although I will return to this point later in the chapter, it should be noted that the broader the geographic boundaries placed on an industry, the larger the number of competitors. However, these boundaries are determined by the nature of competition, which can range from very local (restaurants) to global (automotive).

There are other factors that influence the degree of competition, such as the relative size and dominance of firms. Industries in which the market is dominated by a few firms will tend to be less competitive than one with the same number of firms but relatively equal shares of the market.[10] Another characteristic that can diminish the intensity of competition is differentiation among firms in an industry. So even an industry with many competitors will be less competitive if these firms are different in ways that lead them to appeal to different segments or niches within the market (quality, style, location, service, etc.). Retail clothing—with an extremely diverse universe of product offerings targeted to numerous customer segments—would be an example of this type of industry. In contrast, if there is little differentiation among many equally sized firms, as in commodity markets such as corn, soybeans, or copper, then competition will be very intense.[11]

Having listed the competitors, we next assess the intensity of competition or rivalry in accordance with these listed factors. The more competitive the industry, the lower the overall level of profitability; the less competitive the industry, the higher the overall level of profitability. Although there are a variety of much more sophisticated and precise ways of measuring the degree of competition in an industry, for most managerial (versus academic) purposes, a simple qualitative judgment about whether it is low, medium, or high is usually sufficient.

Competitors in the Nonprofit Context

In the nonprofit sector, the degree of competition is often mitigated by the nature of the relationships among the players. Their interaction may be characterized by cooperation more than direct competition. For example, homeless shelters are likely to cooperate and support one another because they share a common purpose of meeting an important social need. Since the homeless do not pay for shelter, there is no need to compete over customers. There can, however, be competition for funding, but even here there may be joint planning and efforts among nonprofit service providers to optimize the services available to the community as a whole. Despite the image of nonprofits as noncompetitive, there are many areas where competition is fierce. Universities compete for students and faculty; theaters compete with one another for audiences and plays, as well as artists; neighborhood-based organizations compete for public facilities in which to run their programs. Moreover, increasingly we see nonprofits competing with their for-profit counterparts in health care, education, real estate and housing, and arts and entertainment, to name but a few. In these industries, the list of competitors will include nonprofits, for-profits, and even public agencies.

Depending on the nature of demand and the degree to which organizations pursue different strategies, the level of competition can be very high and direct, or the players can coexist quite peacefully. Ultimately, just as in the case of the for-profit industry analysis, we need to assess the degree of competition explicitly rather than simply make a priori assumptions about rivalry.

Substitutes in the For-Profit Context

Substitutes include any products or services that can be used in place of the product or service produced by the industry. Radio broadcasts and newspapers are substitutes for the television industry. Similarly, trains and automobiles are substitutes for airline travel. Substitutes are important because, as the price of a particular product in an industry rises, substitutes will become more attractive alternatives to buyers. Also, as the price of substitutes drops or their performance improves, they become more attractive to buyers. In this sense, the availability and cost of substitutes limit the prices (and hence the profitability) of an industry.

For example, as the price of air travel rises, travelers are more likely to consider other forms of transportation where there are reasonable substitutes. Obviously the substitute must be close to the original product or service in terms of its ability to satisfy buyers' basics needs. For example, this would be true to a greater extent for trains or driving as a substitute for the Boston–New York airline shuttle than it would be for transatlantic flights, where a boat is a much more distant substitute because of the huge difference in travel time. Of course for different buyers, such as those transporting large quantities of heavy goods like oil, ships will represent a much more attractive alternative than planes.

Substitutes in the Nonprofit Context

Substitutes operate in much the same way in the nonprofit sector. For example, musical theater is a substitute for opera, and, as the price of attending an opera performance increases, musical theater becomes more attractive in the eyes of some (though not all) buyers. To an even greater extent than with direct competitors, nonprofits are likely to face competition with for-profit substitutes for their products and services. Again, consider performing-arts organizations such as ballets, symphonies, and theaters, which face indirect competition from a host of substitutes, including sports, movies, recorded music, and television. Each of these for-profit substitutes presents appealing (and often less expensive and more "popular") alternatives for consumers. Indeed, when leaders of nonprofit cultural institutions begin to identify substitutes, the list often expands to include almost every conceivable leisure-time activity.

At the same time, for many social service nonprofits, some of the most threatening substitutes are actually not very "good" substitutes at all, but clients still choose them anyway, for a wide variety of reasons. Consider again nonprofit organizations that run homeless shelters. It seems hard to imagine that sleeping on the street is a preferable alternative, but in fact there are often barriers to accessing and using social services, barriers that may make a city park preferable to the local shelter. Similarly, for a youth development program like City Year, which we used as an example in the last chapter, in addition to college and the military, gangs can serve as a substitute for subsets of the population of young people that the organization hopes to attract.

As with competitors, the key here is to assess the number and relative attractiveness of major substitutes for the industry's products or services, to understand how number and relative attractiveness may be changing, and to think through ways to make the industry's offerings more attractive than available substitutes. In many cases, this is actually a very important opportunity for the increasing overall prosperity of industries dominated by nonprofits, because there is an incentive for all of the competitors to cooperate and coordinate their actions to improve the structure of their industry.[12] And, indeed, because antitrust provisions that preclude collusion among for-profits are less stringent and less vigorously enforced for nonprofits, the opportunities for collective action to deal with the threat posed by substitutes are abundant.

Barriers to Entry in the For-Profit Context

Barriers to entry are those features of an industry or activity that make it difficult for those not already in the industry to enter. Barriers to entry are good for incumbents and bad for potential entrants, although the barriers need not be applicable to every potential entrant. Like substitutes, new potential entrants constrain the value that can be claimed by a particular industry. If prices (and profits) in an industry rise, competing in the industry will become more attractive and new organizations will enter the industry, dissipating profits through increased competition.[13]

If, however, there are structural features of the industry that prevent others from entering, then higher levels of profitability can be sustained. For example, before deregulation of the airline industry in 1978, rules made it difficult for new firms to enter and gain a foothold in the industry. Prior to deregulation, there were nine trunk carriers, four of which held 70 percent of the market.[14] After deregulation, these rules were relaxed and a host of new carriers, such as People Express, appeared, offering lower fares and putting significant pressure on the profitability of industry incumbents. By 1980 there were twenty-two new low-cost entrants in the airline industry. This was, of course, good for buyers (the traveling public), but it was bad for the major airlines, and, indeed, in the aftermath of deregulation, overall profitability for the industry declined significantly, and a number of carriers were acquired or went out of business. Government regulation is a common barrier to entry, as illustrated by this example. Other barriers include access to distribution channels, large capital investment, switching costs, and reputation or well-established brands.

Barriers to Entry in the Nonprofit Context

The dynamics of entry barriers operate in a similar fashion in the nonprofit sector. If there is significant growth in funding or increased demand for a service or product, new organizations will be attracted to the industry. Unless there is some mechanism or check against their ability to enter, there will be an increase in the number of competitors, increasing the degree of rivalry within the industry.

Such barriers to entry are often the same as those for for-profits, although overall barriers tend to be lower in most industries populated by nonprofits. For example, perhaps one of the easiest industries to enter is the theater. Virtually anyone can start a theater by renting a church basement, printing up flyers, and putting on a production. Even finding cast members by recruiting some friends or aspiring actors is relatively easy. But what about a script? If there is not time to write one's own, using one of Shakespeare's plays is ideal, not only because of instant recognition of texts like *Hamlet* or *Macbeth*, but also because these works are in the public domain (and as a result reduce your costs because they do not require royalty payments to the long-dead author).[15]

In such an industry, we would expect to see a large number of competitors (although the attractiveness of the industry to new entrants is limited by the other forces). And indeed, we do. Consider Seattle, a vibrant theater community. With a population of just over 550,000 people, the city is home to 5 major nonprofit theaters and more than 250 total theater groups.[16] Imagine that for some reason the demand for and prices of theater tickets increased dramatically in Seattle. What would happen to the prosperity of the existing organizations? It might increase for a short period of time, but then there would soon be 7 major theaters and 275 theater groups—a result that would divert revenues from existing organizations, decreasing their average prosperity. Thus, the difficulty of entry influences the attractiveness of an industry for those organizations that are already participating in it. From a practical point of view, the key questions are as follows: What barriers exist to entering the industry? How high are they, or what degree of protection do they provide incumbents? How are they changing over time? Finally, just as with the threat of substitutes, incumbents have a shared interest in creating or increasing barriers to entry. A classic example is lobbying for regulation of an industry (as some day-care providers have advocated), or professionalization of an activity (like medicine or law). Both of these approaches create hurdles that new entrants must overcome in order to be able to participate in an industry, thereby enhancing the long-term profitability or prosperity of the industry for those already in it.

Buyers in the For-Profit Context

Buyers are the customers that an industry serves and, importantly, those individuals and institutions that provide money in exchange for the industry's products and services. Sometimes, organizations have multiple categories of buyers. So, for example, Procter & Gamble's buyers (customers) include individual consumers who buy its soap, toothpaste, and other products, as well as the grocery chains or distributors and wholesalers who purchase the product for resale. Similarly, Toyota's buyers are the end consumers who buy the company's cars and trucks, as well as the dealers who stock, sell, and service them. To draw an accurate picture of an industry's structure, it is important to list *all* of an industry's buyers—even if they do not have direct contact with firms in the industry.

Buyers can also extract value from industry players by demanding lower prices (thereby reducing the available profit). Typically, when buyers are powerful vis-à-vis the industry, they will be able to extract such price reductions. Consider Wal-Mart when it is buying product from Proctor & Gamble. With more than 4,700 stores around the globe, and $245 billion in annual sales, Wal-Mart buys a *lot* of products from Proctor & Gamble—in fact, close to 10 percent of Proctor & Gamble's sales. So, when Wal-Mart asks for the best price, Proctor & Gamble has a very strong incentive to keep the retailer happy, especially as compared to the mom-and-pop general store down the street, by giving it what it asks for. Or consider an example of an even more powerful buyer. When manufacturers of commercial aircraft engines negotiate with industry leaders Boeing and Airbus, who control 100 percent of the airframe industry, to sell their product, they do not have many options if one of these major aircraft manufacturers decides not to use their product. Extrapolating from this example, we see the key feature (though not the only one) that determines the power of buyers is how many of them there are. The more buyers, the more options the industry has to sell its product if one turns them down. The fewer and the larger the buyers are, the more dependent industry members are on keeping them happy. This means that the buyers can extract value or profit from the industry by demanding lower prices or more value (costly product or service features) at the same price.

Buyers in the Nonprofit Context

In the nonprofit context, buyer power operates in the same fashion, with the important exception that nonprofits typically have two classes of buyers: *clients* or *users* who actually receive the nonprofit product or service, and *donors* who support or subsidize the provision of the service or the creation of the product. For example, many social service agencies that help the poor or disadvantaged rely on contributions from individuals, foundations, and government to pay for the cost of providing these services. But other types of organizations may derive the bulk of their revenue from fees or payments made by users. Many performing-arts nonprofits are like this, as are hospitals that contract with the government to provide care for Medicare and Medicaid recipients.

This distinction corresponds to Hansmann's typology of donative versus commercial nonprofits, which has long been accepted in the literature.[17] Increasingly, however, most nonprofits rely on a mix of contributed and earned income sources.[18] In principle, we expect that donors support the mission of the organization and want effective and efficient services for the users; however, in practice, there may be needs donors have that are unrelated to the quality of service provided to users (such as a desire for recognition or status). Because of this, it is useful to think about donors as a distinct class of buyer and identify their needs and relative power separately from those of users.

Indeed, one possibility is to put donors into their own category, as nonprofit strategy expert Sharon Oster does in her "six forces" adaptation of Porter's framework.[19] The advantage of this adaptation is that it highlights the distinct needs, preferences, and power of funders. But, at the same time, I believe that it overemphasizes a difference between nonprofit and for-profit industries: that the existence of two distinct types of buyers is somehow unique to nonprofits. In fact, if we recall the discussion of the newspaper and television industries in the introductory chapter, these are clear examples of for-profit settings with two separate buyers (advertisers and viewers). Similarly, in industries with franchise models, notably fast food, companies deal with both franchisees and consumers as buyers. Indeed, in the case of health care, there are *three buyers* (patients, employers, and insurance carriers). An even more pervasive example can be seen in consumer products, in which manufacturers have to think about wholesalers or retail distribution channels, as well as the end consumer. What all of this suggests is that, though the funders and clients for donative nonprofits are clearly different actors, this pattern is not unique to nonprofits.

So how should we deal with the difference? My own view emphasizes differentiating among actors within the broader category of buyers—as defined by their relationship to the industry incumbents, or, in other words, as they choose to purchase, use, or subsidize the industry's products or service—and identifying the unique characteristics of subgroups or segments of these buyers. The key features are needs, preferences, and relative power. Identifying these subgroups or segments is important in virtually all industry analyses, because generally there will be variations among subsets of buyers, variations that will be relevant to strategic choices about scope and competitive advantage.[20] This is true even within a single class of buyers. For example, in fast food there are differences between individual owners who have one or two franchises and those who have large, multifranchise operations.[21] Similarly, to return to the nonprofit setting, even within the class of donors, it is still necessary to differentiate between subsets of these buyers, such as individuals, corporate funders, and private foundations.

Having noted all of this, we must still recognize that competition for funding often occurs over a much different landscape and across a much wider set of competitors than the rivalry that occurs around customers, users, or clients. So to take an example from Oster's text, museums in New York City may compete locally for visitors, but nationally for funding. In this case, according to the national perspective, it is not just the list of donors that will expand, but it is also the list of competitors and substitutes. So, for the Metropolitan Museum of Art, we would have to think about the Getty in Los Angeles and the Smithsonian in Washington, D.C., as well as the other New York museums. Because of the dramatic differences in the analysis, it is advisable to do a separate industry analysis using the broader geographic definition of the industry as based on the donors.[22] Similarly, a careful look at donors and the nature of competition for funding may imply a definition of the industry based on discipline or domain— for instance, environmental conservation or educational reform. Depending on whether the focus is on users (schools or visitors to a natural preserve) or on donors (foundations, government, etc.) the industry definition may vary in breadth. Again, the solution is to conduct two or more industry analyses, but these do not necessarily need to identify donors and users as distinct elements of the industry structure, but rather can treat them as subgroups or segments of the buyer category.[23]

The analysis of buyers focuses first on identifying who they are and what important attributes define key subgroups (or segments). Second, it involves assessing the power that buyers can exert over the industry players. Third, the analysis must examine the question of how strategy can help to minimize buyers' power or deal with their ability to extract value from firms in the industry, or both.

Suppliers in the For-Profit Context

Suppliers sell inputs (services, raw materials, and labor) that are used by firms in an industry in the process of making their products, services, or other outputs. Typically, there are many different kinds of purchased inputs, some of which are generic in the sense that virtually all companies require them. Examples include real estate and facilities, labor, advertising, and legal services. Other purchased inputs are industry-specific. In the case of the automotive industry, for example, these types of suppliers would include steel companies, electronic component manufacturers, fabric and leather manufacturers, glass manufacturers, and tire companies. In analyzing buyers, we typically want to focus on the major categories of suppliers, defined by their importance as a proportion of the total cost of producing the firms product or service, or their importance to the quality of the final product. So, in the automotive example, steel and electronics, manufacturing equipment, and labor would emerge as the primary suppliers of interest.

Suppliers are just like buyers in that they can also extract value from industry players by demanding higher prices for the inputs that they provide (thereby reducing the available profit). Typically, when suppliers are powerful vis-à-vis the industry, they will be able to extract such price premiums for their inputs. Just as with buyers, suppliers are more powerful to the extent that they are fewer in number and larger in size. For example, consider the personal computer industry. Manufacturers of personal computers need an operating system and microprocessors for their hardware to be of value to their buyers. With the exception of Apple, all of the other players have, for all intents and purposes, only one choice with respect to operating system, Microsoft, and a few choices with respect to microprocessors, Intel and one or two other firms whose names are difficult to remember. And, in the case of Intel, the brand recognition of its Pentium processor further increases its power as a supplier by making it more difficult for the personal computer manufacturers to switch to an alternative supplier. This power allows these suppliers to extract value from the personal computer industry and, not surprisingly, Intel and Microsoft are highly profitable as a result. In contrast, the personal computer industry is on average considerably less so, although there are individual firms, like Dell, that have a strong competitive advantage and corresponding above-average profitability.

Suppliers In the Nonprofit Context

In the nonprofit context, supplier power operates in much the same way, although typically the most important supplier tends to be staff (labor), given the labor-intensive character of the industries that nonprofits tend to inhabit.[24] Because labor consists of many individual suppliers, they are powerful only to the extent that they can coordinate their actions and demands on the industry—usually through unionization, although this is a relatively rare but significant phenomenon. For example, the dominant challenge facing the symphony orchestra industry is the cost of labor in the form of musician salaries, which have risen significantly over the last twenty years. This increase is largely the result of the negotiating power of the American Federation of Musicians (the musicians' union). However, for most nonprofits, labor is not organized, and, hence, is less powerful vis-à-vis the industry.

In sum, the analysis of suppliers parallels that of buyers, proceeding through the exploration of three basic questions: "Who are the key classes of suppliers that provide essential inputs?" "How much power can they exert over the industry?" and "What strategic choices can incumbents make that will reduce suppliers' ability to extract value from the industry?"

Complements

Another dimension of industry structure that Porter describes but did not formally include among his five forces is complementary products.[25] The importance and impact of complementary products on industry dynamics are explored in detail in *Co-opetition*, an influential strategy book by Adam Brandenburger and Barry Nalebuff. A complement "to one product or service is any other product or service that makes the first one more attractive [to buyers]."[26] For example, computers become more valuable to consumers to the extent that there is useful and affordable software. The home construction industry benefits to the extent that there are abundant and low-cost mortgages. DVD player sales go up when the selection and availability of DVDs go up and the cost goes down. The addition of the notion of complements is important because it focuses attention on the distinct processes of "cooperation" or "creating a pie," and "competition" or "dividing it up."[27] Where the five forces serve to decrease the profitability of an industry, complements operate as a kind of "sixth force" that can enhance the industry's profitability. Complements are not always a major factor, but, in conducting an industry analysis, one should consider whether or not there are complements likely to influence the demand for the industry's products or services.

Using Industry Analysis to Inform Strategy

Once we have an understanding of the elements of the framework, we can conduct an industry analysis assessing each element (or *force* in Porter's terminology) systematically. This involves identifying the actors (e.g., competitors, suppliers, and buyers) and the features of the industry (e.g., barriers to entry and substitutes), and the power of each element to extract some of the value created by industry players.

We are interested not only in the absolute power of each actor, or magnitude of each force, but also in the rate of change in power or magnitude. Is it stable? Increasing? Decreasing? Understanding these trends provides a guide to threats, opportunities, and critical issues facing the industry, as well as some indication of the future munificence of the environment and hence the overall level of prosperity. At the aggregate level, these trends tell a firm whether the world is getting better or getting worse. This information has direct implications for the firm's performance and, hence, its strategy. To maintain a particular level of performance in a deteriorating industry structure (i.e., a shrinking pie) requires improving competitive advantage. Whether this deterioration stems from increased supplier power (e.g., unionization or consolidation) or the emergence of a new class of substitutes matters in the determination of strategy. In the first case, we may need to consider the impact on cost position of our own organization versus that of our competitors. In the second, we might need to compare our existing competitive advantage to that of the substitutes, as well as the competitors.

On another level, industry analysis informs corporate strategy (the strategy guiding the multibusiness enterprise, which we will address in detail in chapter 5). For the moment, we need note only that this analysis encompasses decisions about whether and when to enter or exit new industries—decisions that must obviously take into account the attractiveness of the overall industry, as well as the likely competitiveness of the entrant within it. In sum, industry analysis is not simply an academic exercise. It has immediate and direct implications for strategy. Thus, it is essential to link the industry analysis framework to the strategy framework. I will illustrate this connection with an extended case, but first we must address some of the practical issues in conducting an industry analysis in the real-world settings.

Practical Issues in Conducting an Industry Analysis

Industry Definition

In practice, an industry analysis begins with identifying the various actors related to each force, starting with competitors. But identifying competitors requires first defining the industry, a task that might seem simple until one tries to actually do it. Imagine, for example, that we want to do an industry analysis for the *New York Times*. Is it in the newspaper industry, or is it perhaps in the wider publishing industry, including magazines like *Time* and *Newsweek*? Or maybe it is also in the information industry, or just the news industry. This latter choice would lead us to include broadcast news competitors such as CNN, NBC *Nightly News*, ABC *World News Tonight*, and any number of other radio, television, and Internet news sources.

Once we include television, we may be tempted to think about *all* forms of entertainment, which would then include the New York Yankees, the New Jersey Nets, the New York City Ballet, and the latest Arnold Schwarzenegger film (or now that he is governor of California, his press conferences). But, actually, this definition *does* seem a bit too broad. So, if we go back to the newspaper industry, what about the *New York Times* Web site, in which the company has made a significant investment in recent years? If we defined the industry strictly as newspapers, we might never have entertained the possibility of pursuing the opportunity represented by creating an online presence. But if we define the industry to encompass electronic media, we have to include Microsoft Network, and America Online, and Yahoo as competitors.

As I noted at the outset, defining which industries an organization does business in is often much more difficult than it appears at a glance. The possibilities of industry definition are daunting indeed. How are we to decide? There are several answers to this question. The first is to apply what a colleague of mine calls the "Goldilocks principle": try on different definitions for size and, by expanding and contracting the breadth of organizations considered, much as we did in the *New York Times* example, arrive at one that "feels just right."[28] Under this approach, the newspaper industry might seem too tight for the *New York Times*, and entertainment might seem too broad. Through this process, we might eventually settle on an industry definition of daily and weekly text-based news and information. Some rivals will be close to one another (the *New York Post* and the *Wall Street Journal*), whereas others, like America Online or *Newsweek*, may seem to be more distant from one another because of differences along various dimensions, such as electronic format versus primarily paper format, or weekly versus daily. A second answer is to define the industry according to the "2:00 a.m. principle." This approach involves listing the competitors about whom the general manager of the *New York Times* worries when he wakes up in the middle of the night. A third answer is simply that "it doesn't matter." Why? Because, if the definition is drawn too narrowly, any organization not included as a competitor will likely crop up as a substitute. Moreover, if you are doing an industry analysis and you are anxious about which definition to choose, another source of consolation is that you can always do multiple analyses and then see which is most helpful. This is a particularly liberating approach that can be used whenever there is enough time and the analysis is more than just an academic exercise.

The issue of industry definition is just as difficult, perhaps even more so, for nonprofits. Consider, for a moment, the example of a musical theater. Is a musical theater in the theater industry, or is it in the performing-arts industry? Or is it, perhaps, in the arts industry in general, or maybe even in the broader entertainment industry? How one defines the industry in which an organization competes will have significant implications for what the industry analysis looks like, as well as how useful the results will be. If the industry is defined too narrowly, the analysis will miss important pressures on an organization's prosperity and may result in a strategy that contains gaps that may render it ineffective. On the other hand, if the definition is too broad, then the nature of critical competitive interactions will be obscured by irrelevant information and peripheral considerations.

Industry Definition and Geographic Scope

Industry definition involves specifying more than just the range of products and services (and, by implication, competitors) to be included. It also entails placing geographic boundaries around the industry, according to an assessment of how broadly competition occurs. Consider, again, our example of the *New York Times*. Let us say that we have decided to opt for a relatively narrow definition of the *Times*'s industry as newspapers. But, though the *New York Post* is an obvious competitor to the *Times*, what about the *Boston Globe* (ignoring for a moment that the *Boston Globe* is published by the *New York Times* Company) or the *Washington Post?* This is the question of geographic boundaries of an industry and, though the answer is sometimes very clear—restaurants in Manhattan do not compete with restaurants in Boston, for example—sometimes the answer is not so clear. But, depending on the customer or cuisine segment, as well as the time of day or week, restaurants in Manhattan may or may not compete with restaurants in New Jersey or in Westchester County and Long Island, New York.

One might think of newspapers as a local business, but today the *New York Times* is delivered to homes and businesses and is available on newsstands around the country and overseas. Nevertheless, though you might find the *Boston Globe* in a few local newsstands that specialize in carrying a variety of newspapers or magazines from around the country, it is unlikely that you will find it delivered to your door each morning, unless your home is within one hundred miles or so of Boston.

So, revisiting the question, in what industry does the *New York Times* compete? My own inclination would be to view the *New York Times* as participating primarily in two industries: metro New York daily newspapers, and national text-based news (online and print). This conclusion necessitates two separate industry analyses, illustrating the point made earlier: when in doubt, do multiple industry analyses, especially when competition for donors is national and competition for clients or users is local.

Substitutes and Industry Definition

Closely related to the issue of industry definition is the distinction between competitors and substitutes. The rule of thumb is that we typically think about competitors as organizations that we would identify by name—for example, competitors for Dell Computer would include Hewlett-Packard, Apple Computer, and Gateway, among others—whereas substitutes are *classes* of organizations. Substitutes for live classical music in New York would, for example, include professional sports, art museums, and Broadway shows.

If we are a theater, we would probably think about other theaters, or perhaps even an opera, by name as a competitor, but it is unlikely that we would think of sports teams as direct competitors. Rather, we would likely think of them as a class of alternative products. So a theater in San Francisco would not identify the San Francisco Forty-Niners, the Oakland Raiders, or the San Jose Sharks as specific competitors. Instead, it would rightly consider sporting activities as a group to be substitutes.

We generally want to define the industry in such a way that, when we start to identify the list of competitors for the organization for which we are performing industry analysis, we capture those rivals about whom it worries on a day-to-day basis. Given the ambiguity involved and the lack of objective criteria, industry definition is ultimately a task that necessarily involves the exercise of judgment.

Industry Analysis and the Dynamics of Industry Evolution

In addition to helping managers assess the overall competitiveness of their environment and prioritize critical threats to profitability or prosperity, industry analysis is an important technique for understanding and anticipating major changes or discontinuities in industry structure (perhaps due to technology or, as in our airline example, deregulation). To do this, we conduct an analysis of an industry at two distinct points in time and compare the overall pattern and level of competition. Then, as part of the process of formulating or evaluating firm-level changes, we try to anticipate, and design an approach that addresses, the implications of such changes. In particular, we need to pay close attention to the impact of such changes on the dynamics of competition in the industry and the viability of historical strategies. The case in the next section offers a dramatic illustration of the impact of industry evolution.

An Integrative Example of the Industry Analysis Framework: The Case of KQED Television

Background

As a way of looking at industry analysis in a concrete and holistic perspective, let us examine an in-depth case study of KQED and the San Francisco Bay Area television broadcasting industry.[29] A publicly supported 501(c)(3) nonprofit, San Francisco's KQED Public Television 9 has for decades been widely regarded as one of the most successful public television stations in the United States.[30] In 2002 it was consistently the most watched public television station in prime time, reaching more than 5 million viewers each month, boasting an impressive 200,000 individual contributing members, and collecting approximately $9 million in corporate donations.[31]

Since the mid-1950s, KQED Channel 9 had operated in the San Francisco Bay Area under a VHF license. This over-the-air "delivery mechanism" remained essentially unchanged until the 1980s, when cable television became an increasingly dominant force on the national stage, as well as in the Bay Area television industry. Cable television originated in Tuckerman, Arkansas, in 1948 as a way for viewers in this remote locale to be able to receive television broadcasts from Memphis, Tennessee, some ninety miles distant.[32] Soon, powerful—and often gigantic—antennas sprouted up across the country, plucking distant stations from the airwaves and then distributing them to communities through proprietary wired networks.

At first, cable television was a boon to television stations such as KQED, because their inclusion on cable television rosters allowed them to reach far greater audiences than their often weak or geographically blocked conventionally broadcasted signals could ever hope to reach. In these early days, cable companies were largely dependent on the relatively small number of broadcast networks (e.g., ABC, NBC, and CBS) that provided the content that cable operators relied on to attract subscribers. In the 1980s, however, power began to shift toward cable operators, as the industry consolidated and as cable-only stations such as WGN (Chicago) and WOR

(New York), and networks such as Cable News Network (CNN) and Music Television Network (MTV), began to spring up. And, with the advent of satellite transmission by the major networks, cable companies could just as easily include a flagship network station from a major metropolitan area—say, KNBC in Los Angeles—in their offerings as they could broadcast a local NBC affiliate such as KSEE in Fresno, California.

Initially, these trends posed less of a problem for local stations like KQED, because cable still had a relatively low market penetration, and the vast majority of viewers still used their own antennas to receive their local stations' broadcasts. However, through the mid-1980s, viewers began to discard their antennas and switch over to cable in increasing numbers, exceeding 50 percent penetration of all households in the Bay Area by 1987. This put cable companies in between television stations and their viewers. And, increasingly, cable operators became interested in replacing local stations with larger stations originating in major metropolitan areas. The only protection for smaller local stations was regulatory. Concerned about exactly this phenomenon, the Federal Communications Commission (FCC) established the "must carry" provision in 1972, which required cable operators to carry local stations in the communities they served. However, by 1987, it was clear that this provision would be repealed, and KQED found itself facing an uncertain future. The problem was particularly acute in the Bay Area, where there were five different public television stations, which in the absence of the "must carry" provision would soon be competing with one another for spots on the lineup of the cable operators.

This dynamic was a source of concern to all public television stations, including KQED. In 1986 KQED's president, Anthony Tiano, mused, "If the cable companies choose to drop our stations from their systems, how can we reach the public with quality television programs?"[33] In reality, if the cable companies chose to drop KQED from their systems, nothing less than the survival of the television station itself would be in grave doubt. The key, then, was to ensure that Bay Area cable companies would see it as in their interest to include KQED in their offerings. By putting ourselves in the shoes of Tony Tiano in 1986, we find that KQED's situation provides an excellent example of the utility of industry analysis. In particular, it is instructive for understanding changes in industry structure to conduct an analysis of the environment *before* cable became a major force in the industry, as well as *after*, and then to consider the implications for KQED's strategy.

Industry Analysis: Before Cable

The first step in the analysis is to define the industry in which the organization resides. KQED might be considered to be in the entertainment industry, but, as in the example of the *New York Times*, this consideration is probably taking too broad an approach. At the other end of the spectrum, KQED might be considered to be in the public television industry but, because viewers (and KQED managers) probably compare and choose between public television stations and commercial stations such as local affiliates of the NBC, ABC, and CBS television networks, this definition would be too narrow. In KQED's case, the most useful (and hence best) definition of its industry would probably be Bay Area television broadcasting.

The next step is to determine who the competitors are. Historically, the Bay Area broadcasting channel roster (including San Jose) included the network affiliates ABC, NBC, and CBS; four public television stations KQED, KQEC (owned by KQED), KCSM, and KTEH; and independent, typically UHF stations. But we also need to determine if other stations are truly competitive. Prior to the advent of cable, not every station on the Bay Area broadcasting roster was a competitor of KQED. So, though it might appear, for example, that KTEH, a public television station in San Jose, forty-five miles south of San Francisco, is a competitor of KQED, this is actually not the case, because few San Franciscans can receive KTEH's signal and few residents of San Jose receive KQED's.

After identifying direct competitors, we next consider possible substitutes. In the case of television, there are many. Television viewers can turn to culture (film, museums, plays, live music, etc.), sports (football, baseball, jogging, bicycling, etc.), sleeping, reading, and indeed virtually any leisure activity as a substitute for watching television. Typically, we are most concerned with substitutes that are relatively similar in terms of their function and characteristics. Thus, one of the substitutes that the general manager of a television station might have been concerned about in the 1980s was the wide availability of movies on videocassette.

Once the potential substitutes for an industry's products or services have been identified, the next step is to consider barriers to entry. Barriers to entry prevent other organizations from getting into an industry and claiming a share of the value created. Barriers to entry are good for incumbents and bad for potential entrants. What are the barriers to entry for the Bay Area television industry? The biggest ones are physical and regulatory. Essentially, the broadcasting spectrum (available channels) is limited, and there are a finite number of broadcasting licenses available from the FCC in any given market. Capital might be another barrier to entry. It takes a substantial amount of money to purchase broadcasting equipment and produce or buy programs. Barriers are high as compared to some other industries, say, for example, the restaurant industry. The cost of starting a restaurant, for example, is likely to be within the reach of many more people than starting a television station. At the same time, the cost of starting an automobile manufacturing company is probably out of reach of all but a very few individuals. Thus, though relatively high, the capital barrier was not insurmountable for a potential competitor with a good idea and a compelling strategy.

The next step in the industry analysis is to identify the buyers. In the case of television, there are two key groups of buyers: viewers and advertisers (or in the case of KQED, donors or members). Advertisers pay money (in the parlance of public television, which once prided itself on being commercial-free, they "underwrite" the station's programming) to get their names and products in front of the public television audience, which tends to be better educated and to have a higher income than the average viewer of commercial television.[34] And, because there are millions of viewers, individually these buyers do not have very much power.

The final step is to identify suppliers and assess their power relative to the industry. Suppliers are the organizations and individuals from which the industry players buy inputs necessary to create and deliver their products. In the case of television broadcasters, the primary suppliers (most significant in terms of the proportion of the budget) would include producers and studios that provide programs, the electronic manufacturers that supply the equipment necessary to operate a station, and the people who provide the labor needed to run the station. Having identified the suppliers, we need to understand how much power they have in their relationships with the industry that purchases their goods and services. Supplier power determines how much value the suppliers can extract from the industry in the form of higher prices or other terms of the transaction. As in the case of buyers, if there are only a few suppliers, and hence fewer alternatives for industry, then supplier power is high; if there are many suppliers, then supplier power is lower, because suppliers will be forced to compete with one another, thereby reducing prices or increasing value provided to the industry. In the television broadcasting industry, there are a large number of content producers, equipment vendors, and potential workers; hence supplier power is relatively low.

Looking at forces or elements of industry structure overall, we can see that before cable the industry was fairly attractive and conducive to relatively high levels of prosperity on average.

Industry Analysis: After Cable

After cable garnered a substantial base of viewers or households, the industry looked very different. Even an unsystematic, intuitive assessment of this situation would suggest that matters had worsened. But can we unbundle this general sense of apprehension and be more precise about what cable did to the structure of the Bay Area broadcasting industry and why? To do so, we need to understand where cable companies fit into this industry and what impact they have.

The role of cable can be confusing. Some students' initial reaction is to categorize cable providers as suppliers of access to viewers. Others see them as competitors offering an alternative to local television stations. But, as a class of actors, cable companies can be in only one box of the framework (although part of the reason this case is so interesting is that, in addition to its primary role, cable actually has a number of other, second-order effects on the industry structure, all of which are bad from the point of view of KQED and its fellow incumbents). First and foremost, cable companies become *buyers* for the industry. They decide whether to purchase the signal or broadcast from stations like KQED and then distribute it to their customers, viewers who formerly accessed KQED and other stations directly over the air. Thus, just as Wal-Mart is a distribution channel (hence a buyer) for Procter & Gamble, Tele-Communications, Inc. (TCI) was a distribution channel and a buyer for KQED. But, unlike Procter & Gamble, KQED did not have many alternatives if in a community TCI decided not to stock its product. This is because, in a local community, a cable operator had a monopoly. Neither viewers nor televisions stations had another alternative, other than over-the-air transmission, which was rapidly becoming obsolete.

So the most important change due to cable may have been the dramatic increase in buyer power. Stations now faced two or three individual buyers overall, and only one in a given municipality, rather than the millions of individual viewers who were choosing whether to tune in before cable. Note that the power of the other buyer, advertisers and sponsors, does not change for the most part as a direct result of cable in this instance.

A second effect of cable is that it reduces the barriers to entry into the industry—Bay Area television. Let us say you manage a station somewhere else in the United States. Before cable, there is no way you can broadcast your signal in San Francisco, unless you want to go to the city, get a license, and put up a broadcasting tower. However, once cable arrives, it becomes relatively easy and inexpensive for a station in, say, Atlanta, to send its broadcast across the country. So barriers to entry into the Bay Area television broadcasting industry declined greatly because of cable. Moreover, the ability to expand to multiple markets almost simultaneously created tremendous economies of scale for stations that enjoyed national distribution through their agreements with cable companies. Costs of purchasing or producing programming could be spread over an exponentially larger number of viewers with the flip of a single switch. The result of lowering the barriers to entry is an influx of new competitors, many of which may be directly competitive with KQED in various programming categories (e.g., the Discovery Channel, Nickelodeon, and CNN).

Another consequence of cable for Bay Area broadcasting was an increase in competition among the existing players. Over and above the new entrants from outside the Bay Area, stations within the market—which did not compete with one another before—did as a result of cable. Remember that, because of the geography of the region (mountainous terrain), an over-the-air signal from San Francisco cannot reach San Jose. Now, stations in different parts of Bay Area would compete with one another for viewers if they were carried on the same cable operator, and more important, they would compete in a given community to be one of the stations carried by the local cable company. This competition would be particularly intense where there was duplication of programming, as with multiple affiliates of the major networks, and even more so with the four public broadcasting stations.

Implications of the Industry Analysis

Since the number of viewers in the market remained essentially the same, between the increase in buyer power, appearance of new entrants, and increased rivalry between incumbents, the structural attractiveness of the Bay Area television broadcasting industry declined dramatically as a result of cable. Hence, we would expect overall prosperity to have declined, as well. So far, what this analysis does is confirm our intuition that matters had just worsened and help us to understand why. But, ultimately, from KQED's perspective at the time, we want the analysis to be helpful to KQED in thinking about what to do, as well. This emphasis leads us back to strategy.

Imagining we are KQED management at the time, we can anticipate the competition will be even more acute for public television stations, most of which offer the same programming, which they purchase from the Public Broadcasting Service (PBS). This was not a problem before cable, when there was no overlap among the stations' viewers, but it is a big problem once there is overlap—especially if the buyer (TCI) is trying to optimize its own offerings and minimize duplication. So let us imagine for a moment that cable takes over every house in a community. KQED now has to sell its signal to cable operators, which have the option (and the power) to decide to carry it, or not to carry it (once the "must carry" provision is repealed).[35] Presumably, TCI is going to carry at least one public television station in the Bay Area, but which one?

As KQED, we need to think about our competitive advantage vis-à-vis the other noncommercial stations. Given our strong and loyal viewer base and high levels of penetration as compared to that of other stations, we have the dominant position and are probably going to do well in the new competitive environment—at least in terms of getting the cable companies to carry our signal. A more interesting challenge is the one facing the second PBS station, San Jose–based KTEH. In terms of competing against KQED, to make itself attractive to cable companies and viewers, it has to differentiate itself in some way that is valuable to at least a subset of the market. And, in fact, this is just what KTEH actually did. It developed a programming niche that was different from KQED's—specifically, one that focused on science fiction (e.g., *Dr. Who*), as well as financial, technology, and business programming that appealed to its Silicon Valley base. This way, even with KQED on a cable operator's lineup, viewers, particularly those in Silicon Valley, still wanted (and demanded) access to KTEH, as well. If KTEH and KQED were the same, KTEH would probably have become expendable both for the cable company and for the viewers.

Ultimately, other public television stations also found ways to differentiate themselves. One focused on programming appealing to minority communities and another on catering to educational institutions. As a result, there were multiple public television entities that remained viable, illustrating an important point about this type of analysis. Strategy is often not as much about how to compete as it is about how *not* to compete. Clear and distinct strategies improve industry structure, making everyone better off. But in order to understand and create such strategies, organizations must understand the environment in which they are operating. This is the fundamental contribution of the industry structure framework.

4

Execution

Translating Mission and Strategy into Action

Strategy, no matter how robust, and mission, no matter how compelling, still provide only a general indication of an organization's direction and goals, and a high-level plan about how to realize these goals. No organization can create social or economic value until it successfully translates these intentions and aspirations into a coherent set of *choices* and *actions* that are executed consistently over a period of time. Both of these elements are essential to the process of creating value. First, as we noted in chapter 2, strategy is fundamentally about choice: the commitment to pursue one path rather than another.

The notion of a path implies that choices involve options that are mutually exclusive, a consequence of trade-offs and the irreversible nature of truly strategic choices.[1] Second, without action, choices have no concrete manifestation and are inconsequential. Moreover, unless actions are executed consistently over time, they will not lead to competitive advantage and will have no meaningful impact on performance. Mission is exactly like strategy in these respects: it requires both choice and action.

Execution can be viewed from multiple perspectives with respect to mission and strategy. The first, a *retrospective* lens, is more reflective of the concerns of scholars of strategic management. It begins with the observation of a firm's performance and, where this performance is superior in terms of profitability or prosperity, it asks, "How are we to understand or explain the performance of this firm?" By looking backward, one can infer an organization's strategy from the pattern of choices it has made over time, a pattern that reveals its plans for competing. By definition, the explanation entails some reference to competitive advantage. As Michael Porter notes, "any superior performing firm has achieved one type of advantage [cost or differentiation], the other, or both." "To say it another way," continues Porter, "superior profitability can only logically arise from commanding a higher price than rivals or enjoying lower costs (including, at a lower level in the causality chain, asset costs)."[2] In this sense, academics view competitive advantage as the "cause" of a firm's superior performance.

Execution provides an explanation for an organization's past and current performance (in particular, prosperity). To the extent that it has an above-average level of prosperity, it must have by definition some form of competitive advantage that represents the aggregate value created by the various choices and actions that the organization is performing at a particular point in time. In sum, execution is "where the rubber meets the road."

The second lens, the one that is dominant in this chapter, is a *prospective* lens. This approach asks, "Given a strategy that outlines how a firm intends to compete (i.e., achieve a competitive advantage within a defined scope), what concrete choices and actions must it take in order to realize that strategy, or to build and sustain that competitive advantage?" Hence, looking forward, strategy should provide a guide to making future choices. It should inform decisions about whether the company should undertake action X or action Y.

To be useful in this regard, strategy (and, as I will argue later in this chapter, mission) must be sufficiently robust and specific to render some choices and actions acceptable, and to exclude others as unacceptable. Choices, by definition, involve trade-offs—the classic guns versus butter choice of economic theory. Although trade-offs may not always be apparent when there is slack in this system, in principle, when organizations are being as efficient as possible given existing technologies, they cannot be low cost and high quality at the same time: achieving more quality is more costly, and reducing costs reduces quality.

The emergence of the notion of strategy in conventional usage was originally linked to military applications. Perhaps the defining feature is that it elevated the status of plans as compared to tactics, as well as the role of the *general* as compared to his or her lieutenants. And, yet, we know full well that tactics, or execution, matter a great deal. In the absence of the execution of tactics, strategy is inconsequential, just like the corporate strategic plan that sits on a shelf in a thick and dusty binder. Similarly, unless mission inspires and shapes the actions of real people, it becomes no more than an eloquently crafted slogan engraved on a plaque that sits prominently, but without significance, on a wall. The strategy may be intended but not realized; the mission, espoused but not enacted.[3]

In this chapter, I begin by exploring the execution of strategy and the role of logic as key elements. I then turn to mission and the parallel logic of "causal models" or "theories of change" and the role they play in the execution of mission. Finally, I illustrate how the choices associated with the execution of strategy and the choices associated with the execution of mission are related to one another. Here it is important to note that just like strategy and mission themselves, the logic of strategy and logic of mission are distinct, but they are also interdependent. Even though they perform different functions and are designed to produce different outcomes (i.e., economic versus social, environmental, or artistic value), each constrains and influences the other.

The Elements of Execution: Policies, Activities, and Resource Allocation

The strategy literature identifies three categories of choices and actions: *policies*, *activities*, and *resource allocation*. We will look at each of these in turn.

Policies

The first category of choices is *functional policies*, rules put into place to govern the kinds of decisions people can make and how they can make them. In one of the early works on business strategy, *The Concept of Corporate Strategy*, Kenneth Andrews highlights the role of policies in achieving a firm's goals. In particular, he notes the role of policies in major functional areas such as marketing, finance, human resources, and manufacturing. Although Andrews does not formally define the term *policy*, his usage is consistent with the common understanding of policy as a "definite course or method of action selected from among alternatives and in light of given conditions to guide and determine present and future decisions."[4]

According to Andrews, "Corporate strategy is the pattern of decisions in a company that determines and reveals its objectives, purposes, or goals, produces the principal policies and plans for achieving those goals, and defines the range of business the company is to pursue, the kind of economic and human organization it is or intends to be, and the nature of the economic and non-economic contribution it intends to make to its shareholders, employees, customers, and communities."[5] Andrews's examples of policies include not accepting product orders that are inconsistent with a company's values, and being responsive to distributors' concerns and complaints. Hence, in the context of a strategy, policies are explicit rules or guidelines that define and govern the range of acceptable behavioral response to recurring choices made by members of the organization.[6]

Consider the following example of the role policies play in the execution of strategy. Southwest Airlines has policies that have done away with assigned seating and that prescribe the use of only one model of plane in its fleet of aircraft (the Boeing 737). These policies are derived from a strategy in which low cost plays a central role, and they limit the choices that managers can make with respect to seating and plane purchasing. They also shape the way Southwest performs certain activities. (We will return later to the relationship between policies and activities.) For example, having only one model of aircraft simplifies and standardizes the maintenance process. Eschewing assigned seating speeds up the process of boarding passengers at the gate. Both of these contribute to lowering Southwest's costs by minimizing the downtime of its planes and maximizing its utilization of these very expensive assets. Thus, we see how individual policies contribute to an organization's ability to create and maintain a competitive advantage.

In addition, the most effective and sustainable strategies are characterized by a pattern of policies that is internally consistent. In the Southwest example, policies about assigned seating and aircraft type both support high utilization and low cost. Recall that one of the key functions of strategy is to provide a basis for integrating and coordinating the actions of people, groups, and departments across the organization. In this light, *every* policy should therefore be evaluated on the basis of its consistency with other policies and with the overall strategy. To the extent that policies are indeed consistent, the execution of the strategy will be more effective.

Activities

The second category of choices is *activities*, the basic ongoing, routinized patterns of behavior that a firm performs.[7] The notion of activities was introduced in Porter's 1985 book *Competitive Advantage*, in an effort to make his original (1980) strategy framework more useful for managers. Porter argued that it was important to disaggregate the firm in order to explain the basis for creating and sustaining competitive positions with greater precision.[8] Specifically, he highlighted the activities that firms must perform to "create, produce, sell, and deliver . . . products or services," referring to these as "the basic units of competitive advantage."[9] Examples of activities include "calling on customers, assembling products, training employees."[10] In essence, activities constitute the elemental tasks involved in production of an organization's output.

Although activities are the elements of competitive advantage, advantage actually derives from the way these activities are *configured* and *performed*. By *configured*, we mean the way activities are structured—when, where, and by whom they are done—as well as what their relationship is in time and space to other activities. By *performed*, we mean how they are done: the essential features of the ways individuals and groups go about executing tasks and activities. For example, to return to the example of Southwest Airlines, activities such as passenger boarding are configured in ways that are simple: there are no seat assignments or tickets (all reservations are electronic); passengers are assigned seating zones (A, B, and C) that are printed on their boarding passes when they check in at the airport for their flight. When the plane is ready, the boarding activity is performed quickly and efficiently, with passengers boarding in manageable groups, in accordance with the letters printed on their boarding passes.[11]

Levels of Activities. Activities can be defined at different levels of specificity. For instance, we might think of sales, calling on customers, and demonstrating product features as discrete activities. Determining the appropriate level of specificity depends on the amount of detail necessary to understand how the activity in question contributes to the organization's competitive advantage. For example, in this illustration, the important attribute of the sales process might be the depth of knowledge and expertise salespeople possess, depth that enables them to educate customers about sophisticated product features through hands-on demonstrations. In this case, it would be necessary to define calling on customers as a distinct activity; defining the activity at the level of sales would not provide the basis for understanding competitive advantage in sufficient detail to guide decisions about configuring and performing the activity.

Depending on the level at which activities are defined, there may be hundreds or thousands of discrete activities that exist. Some subset of these will be critical to competitive advantage. Execution involves identifying exactly which activities are most important, and ensuring that

these are configured and performed in ways that optimize their contribution to an organization's competitive advantage.

Interdependence of Activities. In the last section, I specifically used the term
optimize rather than *maximize* in referring to the contribution of individual
activities to competitive advantage. This is because sustainable competitive
advantage depends on the overall combination of activities and the degree
to which they fit together and complement one another. In other words,
the contribution of the whole system of activities is greater than the sum of
its parts (individual activities), because there are trade-offs associated with
the choices about how to configure and perform individual activities.[12] For
example, the way in which a company decides to manage its inventory (i.e.,
determining what items the company will keep in stock and how much
inventory the company maintains at any given moment) can improve the
speed and reliability with which the firm can fulfill customers' orders. However, these choices will also affect how the company must configure other
activities, such as purchasing, order processing, and delivery.

In addition, the trade-offs and interdependence of activities are what
keep competitors from imitating an effective strategy. Simply copying
individual activities is insufficient and actually undermines an existing
strategy. Copying an entire pattern of activities is far more complicated
and difficult than copying individual activities, particularly when those
activities depend on tacit knowledge and culture.[13] Thinking about how
to optimize the contribution of all the activities, given the overall basis of
the firm's competitive advantage, is key to strategy.

Resource Allocation

The third category of choices is *resource allocation*, primarily decisions about
where and on what the organization will spend money (although time and
attention are also scarce resources, which may be even more important in
nonprofits, where financial resources are often limited). Every organization has to spend money to maintain itself and to achieve its goals. Some
examples of essential expenditures include rent and utilities, payroll, travel,
and administration. But, in the context of strategy, we are primarily concerned not with essential expenditures, but with the distinctive set of
expenditures that drive competitive advantage.

In linking resource allocation to strategy, the objective is to ensure that
the priorities reflected in the overall pattern of resource allocation are

consistent with, and supportive of, the organization's competitive advantage. Part of what makes a competitive advantage sustainable is the fact that it is both unique and difficult to imitate. One of the key ways to create a sustainable competitive advantage is to establish a pattern of resource allocation that is different from that of competitors. Because resources are limited, spending a dollar on one activity or in one way means that it cannot be spent on another activity or in another way.

In effect, there are trade-offs, and trade-offs necessitate choice (a point we made in discussing activities). This is not to say that an organization should absolutely refrain from spending money on things that do not contribute to its competitive advantage, but it *should* spend—as compared to its competitors—more on what does contribute to its competitive advantage than on what does not.

Consider, for example, Apple Computer, which we briefly discussed in chapters 1 and 2. Apple's competitive advantage in the segments that the company dominates is the combination of technical innovation—reflected in product features and capability—with ease of use. We would expect Apple to have a pattern of resource allocation decisions that are consistent with and that would support this competitive advantage. Moreover, this pattern of decisions should be markedly distinct from those of a competitor with a different strategy, such as Dell, which competes on the basis of cost and a direct-to-consumer distribution model. We would expect to find that Apple Computer spends considerably more money on research and development (R&D), particularly in the areas of innovative performance features, as well as user interface features that make the advanced technology easy to use.

Looking at the data, we see that Apple Computer and Dell in 2002 spent almost the same amount on R&D ($446,000,000 versus $452,000,000, respectively); however, for Apple this represented a sizeable 7.8 percent of its annual revenues, whereas the comparable amount represented but a paltry 1.5 percent of Dell's annual revenues.[14] Much of Apple's R&D investment goes into new products, upgrades and innovation of existing products, and product integration so that applications work seamlessly with one another and with new hardware. Dell, on the other hand, invests its resources in ways that reflect its own competitive advantages of cost (due to its direct-sales model and inventory management) and product customization and flexibility (due to its made-to-order approach). Thus, in a relative sense, Dell focuses its resources on its logistics system (order processing and just-in-time assembly).

Finally, though, as this example suggests, an organization's resource allocation priorities should *support* its competitive advantage. This is not to say that *any* investment or expenditure that is consistent with its competitive advantage is justified. To return to the example of inventory management presented in the previous section, if speed of delivery and availability of product are both valued by buyers and are a source of relative competitive advantage for a firm, then the firm should spend more on activities, structures, or capabilities that allow it to sustain that competitive advantage. This plan might include keeping more inventory in stock, which is costly because of the carrying costs, but important for maximizing speed and availability. Similarly, it would include investments in technology to process orders more quickly or in a larger network of warehouses close to customers, which would also be consistent with this competitive advantage.

But, in some instances, there might be cheaper ways to achieve the same level of speed. Consider an investment in express shipping to provide overnight delivery of products. This approach might actually be less costly than keeping large amounts of inventory in multiple warehouses (and, in fact, is an approach that has been used with great success by many vendors in the mail-order computer hardware and software businesses). Similarly, investments in availability and speed beyond a point at which the buyer values them and is willing to pay a premium for them would fail to enhance the competitive advantage, and should therefore not be undertaken. Customers might want and be willing to pay a premium for two-day delivery but be unwilling to pay enough to cover the cost of overnight delivery. In this case, the allocation of resources should be limited to the level that optimizes the competitive advantage, given the cost-benefit trade-offs.

In analyzing the relationship between resource allocation decisions and competitive advantage, we should focus not only on unique and important decisions, but also on large commitments of resources. At the end of the day, an organization should be able to identify specific expenditures in its budget that are distinctive, meaning those expenses that its competitors either would not make or would spend less on.

Execution and Logic Loops

Logic loops are diagrammatic representations of the logic, which is the third component of strategy that we identified in chapter 2. As you may recall, logic is a detailed explanation of why and how the strategy will work. The logic unpacks assumptions about the market, about the firm, and about how the concrete choices made with respect to policies, activities, and resource allocation will create the organization's competitive advantage.

The logic also addresses the assumptions about the causal relationships between these attributes of the firm, or its competitive advantage, and buyers' needs and behavior in paying the firm a premium, or choosing the firm over other firms, because of competitive advantage. The logic needs to make explicit the assumptions about the firm and its environment, and the causal relationships that will lead to greater prosperity or superior profitability, if it is a for-profit organization.

Specifically, logic loops are detailed representations of causal chains that relate resource allocation decisions, policies, and activities to competitive advantage, and relate competitive advantage to the needs and characteristics of specific buyers who will pay to have them met (see figure 4.1). In theory, one could create a large complex encompassing all the elements of an organization's strategy. However, in practice, it tends to be more helpful to unbundle the overarching logic into smaller, more discrete causal diagrams that highlight key elements of a specific strategy. At its heart, drawing logic loops involves making explicit the assumptions about how competition occurs and how the organization is going to be successful as a result of the choices it makes. One can track logic by drawing schematic diagrams with arrows going from one key component to another. These key components could include elements such as what buyers want, or buyer purchase criteria, and what the organization does uniquely well that is valued by customers.

In the case of Apple Computer, we can identify a pool of buyers with a range of needs that include ease of use, cutting-edge technology, advanced performance, and product design that is "cool" and "sexy." For some of these buyers, only one of these criteria really matters, but for others, the combination is important. Yet delivering simultaneously on all three dimensions is difficult because of the trade-offs involved (cutting-edge technology tends to be more complex and difficult to use). Apple's competitive advantage is therefore its ability to deliver technologically advanced but easy-to-use personal computing products in a hip, sexy package. For this ability, the company is able to command a price premium over the Windows-Intel alternatives, although as Porter reminds us, any differentiator must still maintain proximity to its competitors in price.[15]

Following the company's logic loop (see figure 4.2), we find that, as we might expect, Apple spends much money on research and development.

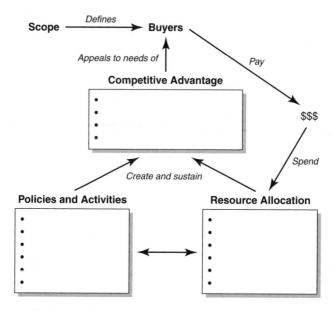

Figure 4.1. The logic of strategy.

The company created a culture that is freewheeling and creative. It spends money on design. Its leadership team made the decision for the company to develop its own proprietary operating system—a very expensive decision, but one that was necessary to create the ease of use that its customers demand. But what are the real choices the company makes that allow it to create this competitive advantage? Logic comprises the assumptions we make about what we do, how we spend our money, and how these answers in turn lead to what we can do better than other organizations. Part of what is interesting and compelling about strategy is that when you can create a competitive advantage that is dependent on a complex setup—policies, behaviors, and cultures—it becomes very difficult to imitate.

Sustainability and Fit: How Do You Know It Will Last?

Part of what makes a strategy sustainable in the face of competition is the inability of competitors to copy the organization's strategy—specifically, their inability to duplicate the sources of an organization's competitive

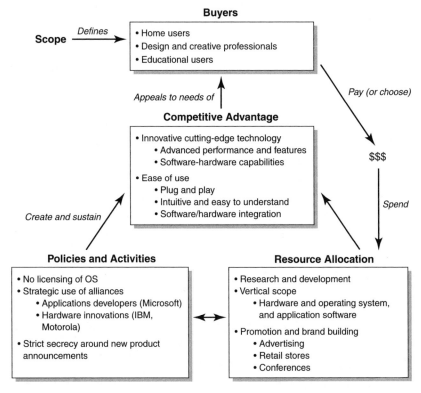

Figure 4.2. Apple Computer strategic logic.

advantage. The more complex and dense the logic loops that lead to the competitive advantage, the more difficult it will be for a competitor to emulate them.

Add to this the probability that there are hundreds of different resource allocation decisions being made at any given time, and hundreds of different policies in place within the organization—any or all of which can contribute to its competitive advantage—and it becomes readily apparent that duplicating this unique mix of decisions and policies is going to be virtually impossible. Conversely, if there is only one thing that an organization does that produces its competitive advantage, it will be far easier for somebody else to copy it. Understanding and detailing logic loops, particularly relatively complex logic loops, is a way of not only guiding the organization's choices, but also ensuring that the strategy will be sustainable over the long haul.

The Relationship between Activities, Policies, and Resource Allocation

We have discussed policies, activities, and resource allocation choices as if they were distinct and unrelated elements of execution; in reality, they are closely related and often indistinguishable. Consider the example we used earlier of a firm that competes in part on delivery and availability, and that structures its inventory management activities accordingly. This same firm might also invest significant *resources* in building warehousing, distribution, and logistic systems to enhance delivery and availability. But it will also perform these distribution and logistic *activities* differently than a company that does not make those investments. Similarly it might also establish *policies* on the permissible level of inventory, or on the handling— or even acceptance—of customer returns, policies based on the nature of these systems.

Interestingly, even a number of the activities used as illustrations in Porter's detailed mapping of activity systems are in fact more like policies. Consider his analysis of the low-cost advantage of Vanguard Group's mutual funds. He lists activities such as "no first-class travel for executives," "no loads," and "low rates of trading."[16] Although this describes the way Vanguard performs activities such as trading, travel, and pricing, it also describes policies that the organization has about the range of choices that managers can make in these areas. Similarly, in Porter's discussion of Southwest Airlines' activities, he lists "no seat assignments" and "no meals" as elements of the organization's approach to customer service. But these elements reflect company policies and also have implications for the allocation of resources. So, rather than spending money on meals or on extra staff to provide seating assignments and other forms of service, Southwest allocates resources to actively monitoring and reinforcing the company's culture and an extraordinarily elaborate and selective recruiting process.[17]

Again, representing the way the system works through a logic loop is an invaluable device for testing and evaluating a strategy and its execution. In figure 4.3, I illustrate a logic for Southwest Airlines: as we can see, policies, activities, and resource allocation decisions often overlap. This is understandable, given that a policy is a rule, which should, when followed, guide the conduct of an activity or pattern of behavior, and often has resource implications, as well. But more important than the overlap is the fact that policies, activities, and resource allocation decisions reflect choices and actions integrally connected to one another, as well as to strategy.

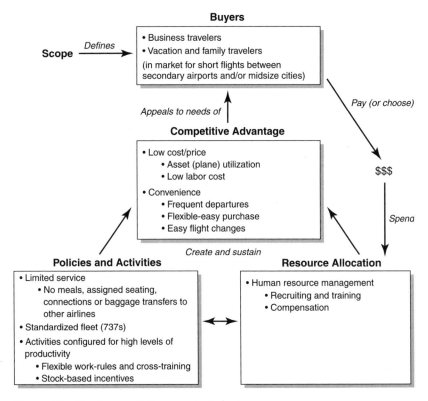

Figure 4.3. Southwest Airlines strategic logic.

Execution in the Nonprofit Context

To the extent that strategy is important for nonprofit organizations, *executing* it must also be important. In the world of business strategy, there is a well-worn adage that a mediocre strategy with great execution will outperform the great strategy with mediocre execution. Execution involves the translation of mission and strategy from intentions, plans, and aspirations into reality through concrete choices and actions.[18]

Execution is where competitive advantage is made or lost. But in non-profits, it is also where the mission is realized: core values are lived (or not), purpose is pursued, goals are achieved, and vision is brought to life. Thus, every choice that a nonprofit makes must be evaluated by the degree to which it is consistent with and advances the mission, just as it must be evaluated by its consistency with the organization's strategy. However, if we compare such evaluation with respect to strategy to the evaluation with respect to mission, we see that the two are quite different.

In the case of strategy, the assessment is based on core concepts of competitive advantage, scope, and industry analysis. Are we making a choice that is consistent with our competitive advantage, given our scope? Or, better yet, does the choice support and enhance our competitive advantage? If the choice represents the pursuit of a new opportunity and expands our existing scope, will we have a competitive advantage in the new domain (service, product, clients, or donors)? Ultimately, the question asked about any choice "boils down" to a judgment about whether it will enhance or diminish an organization's prosperity.

The logic involved in answering these questions with respect to strategy is fairly clear and is based on the framework introduced in chapters 2 and 3. The framework is based on empirical and theoretical knowledge about the causal relationships among critical economic variables. This knowledge provides a manager with a systematic way of analyzing questions and predicting the consequences of a choice for the economic viability of the organization (i.e., what will customers pay, how will they choose, what will be the cost or value of a choice?).

In the case of mission, the core values, purpose, primary goals, and vision are the bases for the tests. Central to execution in the domain of mission are questions like the following: Is a decision right or wrong? Is it consistent with core values? Does a choice serve the purpose or advance progress toward the primary goal and realization of the vision?

Answers to such questions are based on a logic of mission that parallels the logic of strategy. This logic is based on a model (assumptions, understandings, and explanations) of the causal relationships, and the nature of the world and the problems that the nonprofit addresses. In the world of evaluation, these models are referred to as *logic models, theories of change,* or *theories of action.*[19] Such models deal with social, environmental, or aesthetic phenomena that involve not only economic, but also psychological, sociological, and political factors. Typically, the causal relationships in these domains are relatively complex and the state of knowledge available is relatively undeveloped. Thus, the nonprofit manager faces considerably more uncertainty in evaluating key choices with respect to their impact on the organization's mission.

For example, Feed the Children is a "nonprofit, Christian, charitable organization providing physical, spiritual, educational, vocational/technical, psychological, economic and medical assistance and other necessary aid to children, families, and persons in need in the United States and internationally."[20] In evaluating a particular choice about a policy or resource allocation, Feed the Children would need to explore the degree to which the choice would advance its fundamental goal of reducing hunger. Or consider, for example, a nonprofit pursuing education reform based on creating small schools. Will the choice to reduce classroom size result in better learning outcomes, and will we be able to successfully implement a shift, given the current political situation? How will teachers and parents respond?

Despite the complexity and uncertainty, there has been considerable emphasis on the importance and value of making logic models in the social domain explicit as part of the process of evaluation.[21] Explication is important because it makes the assumptions and rationale underlying what an organization does and how it intends to achieve its primary goals transparent. It explains the causal mechanisms through which the activities undertaken by the organization will lead to the creation of social, environmental, or artistic value. Consider a generic logic model (see figure 4.4).

Over and above the challenges associated with logic models in most nonprofit arenas, using them to evaluate choices involved in execution is even more complicated for two reasons. First, depending on the level of specificity with which choices are defined, there will be literally thousands, or even tens of thousands, of choices to be made. So it is essential to identify and focus on a limited number of *critical* choices. This means prioritizing policies, activities, and resource allocation in terms of their importance to both the strategy and the mission. Second, any given choice can be consistent with the mission of an organization, but not the strategy, or vice versa. Hence, where there are tensions between the practical implications of mission and strategy, a determination must be made about how to balance this tension. In the ideal world of perfectly aligned organizations and congenial environments, there would be no instances in which mission

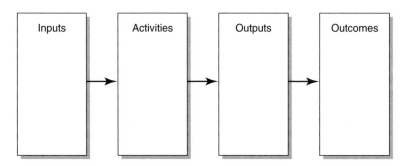

Figure 4.4. Generic logic model.

and strategy would conflict. But, given the harsh realities of a real world that has become more competitive, and where the pressures of commercialism have grown dramatically, the day when tensions between economic, emotional, and moral considerations were rare is now in the past.[22]

Consider the example of the American Repertory Theatre (ART), previously discussed in chapter 1, a leading nonprofit theater based in Cambridge, Massachusetts, at Harvard University. Since its founding in 1980, the ART has had a mission that is as ambitious as it is pure: to nurture artists and art of theater by protecting and insulating them from commercial pressures.[23] In pursuit of this mission, the ART has consistently made a host of choices about policy, activities, and resource allocation. These include choices such as operating as a resident theater, having rotating repertoire, offering training and education, and operating multiple stages and programs. Ask any theater manager about the economic implications of these choices and that manager will tell you that they are all negative in that they are very costly and more likely to reduce prosperity than to increase it. None is "profitable" under typical circumstances facing the average nonprofit theater. Thus, the question arises, how does the ART make it work? How is it sustainable? The answer has to be based on strategy. What are the scope, competitive advantage, and logic such that the ART is able to secure the resources that it needs to survive and even thrive? The strategy is outlined below.

Scope
1. Product
   - Experimental, avant-garde (new plays, reinterpretations of classics, neglected works)
   - Not historical or traditional
   - Larger casts
   - High-quality production values (technical, expensive productions)
   - Audience engagement (forces audience to question itself)
2. Market/geography
   - Greater Boston, especially Cambridge
3. Customer/audience
   - Well educated, affluent, young, elite
   - Arts and theater patrons, aficionados (people who read the text)
   - Theater "hard cores" and "wannabes" (people who want to be hard core)
   - Literati, intellectuals, socialites

- Genuinely curious
- Students
4. Funders
   - Harvard University
   - National foundations
   - Government (federal and state agencies)
   - Individual donors
   - Corporate sponsors

Competitive Advantage
- Reputation for advancing the art of theater and providing a supportive and nurturing setting to develop the next generation of leading artists
- *Quality*: emotionally and intellectually challenging, high-quality production values, high-quality acting
- *Innovator*: fresh approaches to work that is uniquely theatrical, provocative

Given this scope and competitive advantage, we can begin to outline the logic that explains why the strategy works and how the mission is to be realized. In addition, we can also start to understand how the choices that the ART makes to realize its mission also support its competitive advantage.

Nurturing and insulating artists from commercial pressures by providing stable employment by means of the ART's unique resident company fosters innovation and experimentation. This approach also appeals to Harvard University's objectives of basic research and generation of knowledge. The ART's education and training program is consistent with the educational mission of the university. Its avant-garde and intellectual programming appeal to the highly educated community in Cambridge and act as a recruiting vehicle. The investment in artists and developing the art form appeals to major funders who aspire to have an impact not just on individual organizations, but on the field as a whole. The prestige of the ART's affiliation with Harvard reinforces the legitimacy and credibility of the institution with national funders. Grants to the ART, even when they support controversial work, have the benefit of the doubt because of the stature of the theater and its academic base.

Ultimately, these choices result in a strategy that is viable for reasons that are somewhat unique—the ART satisfies the needs of Harvard University and national arts funders such as the National Endowment for the Arts (NEA) and major foundations. But there can really be only one theater with this strategy. Moreover, its continued viability depends on industry structure and preferences of major contributors and buyers.

Around 1992–1994, however, the climate changed. The culture wars, a shift in emphasis at the NEA from elite to popular art, and a number of other factors led to severe financial pressure at the ART. It seemed that its existing strategy would no longer support such an extreme and uncompromising pursuit of the organization's mission. As a result, the ART had to adapt its choices (but not necessarily its strategy) to reinforce its competitive position. The ART decreased costs to levels that this new environment and reduced degree of prosperity would support, and also undertook actions to increase its earned income, such as expanding its scope and—at the margins—broadening its basis of competitive advantage. It did so by programming more popular and less costly productions, devoting more attention to its relationship with Harvard University, and trying to extend the appeal of unique competitive advantage to new donors—individuals and corporations. These changes seem to have worked. Although there is more financial pressure at the ART (as at most theaters) than there was in the past, it still has relative freedom to invest in choices that are costly but advance its mission. It has what we referred to earlier as *control over its destiny*. Still, there are those who have criticized the ART's compromises and accused it of straying from its original mission.[24]

The importance of this example is that it highlights the interdependence of and tensions between mission and strategy when it comes to execution. Balancing these tensions and, in the best of all worlds, diminishing them through creative thinking is a key function of execution. But, given that this is not always possible, we need to reinforce the point made throughout this text: do not conflate mission and strategy.

Evaluation of choices from the perspective of mission should not take economic concerns into account. Questions about the implications of policies, activities, and resource allocation for mission must begin by assuming that the organization has the resources that it needs to undertake the actions and activities. The concern is therefore, "Does this choice directly advance the ends that the organization is committed to pursuing?" We ask, "Will the activity or the intervention produce the results that are implied by the primary goal? And are they consistent with achieving the goal or realizing that goal in a way that reflects all of the elements of the vision that is associated with the goal?"

These questions must be analyzed rigorously and carefully. Just as the assumptions about cause and effect and the state of the world embedded in the logic of a strategy are scrutinized, the validity of the assumptions and claims in a logic model must be examined as well. Nevertheless, it is not the function of mission to ensure or to assess economic implications. That is the role of strategy and its distinct logic. Only after a set of choices has been evaluated and prioritized in terms of their importance should the analysis of those choices from the perspective of strategy be undertaken.

5

Corporate Strategy, Alliances, and Collective Action

Application of the mission, strategy, and execution frameworks is most straightforward in the context of a single, strategically distinct business, or "pure player." Though not easy by any stretch of the imagination, the analysis is less difficult for simple organizations and industries than it is for complex organizations or industries. However, many nonprofits find themselves dealing with problems, pursuing aspirations, and operating in environments that are becoming more and more ambitious and multifaceted. Not surprisingly, this leads to the emergence of multibusiness or multiprogram organizations. Such structures create the need to manage the interaction among autonomous units or divisions within an organization, or what we will refer to as *intraorganizational* relationships.

In addition to these internal challenges, nonprofit leaders increasingly have to deal with cooperative *interorganizational* relationships, such as alliances and partnerships. These bilateral and trilateral relationships tend to arise from strategies that require firms to create or access resources beyond their individual capabilities. As a result, organizations establish formal ties that allow them to combine their resources and expertise in pursuit of shared and individual goals. Thus, the fundamental nature of an alliance is cooperative, as opposed to the competitive interorganizational relationships analyzed in chapters 2 and 3.[1]

Finally, there are some strategic objectives that require even broader levels of collaboration. In particular, large-scale efforts to influence the environment facing an entire class of organizations (e.g., an industry) require coordinated action that not only transcends organizational boundaries, but engages the majority, or at least a critical mass, of industry players. In contrast to alliances, which may involve only two or three parties, these *coalitions* involve dozens, hundreds, and even thousands of independent actors and often arise to improve *industry structure* (e.g., by promoting industry growth or creating barriers to entry). In the case of social-purpose organizations, collective action is also often geared toward advancing system-wide solutions (e.g., through advocacy or policy change).

In all three types of cooperation—multibusiness organizations, alliances, and collective action—the development and execution of strategy and mission become more intricate because of the need to coordinate action across intra- and interorganizational boundaries. This chapter extends the frameworks developed earlier to provide a basis for understanding and managing these three sets of issues: (1) interrelationship within complex multibusiness organizations, the domain of what is called *corporate strategy*; (2) ties that create relationships between two or more distinct organizations (both within and across sectors), *alliances* and *partnerships*; and (3) coordinated efforts to shape the environment through industry-wide collaboration, *coalitions* and *collective action*.

In the pages that follow, we will examine the fundamental questions that need to be addressed when one makes choices about *whether, when,* and *how* to establish and maintain these intra- and interorganizational relationships, as well as some of the challenges associated with managing them on an ongoing basis.

Corporate Strategy: Understanding and Managing Interrelationships

Corporate strategy . . . [i]s the mechanism by which a
diversified firm enhances the competitive advantage of its
business units.
—Michael E. Porter, *Competitive Advantage: Creating and*
  Sustaining Superior Performance

Corporate strategy is distinct from competitive or business strategy. Competitive strategy concerns the positioning of a firm to deliver products or services that satisfy a unique set of needs or customers, over against competitors (existing and potential) and substitutes. But *position* has to be defined within the context of an industry that is clearly identifiable and bounded—not only because this step is logically necessary in order to identify competitors, customers, and other key actors, but also because industries differ and one must understand the context of a business or nonprofit to predict and control its performance.[2] In general, it is more useful to analyze the battered women's shelter industry, or the substance abuse treatment industry, than to analyze the more broadly defined social services industry. Likewise, a nonprofit serving both battered women and people suffering from substance abuse is more likely to organize those activities as separate programs or units, thereby creating the need for corporate strategy.

Corporate strategy arises anytime two or more business units are part of the same company, and it must fulfill at least two critical functions. First, it must provide a rationale for including multiple businesses under the same organizational, financial, and legal structure. Given the choice to do so, the presumption must be that each individual unit is "better off," because its performance is enhanced by its ties either to the corporate entity (parent) or to the other units (siblings). Second, corporate strategy must provide the logic and plan of action for actually creating value at the corporate (family) level. That is to say, it must help the corporate manager figure out what she must do to enhance the performance of the individual units. Clearly, whether in the business arena, or in the nonprofit world, strategy in the context of a multibusiness enterprise becomes much more complicated than one in the context of a single business.[3]

Below, I review three approaches that have dominated the thinking about corporate strategy in the business world at different points in time over the last fifty years or so: *diversification, portfolio,* and *synergy/interrelationships.*

Early Approaches to Corporate Strategy

Early thinking about corporate strategy was dominated by a focus on *diversification,* an approach predicated on the assumption that a multibusiness enterprise with a diverse array of businesses competing in different industries would be less vulnerable to the risks associated within any single industry, risks such as cyclical swings or changing technology. Though this approach drove diversification and the creation of a host of conglomerates in the 1950s and 1960s, eventually, financial economists developed formal models demonstrating that investors could readily diversify *themselves* by assembling their own portfolios of securities. Hence, there was little value in having individual corporations to do this for them.[4] Moreover, subsequent work demonstrated that lumping unrelated businesses under the umbrella of a "conglomerate" actually destroyed value, because the capital market (investors) discounted the value of the diversified corporation as a whole, as well as its units, below its value as a stand-alone firm.[5] Explanations for this phenomenon include the problem that conglomerates obscure the financial and market performance of individual units and may also be more inefficient from an operational perspective.

As experience and research dispelled the myth that diversification and unrelated businesses under a corporate umbrella somehow added value by reducing risk, the era of unrelated diversification ended, and the multibusiness enterprise had to pass the test of adding value. Subsequently, the *portfolio* approach emerged in the 1970s. The premise underlying this perspective was that corporate managers could create value by optimizing the flow of capital among various businesses more efficiently than the external market. For example, the well-known Boston Consulting Group growth-share matrix classified a firm's portfolio of businesses into four categories: *cash cows*, *dogs*, *stars*, and *question marks*. Based on this framework, corporate strategy entailed achieving the right balance in the mix and size of various businesses through acquisition, divestiture, and the allocation of capital.

Work by another consulting firm, McKinsey and Company, with General Electric eventually led to a somewhat more sophisticated version of the portfolio approach, the Industry Attractiveness–Business Strength matrix. Like the diversification approach, portfolio-based corporate strategy eventually came under attack because of the unreliable nature of the classification schemes and argument, its rigidity, and another insight from financial economists: an efficient capital market should be more effective at allocating capital to distinct businesses than corporate managers operating within the firm.[6]

The third approach to corporate strategy that emerged was based on the notion of *synergy*, the idea that a set of independent businesses could benefit from being part of the same corporate structure if they were related in some way. The nature of just what constituted "related," however, was subject to wide interpretation. As a result, a host of mergers, acquisitions, and diversification initiatives were undertaken by corporate leaders confident about the synergy that would be created. Consider, for example, the Cinderella wedding of old-media giant Time Warner (which, at the time, owned magazines such as *Time*, the Warner Brothers movie studio, Warner Music Group, television networks such as CNN and HBO, and a variety of other media and entertainment holdings) to Internet new-media powerhouse America Online (AOL). Valued at $164 billion when it was announced, the deal was the largest merger of all time and "synergy" was central to the stated rationale driving this merger. Robert Pittman, president and COO of AOL at the time, argued,

> If you look at magazine subscriptions and our subscriptions, there are opportunities together. If you look at promoting—remember, AOL has a marketing budget of, what, $800 million a year? We can push that over to Time Warner. Again, those are savings that hit the bottom line. If you look at Time Warner's properties and trying to put them online, we can use our distribution platforms at a price much cheaper than Time Warner trying to do it alone. Even in terms of building the properties, again, you get the efficiencies of the AOL infrastructure now for the advantage of Time Warner. So the dreams and the hopes that the operating executives at Time Warner have had are now enabled by AOL. And I think the hopes and dreams that the senior AOL operators had are now enabled by Time Warner. And we find enormous synergies both on the revenue and on the cost side in this combination.[7]

By the end of 2003, the AOL–Time Warner merger was the poster child for the failure of synergy. Its architects, AOL CEO Steve Case, AOL COO Robert Pittman, and Time Warner CEO Gerald Levin had all been ousted. In the first quarter of 2002 the company generated a $54 billion loss, the largest quarterly loss in U.S. business history, and its share price had fallen from a high of $56 in the month that the merger was completed to a low of just under $10. The merger was the subject of a number of books exposing the conflict and flawed thinking of the deal-makers.[8] Perhaps the ultimate acknowledgment of the ill-fated deal was that, in an effort to restore investor confidence, AOL Time Warner shed the "AOL" from its name, becoming just Time Warner.

In the academic world of strategy, synergy, just like the logic of diversification and portfolio analysis, has fallen out of favor. In part, this is due to its abstract and ethereal nature, as well as the lack of clear conceptual models for how to evaluate or create it. In reality, synergy is as elusive as the Easter Bunny—it *sounds* good but is no more real than a fairy tale. Porter notes that creation "of value through synergy was widely accepted . . . in the 1960s and 1970s." "By the late 1970s, however, enthusiasm for synergy had waned," Porter continues. "Synergy it seemed was a nice idea but rarely occurred in practice."[9] He further argues—basing his views on a subsequent study of *Fortune* 500 companies—that "the track record of corporate strategies has been dismal." "The corporate strategies of most companies," he elaborates, "have dissipated instead of created shareholder value."[10]

Still another problem with synergy is that, by definition, it lacks the possibility that the effects of one business unit on another—or the effect of the corporate entity on a business unit—could be *negative*, meaning that whole would be less than the sum of the parts as stand-alone entities (in effect, value is destroyed). This negative effect can occur because of conflict between units or inconsistencies in their competitive strategies and markets, as when a high-end brand and a low-end, or value, brand are part of the same organization. This is the difficulty that some low-cost brands, such as Gallo in the wine industry, faced when attempting to move up-market, even in the face of dramatic improvements in product quality.[11]

From Synergy and Portfolios to Interrelationship and Spillovers

Advances in the area of corporate strategy eventually added rigor to the meaning and process of adding value to business units. Specifically, the notion of interrelationships among strategically distinct businesses and between parent and division took form. Contemporary work on corporate strategy has focused on more concrete and tangible mechanisms of value creation, specifically, *interrelationships* and *spillovers*.[12]

In the context of corporate strategy, value creation means that performance of the whole is greater than performance of the sum of the parts (units) operating alone. Such value arises because one unit (including corporate) enhances the competitive advantage and, hence, the performance of another unit.[13] Given this basic mechanism, two matters become clear: (1) that business strategy is the foundation for corporate strategy and (2) that the beneficial effects of interdependence between units are the rationale for the existence of the multibusiness enterprise. The independent contribution of these factors to business unit performance is supported by empirical studies of the determinants of business performance. Approximately 32 percent of the variation is explained by business unit, or segment, competitive position; 20 percent, by industry structure; 2 percent, by yearly macroeconomic factors; and 4 percent, by corporate-parent factors.[14]

Interestingly, the number of multibusiness enterprises and the extent of diversification belie the actual magnitude of the effects of corporate strategy on performance. Given the zeal with which managers pursue diversification, and the level of mergers and acquisition activity, one would expect to see more evidence that, overall, it actually makes a difference.

Types of Interrelationships and Spillovers

Porter identifies three key types of interdependence between units of a multibusiness enterprise: (1) intangible interrelationships, (2) tangible interrelationships, and (3) competitor interrelationships. Each of these interrelationships can have positive effects (enhancing competitive advantage), negative effects (eroding competitive advantage), or both on an individual unit. In looking at a pair or group of units, one should note that their net impact need not be symmetric; that is, they could be good for one side and not for the other. Intangible interrelationships involve sharing of knowledge and expertise across business units—for example, using marketing or manufacturing knowledge developed in one unit to strengthen another. Tangible interrelationships involve sharing activities among business units. For example, the development of technology that can be applied in two or more units may be conducted jointly or by corporate headquarters.

Johnson & Johnson, the health care leader, fostered this type of sharing when it centralized research and development on absorbent technology for five of its 150 divisions in the 1980s. Creating these interrelationships led technology advances in the area of absorbent materials to be used by the different divisions responsible for manufacturing diapers, sanitary products, and some hospital products. Moreover, in addition to developing new technology that could be used across the organization, the costs borne in their creation could be shared across multiple business units.[15] To contribute to a viable corporate strategy, the sharing must result in either lower costs or improved quality for the individual units. Costs can be lower if there are advantages of scale in performing the activity in larger batches. Again, Johnson & Johnson's decision to centralize certain activities provides an example. During the 1980s, the company consolidated advertising for its major consumer goods divisions in a central location, not only allowing the corporation to perform the activity more efficiently, but also giving it greater leverage to negotiate the best terms and prices for media buys.[16]

As this example illustrates, the value created through interrelationships can stem from reduced costs, but it can also come about as a result of increased differentiation (that is, if shared activity can be performed better, in ways that buyers value). In fact, *both* can occur, when sharing saves resources, which are then available to be invested in building other capabilities. These new capabilities can then benefit multiple units.[17]

Competitor interrelationships arise when multiple units of one entity simultaneously compete with multiple units of another multibusiness rival in different industries. The hallmark of this type of interrelationship is competitive interdependence, where competition in one industry may affect the behavior of rival units in other industries. There can also be competitive spillovers, as is the case with Microsoft's selling its computer operating systems (particularly, Windows) to support the advantages of its application software (Word, Excel, PowerPoint, and so forth). Of course, one unintended side effect of Microsoft's approach is the trouble it has had over the last ten years with U.S. Justice Department allegations of antitrust violations.

The Negative Consequences of Interdependence

All three types of interrelationships create interdependence among multiple units. Although this interdependence is the basis for sharing and coordination, it also comes with costs. Porter cites the costs associated with "coordination, compromise, and [loss of] flexibility."[18] These costs can stem from organizational dynamics, as well as from physical or economic constraints.

So, for example, the difficulty in coordinating shared activities often is the result of conflict in the way the units see and value the shared activity. Economically suboptimal choices are made because it is easier to compromise when there are different perspectives on how to configure shared activities. And structuring activities in order to serve multiple units may limit strategic flexibility by making it more difficult for an individual unit to change tactics in the future if these are dependent on the shared activity. Saloner and colleagues also point out that managers tend to focus on the positive benefits of sharing and ignore the costs—and, especially, the organizational challenges—involved in achieving these benefits.[19]

Neglect of the negative impact of interdependence is not surprising, given that, historically, the multibusiness or multidivisional enterprise emerged during the diversification era of corporate strategy. Documented in the classic work *Strategy and Structure* by Alfred Chandler, this organizational form was predicated on increasing independence of units (initially product or geographic divisions), freeing up corporate managers to focus on expansion into new markets and the allocation of resources among divisions (in effect, a diversification and portfolio logic). This perspective largely ignores interrelationships (and their costs) and, hence, provides little guidance about how to manage them.

Later work, building at least in part on the Chandler tradition, identified more explicitly the very real costs associated with interdependence, and more generally with any form of transaction. Transaction cost economics (TCE) explains when and why interdependence, in the form of an organization (i.e., hierarchy) would be a more efficient means of regulating exchanges than independence (i.e., market).[20] While a detailed description of TCE is well beyond the scope of this chapter, its importance lies in the contribution that it makes to understanding and thinking systematically about the costs, as well as the benefits, of interdependence.

Mechanisms for Managing Interrelationships

If interdependence in the form of interrelationships is critical to the effectiveness of corporate strategy, it therefore becomes essential to understand how to deal with interdependence. In particular, having recognized the costs and benefits of interdependence, we need to know something about how to manage them. Specifically, from a managerial perspective, rather than accept costs and benefits as given, we want to identify ways we can maximize benefits and minimize costs.

Although there are a host of specific tools and mechanisms for doing this, there are essentially two generic categories: *processes* and *structures*. Key processes include resource allocation and human resource management, and strategic planning. Structure relates to the design of an organization, particularly the formal mechanisms for coordination, communication, and integration across units, but including informal structure like culture as well. Different theorists emphasize different mechanisms. For example, Saloner focuses on resource allocation and organizational architecture (specifically, structure), with respect to which activities are performed centrally and which activities are decentralized.[21] Porter, on the other hand, focuses on the processes of strategic analysis and strategy formulation, and structure in terms of how business units are organized within the corporate structure, the nature of incentives and rewards, and the role of the corporate general manager.

Why is the interrelationships framework important? Just as with business or competitive strategy, managers need a disciplined approach to guiding the direction of their organization, one that ensures they are not fooling themselves about the likely performance consequences of their decisions. This is even more important in the domain of corporate strategy, because managers must overcome the long tradition of denial, self-deception, and wishful thinking that has led legions of corporations to undertake costly, even disastrous, acquisitions and diversification initiatives under the flag of synergy.[22] Moreover, the tendency to make these errors is exacerbated by psychological biases toward size and growth, independent of performance (whether profitability or social value).[23]

Corporate Strategy in the Nonprofit Literature

The central concern of corporate strategy—how to make the whole more than the sum of the parts—is the same for nonprofits as it is for for-profit organizations. And, increasingly, as organizations in the sector pursue growth, both in size and in the number of programs they undertake, we see an increasing number of nonprofits with multiple and distinct subunits.

However, even more so than business strategy, corporate strategy has received relatively little attention in the nonprofit strategic management literature. An early article by Ian McMillan draws attention to the need to evaluate the relative importance of programs within a multiprogram nonprofit and to match the allocation of time and money to those programs that are most critical. However, the basic approach still draws on the portfolio perspective by emphasizing the allocation of resources among distinct programs or businesses.[24] Just as in classical portfolio frameworks, this perspective focuses on decisions about acquisitions, divestitures, and investment, which, though deserving of attention, are less relevant than the challenge of synergy: making the whole more than the sum of its parts through the management of interrelationships in ways that build the competitive advantage of individual units.

As in the for-profit world, corporate strategy in nonprofits requires that each program or unit have its own viable competitive strategy, as well as a role within the overarching mission of the organization. But it also requires the organization to identify ways to take advantage of the interrelationships between its different parts or businesses. In essence, the question that must be answered when different businesses, entities, or programs exist under the umbrella of one nonprofit is this: how do they support one another as part of the same organization?

Without an understanding of the costs of interrelationships, organizations can expand in ways that ultimately destroy social and economic value, leading to the failure of an otherwise viable and successful individual enterprise.

Consider the example of the Career Action Center (CAC). Founded in 1973, CAC was at one time Silicon Valley's only source for job listings and career advice. During the 1980s and 1990s the organization grew dramatically, broadened its clientele and services, and achieved national recognition for its unique emphasis on self-reliance in career development. Despite this, after a protracted six-year decline, CAC closed its doors in 2002. This respected nonprofit was felled by the negative impact of interdependence between different programs under the same corporate umbrella that, over time, undermined the competitive advantage of each individual program. News reports on CAC's closing noted the organization was "torn between conflicting needs: those of individuals exploring career change, and those of corporations retraining employees as business changed."[25] In effect, the part of the organization serving the for-profit world could not coexist with the part that provided the traditional nonprofit social services. The combined corporate entity was what Porter refers to as "stuck in the middle" and hence unable to compete effectively in either business.[26]

Rubicon Programs: Corporate Strategy

Fortunately, however, there are also many examples in which the coexistence of different programs under the same roof has led to a whole that is greater than the sum of its parts. One such example is Rubicon Programs, a social service agency in Richmond, California, that serves the entire San Francisco Bay Area. Founded in 1973, Rubicon was originally started as an agency to provide services to mentally ill Californians deinstitutionalized after passage of the Lanterman-Petris-Short Act of 1967. From these humble beginnings, Rubicon grew into a multifaceted social enterprise that provides job training, counseling, and employment; delivers mental health and other supportive services; and builds and operates affordable housing for more than four thousand disabled, homeless, and economically disadvantaged people each year.

As a way of fulfilling the organization's mission while generating revenue to support its service activities, Rubicon Programs Incorporated started three revenue-generating enterprises (all residing under the umbrella of Rubicon Enterprises Incorporated), which together produce about 50 percent of the funds that are necessary to support the social service side of the organization. These three businesses are a landscaping business (Rubicon Landscape Services), a bakery (Rubicon Bakery), and a home health care agency (HomeCare Consortium, no longer active). The combination of a traditional, social service agency with entrepreneurial, money-making businesses has been a fruitful pairing for Rubicon and its clients. In 2002 Rubicon Programs placed 432 people in jobs through its employment program, directly employing 280 people, many of whom are clients of the organization. Rubicon's business enterprises currently employ 129 people.

For Rubicon, starting and operating revenue-generating enterprises offered the organization many benefits. First, there was the obvious benefit of the generation of revenues and "profit" to help defray the expenses for the social services that it provides to its target client base. Second, clients—many of whom were economically disadvantaged, disabled, or homeless, and who had little opportunity to find meaningful employment—would have quality employment opportunities unavailable to them elsewhere. Third, as these enterprises made their mark in the community (Rubicon Bakery, for example, is famous in the Bay Area for the quality of its products), the Rubicon "brand" would be enhanced in the public eye, attracting more attention and more funding to the entire organization, from public and private donors and sources. Rubicon Enterprises does in fact provide a generous contribution to support the organization's social programs. The enterprises are able to accomplish this because they offer high-quality products that clients and customers are willing to pay for, and they are able to keep expenses below the revenue that they generate, resulting in a surplus (or, a *profit*, for the corporate entity).

One of the advantages of being in an organization with multiple units is that, by cooperating with their sister business units and with the corporate parent, individual units can gain a competitive advantage in the market-place. For Rubicon, the potential advantages are numerous. For example, by running accounting and payroll out of the parent organization, Rubicon Programs Incorporated, each business unit can utilize these services at considerably lower cost than if they were to establish their own in-house accounting and payroll department, or to outsource to a bookkeeping or accounting firm. Similarly, human resources functions—recruiting and hiring new employees, administering benefits programs, ensuring compliance with labor laws and regulations—can be centralized within the corporate parent, allowing the individual businesses to once again avoid the additional expense of establishing their own human resources departments or outsourcing to a contractor.

Rubicon Landscape Services is able to draw from a ready pool of pre-screened people (developed and maintained by Integrated Services, its sister organization on the social services side of the house) when it needs trainees or temporary workers to fill an immediate need. This ability to draw workers from within the organization saves Rubicon Landscape Services the time and expense required to recruit and screen its own employees—a significant savings. Likewise, each of the organization's businesses benefits from being part of the whole by enjoying access to a pool of trained labor and the necessary employee support systems for those businesses. Moreover, each supports the organization's core programs in human services and individual development by creating opportunities for the people who are being served by the social service part of the agency.

In its early days, there was little thought given to the potential for applying corporate strategy in leveraging Rubicon's business units. Originally, the primary purpose of these enterprises was training clients and providing them with meaningful employment opportunities, not to generate revenue for the organization's social programs. As a result, Rubicon experimented with a variety of different enterprises, including a retail nursery, building and grounds services, a café, and a catering service, before settling on the landscaping, bakery, and home health care ventures.

Rubicon has built an organization that has received much positive publicity as a model of social entrepreneurship and as a successful provider of social services to its Bay Area clients. In addition to serving as the subject of a PBS program, *The Visionaries*, Rubicon has been profiled in *Harvard Business School Working Knowledge*, the *Christian Science Monitor*, *U.S. News and World Report*, and the *Chronicle of Philanthropy*. The Rubicon brand carries a lot of weight in the Bay Area—and across the nation—and this weight benefits not only the parent corporation, but also the individual enterprises within it. Not only are customers drawn to Rubicon's products, but potential funders (philanthropists, grant-makers, government agencies, private-sector partners, and others) are, as well.

A successful corporate strategy requires getting strong initiative out of individual units, as well as getting cooperation across business units.[27] This is just as true for a nonprofit organization such as Rubicon as it is for a for-profit organization such as IBM or General Electric. Early on there was good cooperation across Rubicon's business units, as well as a high level of initiative, both of which helped to make the individual business units more competitive.

For example, because the organization knew the property management business as a result of its work in that area, Rubicon became a better developer of low-income and special-needs housing when it became a player in that market. And, though not the final determinant of whether or not customers purchase their products (price and quality are higher on the list), the high regard in which Rubicon's social service programs are held rubs off positively when salespeople for the Rubicon Bakery go calling on a new retail account. And, of course, the revenues generated by the enterprises can be used to invest in new facilities and capital equipment, something a smaller enterprise might not be able to afford.

But, as Rubicon's enterprises matured, a natural tension began to grow within the organization, pitting those running Rubicon's social programs against those running its enterprises. Although the social programs depended on the enterprises to train and place their clients, many of whom had very little work experience and may have taken much time to train to a minimal level of performance, the enterprises in some cases preferred to hire people who were proven to be stable employees and who could perform at a high level of productivity. Within the organization, balancing the need for production versus the need for support and training became a delicate act.

This balancing act was amply illustrated in a Roberts Foundation report. According to this report, at Rubicon,

> The business staff feel that the businesses have production
> requirements to meet and only want to meet with vocational
> counselors when a problem presents itself. Vocational counselors
> feel the participants are people who have not fared well in the
> workforce because of a wide range of problems; without ongoing,
> active support, participants are at risk for failure at Rubicon. A

conceptual agreement exists that the employees/participants need some kind of additional support. However, the additional support is sometimes in direct conflict with site productivity.[28]

But corporate strategy requires hard choices. Partly because it was unable to integrate the division into its corporate strategy, in 2003 Rubicon closed down HomeCare Consortium, one of its three commercial enterprises. Despite having provided more than twelve thousand hours of care to clients in the community in 2001, the enterprise could not overcome a competitive disadvantage, an unattractive industry, and the absence of any substantial benefits from interdependence with the other divisions and the corporate parent.

Interestingly, this decision can be viewed as both a failure and a triumph of corporate strategy. On one hand, Rubicon had invested significant time, energy, and money in the division that was unable to create social or economic value to justify this investment. On the other hand, the discipline of an explicit analysis of its corporate strategy led to a difficult, but value-enhancing, choice. This is the power of a robust normative framework.

Alliances, Partnerships, and Joint Ventures

Managing alliances, like managing the multibusiness enterprise, requires a focus on the structures and processes that coordinate the actions and manage the relationships (i.e., interdependence) between independent entities. Making alliances and partnerships effective requires an expansive conception of strategic action. Specifically, we need a framework that informs our advancement of strategy with design of activities that transcend the boundaries of the strategic business unit and guide the building of competitive advantage through relationships with other actors.

When these actors are within the same parent organization, the relationship falls within the domain of corporate strategy. When the actors are outside the boundaries of the parent (multibusiness enterprise), the relationship falls within the domain of alliances and partnerships. Herein lies the unique challenge of such relationships. Because partners are by definition located outside the boundaries of the organization, unlike hierarchal divisions within corporate strategy, an alliance engenders questions about how to design ways of coordinating the action of autonomous actors. Partners have to design the terms of the alliance so that it advances the interests of both parties. The calculus involved in solving this problem is more complex than that involved in trying to maximize the welfare of a single entity—even if it is a heterogeneous one, as in the case of the multibusiness enterprise.

It is therefore necessary to develop new concepts for thinking about strategy and its relationship to organizational performance. Ultimately, alliances must pass the same tests as corporate diversification; that is, they must answer the question, how is each entity better off by virtue of its association with the other? But they must also pass this test at a higher level, because cooperation cannot be enforced through authority or hierarchy as it can in the case of corporate interrelationships. As we shall see, nonprofit alliances can involve another nonprofit, a for-profit, or a public-sector entity. While each type of partnership raises unique challenges, all of these alliances must pass the "better off" test. In addition, they all raise similar interorganizational relationship issues that can be analyzed with use of a common framework.

Types of Alliances and Partnerships

There are three distinct kinds of alliances that are becoming more common in the nonprofit world. The first is a partnership between two or more organizations within an industry created for the purpose of delivering products or services that the organizations would not be able to create on their own. In the performing-arts world, for example, the growing cost of mounting productions is leading some theaters to coproduce shows with "competitors," sharing the costs and risks, as well as the benefits. It also allows them to produce a play that may be too large, complex, or expensive for either one to do independently. This kind of alliance allows the partners to draw on each other's unique capabilities. Noted expert on nonprofit alliances Jim Austin refers to this type of relationship as "intrasector cooperation."[29]

Another advantage of these alliances is that they reduce the degree of competition that would exist if each organization tried to produce the same type of event or show on its own. For instance, in social services, budget pressures can lead to rationalization—the elimination of capacity from the industry—which reduces the level of rivalry. For example, multiple homeless shelters in a city may agree to merge their facilities and services for the sake of efficiency or to better serve their clients in the face of diminishing resources.

A second type of partnership is the ubiquitous alliance between nonprofits and corporations. Given the focus of this text, we are concerned with relationships that are "strategic," meaning that they go beyond sponsorship or corporate philanthropy. The alliance must create some kind of shared activity that is intended to benefit both the company and the nonprofit. Typically, these alliances involve line managers and operational units (signifying the fact that they are true *working* relationships), rather than the corporate philanthropy or community relations departments.

According to Austin, alliances typically pass through three stages of development he dubs the "Collaboration Continuum": These stages are philanthropic (where the relationship is for the most part between a charitable donor and a recipient), transactional (where the partners exchange resources through specific activities, such as event sponsorships or licensing), and integrative (where the partners' missions, people, and activities experience more collective action and organizational integration than in the other two stages).[30] That alliances between nonprofits and for-profits are becoming more frequent, and more important to the parties that participate in them, is clear. Austin notes, "Cross-sector collaboration between nonprofits and businesses has been growing, and this trend will accelerate as we enter this new century. These alliances are becoming of strategic importance to the partners."[31]

The third type of alliance is with a public entity. But, here again, the new alliances go beyond the traditional relationships of contractor–customer, funder–grantee as in the case of social services, or National Endowment for the Arts funding, respectively. Just like nonprofit–private sector alliances, alliances with public entities involve joint production or delivery of a social good or service while advancing the distinct interests of both organizations. In the case where the alliance advances a *shared* interest, it should involve substantial and meaningful contributions by both (or all parties), as well as active collaboration.

The Growth of Alliances among Nonprofits

Accepted as strategic tools in the world of business for many years, alliances and partnerships have become important to nonprofits, as well, for reasons that we shall discuss shortly. Essentially, an alliance is a bilateral, or occasionally trilateral, relationship that is created to advance the strategic interests of the parties involved.[32] These relationships can be with other nonprofits, businesses, or government agencies. Although there are some common themes among these different types of alliances, the forces driving each are largely distinct.

Nonprofit-Nonprofit Alliances. In the case of alliances among nonprofits within an industry, the most prominent reason for their creation is to deal with increased competition. This competition stems from a combination of the growth in the number of organizations, and declining resources and support. In many cases, an alliance with a similar organization provides a way to cut costs through sharing, reduce duplication (and competition) by consolidating programs, or deliver original or superior products and services by combining expertise and resources. The competitive pressure that nonprofits feel is very real, and alliances can improve efficiency, enhance competitive advantage, and even reduce the level of competition between existing organizations directly.

Even when these reasons are not enough to entice nonprofits to pursue such alliances on their own, they may be pushed into relationships by funders who see (or suspect) duplication and inefficiency, and who view alliances—and even outright mergers—as a way to address this problem. And, in the case of large-scale problems such as AIDS, education, and environmental protection, funders often view forced collaboration as a way to maximize impact and encourage more coordinated or holistic solutions and approaches.

Nonprofit-Business Alliances. With respect to alliances between nonprofits and business, a critical enabling factor is the increased receptivity and interest on the part of businesses because of the recognition that perceptions of their corporate citizenship, contributions to communities in which they operate, and social responsibility can positively impact their firms' performance.[33] And, at the same time, these "nonmarket" forces can also constrain a firm's strategic options, a fact that has led to the emergence of interest in the political environment of business.[34] Sometimes, these effects occur as a result of regulatory action by the public sector.

An excellent example is in the area of retail banking, where waves of acquisition and growth in the industry during the 1980s and 1990s often engendered resistance from communities and activists unhappy with the lending practices of some acquiring banks. The result was the Community Reinvestment Act, which requires banks to work to meet the credit needs of the *entire* community in which they operate—not just the more "attractive" middle and upper income members of the community, but lower income members, as well. As the price of gaining approval for a number of its acquisitions of smaller, local banks, New England–based Fleet Bank (now known as FleetBoston Financial Corporation) had to make a real and demonstrable commitment to invest in lower-income, predominantly minority communities to support urban economic development. Would the bank have undertaken these investments without the pressure of regulators? Perhaps, but it is clear that regulation helped motivate their actions.

Sometimes, perceptions of corporate citizenship can impact the bottom line (or at least appear to, based on press coverage) by generating an appeal with groups of consumers who find social responsibility or activist agendas attractive. Consider the Body Shop or Ben and Jerry's, businesses that have carefully cultivated socially conscious or progressive reputations to build their brands. Even in the often maligned oil industry, British Petroleum (BP) pursued aggressive environmental policies, in part as a way to differentiate itself across the world. In 1998 Lord Browne, BP's Group Chief Executive, asserted that the firm would reduce its emissions of greenhouse gases by "10 percent from a 1990 baseline over the period to 2010."[35] Five years later, he announced that the company had achieved its goal well ahead of schedule and with no incremental financial cost.[36]

Alliances with nonprofit environmental groups were instrumental in BP's ability to achieve these results. In particular, the company relied on an internal emissions trading program developed in conjunction with the Environmental Defense Fund (EDF). Emissions trading is "a market mechanism that allows emitters (countries, companies or facilities) to buy emissions from or sell emissions to other emitters." It helps to facilitate cost-effective reduction of overall emissions "by allowing those who can achieve reductions less expensively to sell excess reductions (e.g., reductions in excess of those required under some regulation) to those for whom achieving reductions is more costly."[37]

BP's initiative in this area garnered it praise for its leadership. EDF executive director Fred Krupp called BP's commitment "a really magnificent example of a corporation acting responsibly . . . [that would] set up a whole new level of expectations for other corporations within the oil and gas industry."[38] In addition, BP partnered with the Pew Center on Global Climate Change, a nonprofit whose mission is "to provide credible information, straight answers, and innovative solutions in the effort to address global climate change."[39] Through the Pew Center's Business

Environmental Leadership Council (BELC), BP works with other companies to explore and share insights and best practices about practical solutions to environmental challenges. It is critical to note that, in the partnerships with both EDF and the Pew Center, no financial contributions or exchanges occurred. Both relationships were based on the exchange of ideas and expertise that advanced the strategic objectives of both parties.

Alliances with nonprofits can also be a way for corporations to expand into new markets—markets that might have been considered too risky or unprofitable to serve in the absence of such an alliance. Consider, for example, the Ford Foundation's efforts to bring mortgage lending to poor communities by partnering in 1998 with mortgage lending giant Fannie Mae and North Carolina nonprofit Self Help. By using the foundation's money to take positions that helped to cover some of the commercial banks' early risks, Ford was able to leverage $50 million in funding into $2 billion in affordable mortgages for 35,000 low-income homebuyers nationwide.[40]

Ford Foundation president Susan Berresford described the convergence of interests between social purpose organizations and businesses:

> I don't think there's anything inconsistent with the profit motive
> and interest in social improvement and making people's lives
> better. Sometimes those things are in opposition to each other,
> but they don't always have to be. One of the areas of work that
> the foundation has begun to do in recent years is to support
> people who are trying to find ways that the for-profit side of
> businesses can have a more powerful impact in low-income
> communities in a positive way. For example, we had been work-
> ing with financial services companies, banks principally, trying to
> work out with them some innovative loan products that bring
> homeownership to lower income people and minority groups who
> have been closed out of the mortgage market. The banks see this
> as a possible new market for them. We see it as a way to build
> assets in poor communities, and assets make a difference in poor
> communities, and give people opportunities.[41]

Similarly, Michael Porter points out how targeting underserved populations in the inner city can bring prosperity to these communities and at the same time generate profits for the companies that move into these markets.[42] Often, penetrating such underserved markets is undertaken as part of alliances and partnership, as in the Ford Foundation example. Beyond their immediate benefits, such alliances can also help companies develop and refine new ideas and build new capabilities.[43]

From the nonprofit perspective, the appeal of these relationships is that the more instrumental they are on the part of the corporations, the more stable the relationship is and the greater the potential for growing the joint activities associated with them may be. So long as the benefit exists, the exchange is likely to be secure. In contrast, contribution and sponsorships are subject to unpredictable shifts in the philanthropic or marketing priorities of the corporate partner. As they evolve, such relationships also tend to become more focused and specialized, and as a result both partners' ability and incentive to switch are reduced.

Separate from the stability that results from nonprofit-business alliances, the revenue streams associated with noncharitable partnerships are viewed favorably by philanthropic funders who have come to embrace sustainability and social enterprise. It makes nonprofits seem more business-like, less dependent, and more entrepreneurial—traits that appeal to funders in their own right.

Nonprofit-Government Alliances. In the case of nonprofit-public alliances, part of the shift appears to be related to changes in the nature of the relationship from "contracting" to "partnering." This change represents a ceding of control over, and responsibility for, social needs and problems from government to the nonprofit and private sectors. This outcome is consistent with the philosophy driving the overall downsizing of government: the belief that large bureaucratic government agencies cannot achieve the levels of efficiency and innovation of smaller networks or autonomous providers. The resulting desire to privatize, localize, de-bureaucratize, and deregulate services creates conditions that favor the formation of alliances and partnerships.

On the nonprofit side, there has been a parallel shift from viewing government as just a source of funding to viewing it as a powerful vehicle for taking social innovations to scale. This is because government agencies often control the facilities and infrastructure necessary for widespread distribution of aid or services, or implementation of programs on a large scale. In addition, government can often provide an infusion of resources along with legitimacy and connections to take programs to a national level, as it did for City Year's agenda of national service through the creation of AmeriCorps. Moreover, as nonprofits have become more politically sophisticated and savvy, they have come to recognize the role that the public sector plays in shaping the context in which they pursue social objectives (that is, the legal and regulatory environment). The importance of relationships with government becomes increasingly clear as one understands the ways in which they can and do influence the incentives of donors and clients through public policies.

Another, less salient, but equally important, set of forces has to do with ideas and ideology, specifically, the penetration of business ideas and values into the nonprofit sector. While the reasons for this penetration are complex and multifaceted, they include concerns about the effectiveness and the efficiency of longstanding investments in nonprofits and the social programs and services they provide.[44] The solutions range from new approaches to philanthropy and grant-making, to ideas about earned income, sustainability, and entrepreneurial orientation. However, all implicitly or explicitly involve an increased focus on efficiency and effectiveness, both of which mitigate for consolidation, cooperation, and better allocation of resources across organizations and, hence, alliances. These largely instrumental forces add to the existing moral forces driving collaboration, forces which are already embedded in the nonprofit ethos of inclusiveness, community, and the pursuit of larger purpose, and which create natural inclinations toward cooperation.

A Strategic View of Alliances

Just like the logic of corporate strategy, the logic of alliances can be best viewed in the context of the fundamental principles of competitive strategy. The key question is this: What is the contribution of any given alliance to the competitive advantage of the organization or its operational units? For nonprofits, an equally important question is, what is the contribution of any given alliance to achieving the organization's mission?

The challenge facing nonprofit leaders with respect to any alliance is (just as it is for business leaders) to rank, integrate, and align the partnership to maximize an organization's impact over the long run. *Ranking* existing or potential alliances according to this criterion provides the basis for evaluating and prioritizing the resources or attention a given alliance is entitled to. *Integrating* involves managing tensions and trade-offs between the strategic value of any given alliance and its contribution to advancing the mission (that is, the economic and psychological logics). *Aligning* involves actively shaping the internal and external context in order to reduce the inevitable tensions. This might, for example, entail shifting public opinion, the expectations of an alliance partner, or staff perceptions in order to create closer alignment between the financial contribution of the alliance and its mission-related contributions.

At the end of the day, strategy has to inform choice. Business strategy guides choices about resource allocation within a business unit or program. Corporate strategy should inform choices about resource allocations outside or across units. An alliance (just like an acquisition, in the case of corporate strategy) represents an external allocation of resources. Indeed, alliances and acquisition are alternative ways of pursuing organizational goals. But, although an alliance is less permanent (or is reversible) and more flexible than an acquisition, it provides the organization with less control over the activities.

Ultimately, the choice between an alliance and an acquisition (or, for that matter, building an activity or division de novo) will depend on the costs and benefits associated with the particular situation. Nevertheless, alliances should be evaluated according to the same criteria as an acquisition. Will the organization be better off from a competitive standpoint? If so, will the competitive gains be sustainable? And, finally, do the gains exceed the financial (or mission-related) costs of establishing and maintaining the alliance?[45] Moreover, if, as is usually the case, resources are limited and the possibility of multiple alliances exists, the framework needs to tell us how we choose. Does Alliance A advance the strategy and mission, and if so, does it advance them more than Alliance B, C, or D?[46]

Thinking Strategically about Alliances and Partnerships

As we have noted, a host of factors are driving nonprofits to establish alliances with other nonprofits, businesses, and government. The basic presumption behind these alliances and partnerships is that they represent significant opportunities to leverage economies of scale, synergies, learning, transfer of ideas, and ability to draw on the unique capabilities of each of the different sectors. But, as we know from the literature on alliances in the private sector (and our exploration of interdependence), these collaborations come with significant coordination costs. These costs can sometimes far outweigh the benefits of such unions.

In the case of cross-sector alliances, questions can arise about consistency of core values, purpose, goals, and vision between the organizations, especially when they are from two different sectors of the economy (private, nonprofit, or public). We need to understand the answer to this question: is the psychological logic of the two partners compatible? Even if the goals are the same, how they go about reaching these goals could be a major source of conflict. Similarly, there are strategic questions that need to be answered with respect to any alliance or partnership, having to do with the impact of that alliance—specifically the shared activity or program—on the competitive advantage of, and mission of, each of the respective organizations.[47] So, rather than assume that alliances and partnerships are good or create value per se, we should analyze them carefully using the logic of both strategy and mission. This is true even in settings where collaboration may be valued for its own sake. Ultimately, the alliance has to pass the test of value creation, whether social or economic. The City Year example referred to earlier provides an illustration of the strategic implications of alliances. In the early 1990s, City Year accepted a large grant from the federal government to support and expand its program. Prior to this infusion of public funding, its financial support had come primarily from the private sector. This new source of money seemed to be a windfall, as well as a testament to the appeal of the young nonprofit. It was also the first step in the development of a relationship with the government that would eventually lead to the formation of a national service entity, AmeriCorps.

On its face, this alliance advances the strategy and mission of City Year (increasing geographic scope and moving toward its goal of influencing a national program), but the relationship had other equally dramatic strategic implications. First, it increased buyer power significantly as government funding jumped to close to 50 percent of the organization's revenues. Second, it expanded City Year's competitive scope to include the public sector. Such expansions always raise the question whether the competitive advantage of the organization applies to the new set of buyers. In this instance, difficulties arose around government expectations about financial accountability. Known for detail-oriented reporting requirements, the federal government had buyer needs (specifically, a detailed accounting of expenditures of taxpayer funds) that City Year was not configured to meet. As a result of a government audit, in 1996 the organization was cited for failure to document expenses and for misallocating grant funds.[48] This was not a case of impropriety, but simply a failure to satisfy the unique expectations of a particular buyer—but a very powerful one.

Yet, while City Year's relationship with the government deepened through the creation of AmeriCorps, even this path proved to be fraught with other perils as ideological battles arose in Congress over the true nature of "service." Disputes over the role of compensation threatened the federal funding for City Year and other youth service organizations. In addition, cofounders Michael Brown and Alan Khazei had to spend considerable time lobbying in Washington. The more time they spent in Washington lobbying their government sponsors, the less time they had to devote to running the organization.

All in all, it is not that the partnership was necessarily bad, but it did involve costs and require shifts in the execution of City Year's strategy. Neither of these consequences appears to have been anticipated on the front end. Herein lies the lesson of this section: alliances, no matter what benefits they bring, have to be entered into with a clear understanding of the costs and strategic implications of the relationship.

Industry-Level Collaboration: Collective Action

Collective action at the industry level is, in effect, a larger and broader-based intrasector alliance. However, because it serves a fundamentally different strategic function, we will treat collaboration among a large number of players within an industry as a distinct phenomenon. To be more specific, coalitions among multiple "competitors" in an industry typically form in order to shape the political, economic, or social environment in which they reside. Such collaboration is a form of *collective action*, a mechanism through which individual actors coordinate their choices and actions in order to improve their collective welfare. In the absence of such coordination, the improvement (creation of value) would not occur. Though it seems eminently sensible, this type of coordination is notoriously difficult to achieve.[49]

A Proactive Stance toward the Environment

The target of collective action in the context of strategy is industry structure. To see the possibilities and potential of collective action, we need to recognize that industry structure is neither fixed nor static, though we typically treat it as such in developing the competitive strategy of an individual business. Recall that the analysis of industry structure is a way of assessing how hospitable an environment is, and it provides a methodology for evaluating the forces that determine the level of profitability or prosperity an industry can support. Some industries are more attractive (support higher levels of prosperity on average) than others. In addition, industries change in attractiveness over time. Indeed, in some cases, the transformation can be dramatic and rapid. Recall the impact of cable on the television industry that we analyzed in the KQED and public television case of chapter 3. Or consider the impact of deregulation in the airline or telecommunications industries. Thus, the environment in which an organization competes is a key determinant of its performance and prosperity.

Why is collective action at the industry level important? It is important because industry structure, and the environment more generally, are shaped by a variety of external and internal forces that can be actively influenced—but usually not by one competitor unilaterally. And, especially for nonprofits, coalitions and collective action focus on the nonmarket (political, legal, regulatory, and social) environment, as well. In contrast to competitive strategy, corporate strategy, and alliances, which place the focus on the positioning of the business unit and the firm, coalitions and collective action focus on industry structure.

So what does one do upon finding oneself in a structurally unattractive industry, or in an industry whose attractiveness is declining? These questions are particularly relevant to nonprofits because they often inhabit industries that by their very nature are relatively unattractive and that tend to be avoided by profit-seeking enterprises.[50] Even though private-sector players have entered fields like health care and education, not many for-profits are clamoring to break into the business of feeding the homeless or training disabled veterans.

The question itself evokes the possibility of being able to "do something." This necessarily implies that industry structure (or the environment more generally), rather than being taken as a given, can be changed. And, indeed, much of what happens through industry association and professional groups is fundamentally designed to shape industry structure. Perhaps the classic historical example of this is organized labor. By forming a union, workers dramatically increase their supplier power vis-à-vis an industry. This makes all of the workers in the union better off because of their collective ability to claim more of the value created by the industry. But in order to do this, they must coordinate their actions.

Another contemporary example is the pharmaceutical industry and its efforts, largely through its industry association, the Pharmaceutical

Research and Manufacturers of America (PhRMA), to influence the regulatory, legal, and political environment in ways that preserve the attractive structure of the industry (the pharmaceutical industry has consistently been the most profitable in the United States). Particularly, legislation to provide a prescription drug benefit for Medicare was shaped in ways that leave the industry better off.[51]

So, in the best of all possible worlds, the desideratum is to make the environment better for everyone, or at least for competitors or incumbents. As we will see, this is not always easy, nor should we expect it to be. But, in a large number of settings, collective action, especially for nonprofits, can provide a basis for ensuring that the environment does not worsen.

Defensive Collective Action: Dealing with Threats to Industry Structure

There is a host of players outside an industry whose actions can contribute to deterioration of its structure. In some cases, these actions are intended to have this effect. For example, producers of a substitute product want to "eat your lunch." In other cases, the damage is unintentional, and, in fact, the actors may be trying to help but inadvertently end up harming the industry structure.

Two key groups that exert powerful influence on the structure of industries inhabited by nonprofits are government and philanthropy. Government has a major impact, both as funder and as regulator. Grant-makers—both organizations and individuals—contribute cash to nonprofits to enable them to carry out their stated missions. But, at the same time, their overall patterns of funding decisions can have a dramatic and long-term impact on the industry structure of their grantees, and some of these effects are unintended and poorly understood.

One example is the diffusion of focus engendered by funders that try to push the latest trend, fad, or "cause of the month" onto their grantees. The problem with this is that it contributes to "mission creep," which eventually undermines differentiation among organizations, increasing competition and weakening organization-level competitive advantage. Organizations without a clear and well-understood competitive advantage find their efforts fragmented and become even more prone to opportunistic money-chasing behavior—outcomes that make it more difficult rather than less difficult for organizations to create social value. Development of new programs to appeal to funder enthusiasms also creates more overhead and more infrastructure within these organizations, which need to be supported with additional general operating funds, which are often not linked to these one-off initiatives.[52]

A second consequence of funding trendiness is the creation of new organizations during periods of excitement and exuberance. The amounts of funding can lead to growth in number and size of organizations, eventually creating overcapacity when the funding community moves on to a new enthusiasm. Overcapacity in the arts or youth programs has the same adverse effects that it does in the airline or steel industries: it dramatically increases competition and decreases the average level of prosperity of all incumbents. These effects are exacerbated by the high psychological barriers to exit in many nonprofit industries.[53]

Mechanisms Driving the Deterioration of Differentiation

The most pernicious of mechanisms leading to the deterioration of industry structure stems from policies and practices by funders or government that increase competition by homogenizing the existing population of organizations. Again, as I noted earlier, this effect, though unintended, is common enough that I want to illustrate it with a few examples and suggest how collective action by industry could provide a means for challenging funder practices or government policies that contribute to this problem.

PBS Programming. The Public Broadcasting Service is a private, nonprofit corporation composed of approximately 350 members, or public television stations, in the United States. During the 1980s, PBS began to evolve from a decentralized trade association into a more distinct and independent corporate entity. During the course of this evolution, decision-making authority for the core PBS schedule shifted from what was essentially a decentralized market-based mechanism, to a more centralized PBS staff function.[54]

Initially, member stations could purchase programs on an individual basis, in effect using any percentage of the PBS program schedule that they wanted. Not surprisingly, many stations began to "cherry pick" a select number of programs with the highest ratings. As a result of this fragmentation, many programs in the PBS pool became "unprofitable": the overall revenue from the total number of stations purchasing them was insufficient to cover the cost of producing these shows. Given the noncommercial mission of public television, the potential impact of this trend on quality and breadth of programming raised concerns within the PBS leadership.

In response, PBS introduced a new system that required all PBS member stations to purchase either 100% of programming (core stations) or no more than 25% (Program Differentiated Provider, or PDP, stations). In most cases, the PDP stations were the secondary or tertiary PBS station in multistation markets—large metropolitan areas where there were two or more public television stations.

Although this policy addressed the problem of "cherry picking," it created a new problem for multimarket stations in particular: it constrained their ability to select a menu of programs that would allow themselves to differentiate themselves from other PBS stations in their market. Recall that this was exactly the challenge noted in the case example of KQED and KTEH in the San Francisco Bay Area (see chapter 3). To the extent that the programming of KQED is essentially the same as KTEH, there is little incentive for a cable operator to carry both of them, much less the other two public television stations in the market.

Not surprisingly, PBS member stations complained bitterly, and there were some modifications and exceptions made to the policy that allowed some stations to get as much as 35 percent of the PBS schedule. Although this is an example of a coordination among multiple industry actors, the long-term collective action strategies of PDP stations have proven even more beneficial. For example, through an alliance called the Program Resources Group, they have been able to pool their resources and viewership to acquire or develop exclusive programming that is available only to members of this group. Hence, it facilitates their ability to differentiate themselves from primary or core PBS stations, and reduces their overall program acquisition cost.

Lila Wallace–Readers Digest Audience Diversification Program. Another example of practice that inadvertently undermined differentiation comes from the nonprofit theater industry. In the early 1990s, the National Endowment for the Arts and a number of foundations, notably the Lila Wallace–Readers' Digest Foundation, provided a significant number of large grants to encourage and help theaters to diversify their audiences, in particular to attract ethnic minorities who were underrepresented among mainstream theatergoers. Interestingly, the Wallace funding, $27 million in total, was directed through two separate programs toward both smaller community theaters and large, established institutions.[55] Both were intended to bring new audiences to the table and bring the complexion of theater audiences in line with the changing face of the American population. As a result, major mainstream theaters that received the money introduced plays by minority artists or that dealt with themes of ethnic relevance. In addition, smaller community theaters that had been located in and catered to minority audiences not only expanded their seasons to offer more work, but also presented more conventional work in an effort to broaden and expand their own audience base.

On a values level, both of these trends would seem to be appealing—to our sense of egalitarianism, access, and pluralism—and on an economic level to be reducing the dependence of individual arts organizations on any one audience base. But from the perspective of strategy, the result is problematic in at least two ways. First, it has the unfortunate side effect of bringing established institutions and community, smaller-niche theaters (often minority operated) into direct competition with one another. In the process, the niche players, in particular, began to lose their unique identities. And, of course, in many markets, previously well differentiated theaters began to look like one another, dramatically increasing the level of competition and reducing the attractiveness of the industry as a whole. The second problem is that, to deliver on these new initiatives, theaters built infrastructure, adding staff, space, and assets that increased their overhead. But, once the grants ended, the theaters were left with this infrastructure and general expenditures required to support it, but they no longer had a corresponding source of revenue. Ultimately, this left effect them worse off than they were before the infusion of audience diversion funds.

Although the critical factor precipitating the erosion of differentiation in these two examples stems from the actions of groups outside the industry, the same outcome can also be produced by the industry players themselves. There is a host of behaviors that can cause deterioration of an industry, but many fall under the rubric of failing to anticipate and consider the implications of competitor actions and reactions (for example, adopting costly but easily imitable strategies or expanding programs and adding capacity). To realize how powerful this insight is, one has only to look at the range of industries that suffer from what can be characterized only as self-inflicted wounds, such as the creation of tremendous overcapacity in the steel industry, or the introduction of double and triple frequent flyer miles in the airline industry during the 1980s.

All of these examples beg the question of what incumbents in an industry can do in the face of intended and unintended threat to the structure of their industry. The first step is recognizing the consequences for industry structure of policies or choices initiated either by outsiders, or by themselves. The second step is overcoming traditional notions that equate "winning" with beating the other guy. This is much easier for nonprofits for two reasons. First, as I noted earlier, the sector is naturally inclined towards cooperation and seeing fellow industry players as pursuing shared objectives. Second, the antitrust laws that govern collusion and anticompetitive behavior are applied differently to nonprofits. Communication designed to coordinate market behavior that would be illegal for for-profit businesses is typically allowed for nonprofits because of their social mission and the nondistribution constraint.[56]

The third step is finding a venue in which to engage in conversations about the types of alternative policies or practices on the part of funders or policy-makers that would serve the ultimate goal (e.g., audience diversification) while preserving the healthy structure that will support sustainable levels of prosperity for all the organizations in the field.[57] Finally, incumbents must create structures and mechanisms that facilitate a coordinated response to the relevant constituency, whether this is lobbying or engaging funders in a dialogue about how to protect industry structure while achieving the primary objectives. These mechanisms may already exist in the form of industry or professional associations, or even informal networks. The challenge is to identify the shared interests and figure out how to separate conflicting or competitive interests clearly enough to enlist the support of a critical mass of incumbents to present a credible case to the external constituency.

The Possibilities: Collective Action to Improve Industry Structure

Just as collective action on the part of players in an industry can provide a means of resisting potential threats to industry structure, it can also serve as a way to improve the attractiveness of an industry in a proactive fashion. However, perhaps because such opportunities are difficult to recognize, they are also relatively rare. Hence, a number of the examples in this section are hypothetical.

In thinking about the attractiveness or potential of an industry to support prosperity, Saloner and colleagues use the metaphor of a pie, but this is also an acronym for potential industry earnings (PIE).[58] To the extent that an industry is growing or becoming larger, it reduces competition and provides more opportunity for the incumbents. A key determinant of the PIE is the availability and attractiveness of substitutes. Herein lies an interesting opportunity for nonprofit arts organizations.

In most cities, there are many substitutes for the live arts, including out-door activities, the Internet, sporting events, television, DVDs, films, and so on. In a few communities, arts organizations have banded together to promote arts education programs that are directed toward shifting the preferences of the new generation of buyers, students in schools, away from these substitutes and toward the arts. They accomplish this goal by increasing young people's appreciation for the arts as an area of endeavor relative to the many substitutes available to them. And, by collaborating to support arts education in schools, arts organizations in these communities have been able to sow the seeds for growing the future markets, as well as potentially shifting the preferences of the buyers in those markets by early exposure. Another way that incumbents can influence the industry structure is by engaging in market development activities and shaping buyer preferences. Organizations can do this by increasing the demand for their product, either by increasing the amount of money available, or by influencing the preferences of buyers so that they are more attracted to the industry's products and services, compared in particular to substitutes.

Consider, for example, the performing arts. One of the biggest threats to the health of many arts communities is the aging of their core audience: symphonies and classical dance companies tend to attract an older demographic than, say, popular films or video game arcades. This is compounded by the decline of arts education in schools, which are strapped for funding themselves and no longer able to afford "nonessential" educational programs. The disappearance of arts from the curriculum of public education directly impacts the development of the next generation of arts patrons.

Although some performing-arts nonprofits do outreach and education on their own, consider the potential impact of an entire community of performance-arts organizations rallying for funding for arts education in the curriculum and participating to support teachers in delivering this curriculum. This would simultaneously increase future generations of audiences, change attitudes toward the arts, and raise the visibility of the arts in the community. Moreover, as more kids became engaged in the arts, their interest would give them and their parents an immediate reason to go see the symphony or the ballet. Ultimately, more sophisticated and better-educated young people would be more likely to appreciate the value of art over popular substitutes such as movies and video games.

Educating buyers and shaping their preferences can be a powerful way of improving the structure of the industry. To the degree that performing-arts organizations can come together to influence people's appreciation of art, they increase the likelihood that art will gain distinct value in comparison to the substitutes that consume so much of people's time, attention, and money (entertainment such as films, sports, and television). Such coming together makes everybody in the industry better off.

Education provides another example. One of the biggest strategic issues for public schools and districts is not competition from other public schools or even private schools; it is reductions in the overall level of funding to the entire population. These schools might be better off investing resources and energy in lobbying for higher levels of funding for their entire industry rather than competing to protect the funding for their district in competition with other districts. Why not raise the ocean—and all the boats within it—instead of hoping that your boat alone will be the one that rises with the next tide?

Legal Barriers to Collective Action

Earlier, I alluded briefly to an important difference between nonprofits and for-profits that is critical to the phenomenon of collective action: that, in general, the antitrust prohibitions against talking to one another or engaging in coordinated action historically are not applied as stringently to nonprofits as they are to for-profits. This means that they can engage in coordinated action, which would help to improve the industry.

There are exceptions to this general principle, however. For example, coordinated action that involves agreements around pricing has been questioned. A number of elite universities, including Massachusetts Institute of Technology, Harvard, Stanford, Berkeley, and Columbia, were colluding on the amount of financial aid they would offer different students, as well as the amount of tuition they would charge. In this case, the U.S. Department of Justice decided that this practice constituted price fixing and was illegal. The position of the universities was that they were acting in the public interest and that they were not price fixing, because they could not take the money they made and give it to their shareholders (of which they had none). Similarly, mergers and consolidation that increase the market power of nonprofits, particularly in the health care industry, have tended to be scrutinized in much the same way as mergers among for-profit counterparts.[59]

Despite these exceptions, there is a host of cooperative activities among nonprofits, activities that present opportunities for collective action and that are not available to for-profit enterprises. There clearly are ways—such as buyer preferences or funding for the industry, which are not subject to antitrust regulation—in which nonprofits can collaborate in an industry to improve aspects of industry structure. In fact, for-profit organizations have long used industry associations to lobby the government, other organizations, and the public to influence industry structure. As mentioned earlier, the pharmaceutical industry has a number of associations, including the very influential PhRMA, that have lobbied to prevent price regulation, extend patent protection, and do all sorts of things that help everyone in the industry be better off. Nonprofits can learn from this example and apply the lessons learned to the benefit of their own industries.

Strategy and Interdependence

When an organization expands into a multibusiness enterprise, establishes an alliance, or participates in some form of collective action, it does so in order to enhance the performance of one or more distinct business units. For nonprofits, performance includes two types of value: economic (or strategy related) and social (or mission related).

All three of these vehicles work (at least in theory) by creating between separate entities interdependence through formal and informal ties that provide the basis for cooperation and coordination. This cooperation and coordination produce (again, in theory) an overall net benefit. I say "net" benefit because there are costs associated with interdependence that have been enumerated extensively in the field of transaction cost economics as part of a theory of when transactions will occur through markets versus through hierarchies (that is, within a firm).[60] In addition, in the case of alliances and collective action, there must be a net benefit to all parties (although this need not necessarily be an equal benefit, just greater than the other alternatives available to that party).

In the case of the multibusiness enterprise, the ties between business units are relatively strong.[61] Corporate strategy provides the logic that guides the creation of benefit. The mechanisms through which this happens are interrelationships, shared activities, knowledge, and improved positioning vis-à-vis multimarket competitors.

In the case of alliances, the ties (which, by nature, are weaker than in multibusiness enterprises) can be with related entities (competitors) or with unrelated or more distantly related entities. In the former case, the alliance is an alternative to an acquisition and provides some of the benefits of interdependence while preserving flexibility and limiting some costs.

In the latter case, the ties can be with unrelated nonprofit, business, or governmental organizations, but they must provide some opportunity to create value through interdependence (versus market transactions). Thus, there often is overlap in customers, stakeholders, services or products, objectives, geography, or values that provide the basis for pursuing shared or complementary interests or objectives.

In the case of collective action, ties are formed to a broad array of similar others, usually nonprofits within the same industry or discipline, and are even weaker than in the case of multibusiness enterprises or alliances. Value, or the net benefit of the interdependence, is realized by the parties' actively changing the overall environment (industry structure, for example), the problem, or the solution. Each one of these approaches usually involves a paradigm shift of some degree. In the case of environment, the shift is to view the context as malleable rather than given and static. Or, in the case of solutions and problems, the shift may entail redefining the problem or need in ways that lead to more holistic or fundamental interventions that get at root causes. In some cases, it may lead to the creation of action at a scale that produces a quantum shift in the impact, but which is beyond the scope of individual organizations (for example, in the case of climate change).

Important to note about all of these vehicles is that they are fundamentally mechanisms for creating interdependence that generates a net benefit in performance. In all cases, the critical analysis involves identifying the costs and benefits of interdependence, choosing the mechanism for creating interdependence, and managing and sustaining the interdependence to ensure net benefits are realized. Benefits can be defined only in terms of economic value (and, hence, strategy and competitive advantage, or industry structure), or in terms of social or environmental value (and, hence, mission and, particularly, to primary goals). Thus, corporate strategy, alliances, and collective action must be built on and tied to the foundation of the frameworks we introduced earlier.

6

The Role of Leadership in Mission, Strategy, and Execution

Although the core of this book is mission, strategy, and execution, and their importance as determinants of organizational performance, any prescriptions related to them beg the questions, who has responsibility for overseeing and conducting these activities? and who needs to understand and employ the mission and strategy frameworks? On a more personal level, one might also wonder, who is the reader to whom the ideas in previous chapters are directed?

This chapter represents a fundamental shift in the focus of this book, but one that is of significance to the practical utility of the material in the previous chapters. Let me explain. In the educational settings that led to the development of these ideas, the audience consisted of the senior executives of the kinds of nonprofit organizations we have examined throughout this text. Whether we call these individuals "leaders," "managers," "executives," or "social entrepreneurs" is immaterial. The fact is that, regardless of what label we choose, they are the ones who have assumed, or been charged with, the responsibility for shaping and evaluating the organization's mission and strategy, and ensuring the execution of both. That they may do this in ways that involve considerable delegation, empowerment, or self-management is also immaterial. Ultimately, the primary organizational stakeholders—be they shareholders in the case of a for-profit entity, or the public as represented by the board of directors in the case of a nonprofit entity—look to these individuals as the stewards of the organization's performance. Hence, they are the agents responsible for integrating mission and strategy and ensuring their execution.[1] For simplicity, I will refer to them as *leaders*, even though doing so means dealing with a host of thorny conceptual problems.

The Problem with Leadership and Its Relevance
to Mission, Strategy, and Execution

Of all the hazy and confounding areas in social psychology,
leadership theory undoubtedly contends for top nomination. . . .
Ironically, probably more has been written and less is known
about leadership than any other topic in the behavioral sciences.
—Warren G. Bennis

There are almost as many different definitions of leadership as
there are persons who have attempted to define the concept.
—Ralph M. Stogdill

Leadership has historically been both one of the most studied *and* one of
the most important areas of inquiry in the field of management—but, at
the same time, one of the most flawed and problematic. Even contemporary reviews of the literature on leadership conclude that the topic is a
conceptual mess.[2] In a nutshell, the problem is that over the last fifty years
there has been little consensus, coherence, or generalizability across theories of leadership. Senior managers consistently cite leadership as critical
to their organizations, yet the advice contained in the literature (both
academic and popular) is as fragmented and disjointed as it is copious.
Rather than contributing to the proliferation of leadership theories or ar-
bitrarily invoking a particular theory of leadership, I draw on two overarching perspectives for *how to think about* leadership. We can think of
these perspectives as "metatheories," or fundamental principles for developing and evaluating specific leadership theories. They provide the basis
for exploring the roles and process through which mission, strategy, and
execution are actually enacted.

Linking Leadership to Mission and Strategy

Before introducing these perspectives and using them to link mission, strategy, and execution to the notion of leadership and the actions of leaders,
we benefit by reflecting on some of the key issues in and problems with
the field of leadership.

Two phenomena reside at the core of leadership. The first, of interest
primarily to disciplinary academics (e.g., psychologists and sociologists),

has to do with interpersonal influence within organizations. The second, of interest to applied scholars and practitioners in the field of management, concerns individuals' (i.e., leaders') influence on organizational performance. With respect to the academic phenomenon, the question is, how useful is leadership as a way to understand interpersonal influence in organizations? The answer is that leadership appears to add little value to analyses focused on more basic (and well-defined) social-psychological processes, such as power, authority, and social influence.[3] With respect to practitioners, the question is, how much, if at all, does leadership matter for organizational performance? From the perspective of managers, there is good reason to be circumspect about the likelihood that it matters at all. Over the last twenty-five years, a host of other constructs have attracted attention as important drivers of organizational performance and as useful guides to managerial action. For example, notions such as innovation, entrepreneurship, culture, decision making, learning, change, vision, organizational architecture, and, yes, even the well-worn concept of strategy have gained ground against leadership.[4]

From an academic perspective, the assumption that leadership influences organizational performance underlies the interest in doing research on the phenomenon. The difficulty with the premise, however, is that there are a host of reasons that leaders might be limited in their ability to influence organizational performance. Pfeffer makes this point in an insightful critique of the field, highlighting three issues: (1) there are powerful external, or environmental, factors that impact organizational performance; (2) leaders are often constrained in their ability to manipulate internal, organizational (or theoretically controllable) factors; and (3) even when leaders are not constrained, the number of individual variables that could affect organizational performance is staggering, creating unmanageable complexity.[5]

This third difficulty is where frameworks come in. Frameworks help leaders to make sense of this complexity. They tell them what to pay attention to, how to understand the mechanisms producing the effects of the levers (variables) that they can control, and how to prioritize efforts to manipulate these levers. But the problem remains: which frameworks should we use? Although the competition among ideas and among related frameworks mentioned earlier (culture, innovation, architecture, etc.) is fierce, my own view, reflected in the focus of this book, is as follows:

- *Mission*, especially for nonprofits, is the most useful lens for understanding the psychological and motivational determinants of

performance, particularly the moral and social-purpose significance, meaning, and, ultimately, *value*, of an organization's
aspirations
- *Strategy* is the most powerful and robust conceptual framework for
understanding the dynamics of competition and the economic
dimensions of performance
- *Execution*, analyzed in terms of activities, policies, and resource
allocation—and their relationship to mission and strategy—is the
most useful way to understand and manage the process of translating intentions into action

In support of these claims, I think it is worth noting that many of the constructs like culture, architecture, and innovation can be subsumed under
execution and are even more powerful tools for managing organizational
performance when they are linked to strategy. For example, culture in the
service of competitive advantage, architecture that complements and supports strategy, and innovation that takes account of industry and competitive dynamics will be more effective guides for managerial action than when
these constructs are not linked to strategy.[6]

Given this argument, *organizational performance* becomes the fundamental point of convergence between *leadership* and *mission, strategy,* and *execution.* Strategy identifies the major classes of determinants and choices
that affect economic performance, and it provides a logic for understanding these effects. Mission provides a psychological and emotional logic and
defines the noneconomic or social and moral dimensions of performance.
Execution provides a framework for identifying, integrating, and prioritizing the large number of choices about organizational structure and
process that determine the efficiency and effectiveness with which the organization can translate inputs into the desired outputs. Over time, these
outputs create the ultimate outcomes that represent the realization of strategy and the fulfillment of mission.

Thus, to the extent that we accept the possibility that leadership matters
(i.e., affects organizational performance), we need to make sense of a broad
array of variables that the leader can use as levers to influence performance.
This leads us back to the three key leadership functions mentioned in the
introduction: *direction, motivation,* and *design,* and, subsequently, to the
frameworks of *strategy, mission,* and *execution,* which provide the conceptual
foundations for guiding leaders' efforts to shape, evaluate, and, when necessary, change the individual elements of mission, strategy, and execution.

An Alternative Perspective on Leadership

The first and perhaps one of the most intuitively compelling ways of rec-onciling the variegated array of leadership theories is the *situational*, or *contingency*, approach, which contends that effective leadership depends on the situation or context in which it occurs.[7] In effect, this approach rejects the possibility of a universal model of leadership and holds that the behaviors that constitute effective leadership depend upon the situation. Despite its intuitive appeal, the challenge for a contingency ap-proach is to go beyond the liberating, but incomplete, answer that "it all depends" and provide concrete guidance to leaders about how to be effective.

Enter the second perspective, known as the *functional* approach to lead-ership. The contribution of this perspective is that, rather than prescrib-ing a detailed list of leader traits (e.g., charisma, vision, intelligence) or behaviors (e.g., goal setting, communication, coaching, analyzing), it de-fines the responsibilities of a leader at a sufficiently high level of abstrac-tion that those responsibilities guide thinking about what the leader must do in any situation. One of the earliest and best-known articulations of the functional approach to leadership is Chester Barnard's classic 1938 work, *The Functions of the Executive*.[8]

Combining the contingency approach with the functional approach leads to a perspective predicated on the assumption that there are basic functions that the leader must fulfill in all situations, but that the specific behaviors appropriate to accomplish a function in any given situation will depend on the features of that situation. Although this perspective does not provide specific prescriptions about what leaders should do, it can guide leaders' thinking about where to direct their attention.

A Functional Approach

The functional approach to leadership assumes that leadership cannot be disaggregated to atomistic behaviors, but rather that it is best defined in terms of the functions that must be fulfilled if the organization is to sur-vive and thrive. At the most basic level, McGrath notes that "the leader's main job is to do or get done whatever [needs to be done]."[9] Building on this tradition, Hackman and Walton note, "The emphasis is not so much on what the leader should do as on what needs to be done for effective performance. . . . [T]he functional approach leaves room [as to how] to get critical functions accomplished."[10] Again, Barnard's classic treatise on the functional approach captures the unique role of leadership elegantly: "Executive work is not that of the organization, but the specialized work of maintaining the organization in operation."[11]

If the functional approach were to stop here, it would not be particularly helpful. Since it leads us to eschew attempts to specify leader traits or behaviors, the approach must rely on another means to enhance leadership effectiveness. This entails identifying the fundamental functions that have to be fulfilled if the organization is to survive and thrive.

In the introductory chapter, we drew on Barnard's classic formulation of the three basic leadership functions: *direction*, which is to "formulate and define the purpose, objectives, and ends of the organization"; *motivation*, which is to "promote the securing of essential efforts"; and *design*, which is to "provide the system of communication."[12] These three key leadership functions are echoed and elaborated by a host of contemporary writers on leadership and management. They can be seen in best-selling business books over the last twenty-five years (e.g., *In Search of Excellence*, *The Change Masters*, *The Fifth Discipline*, and *Built to Last*) that highlight the role leaders play in designing organizations, shaping culture, inspiring followers, and setting strategy.[13]

Harvard Business School professor and leadership guru John Kotter distinguishes between leadership and management by defining the key concerns of the leader as "setting direction," "aligning people," and "motivating and inspiring."[14] These are almost identical to Barnard's classic functions, which have also been central to influential academic theories of organizations.[15] In sum, despite different emphases, much of the contemporary prescriptive literature on leadership implicitly or explicitly identifies functions that fall directly within the span of Barnard's original model.

Direction

Direction is often framed in terms of strategy and mission. When people describe the role of the general manager or CEO, shaping the organization's strategic direction or vision is invariably named as one of his or her primary tasks. So, while the organization's task is to actually execute this strategic direction, the leader's key challenge is setting and monitoring the basic direction. There are a number of ways of framing and talking about direction, but all deal with basic questions of ultimate ends: What do we do and why? Or, where are we headed?

Motivation

One of the hallmarks of an organization is coordinated action in the service of goals that could not be achieved by an individual or a group. For coordinated action to occur, the interests and motivations of individuals have to be aligned with that of the collective. One of the key requirements for getting work done, therefore, is *motivating* or inducing people to exert effort in the service of the organization's goals.

In the for-profit sector, the primary basis of such motivation is economic in nature: we reward people if they behave in the desired manner. Chief among these rewards is money, whether it is given to employees through wages, salary, stock options, or bonuses. (Although other rewards, such as career advancement, satisfaction, and power, also play a role, cash is highly motivating to most employees.) In rewarding people, we create the conditions necessary for high levels of motivation to exert effort and to act in ways that advance the organization's goals.

In the nonprofit sector, norms and resource constraints limit compensation. By their very nature (the tax status of nonprofits precludes them from granting individual ownership of equity or a share of profits), nonprofits are unable to use the most powerful financial inducements used by for-profits as the primary basis for motivating individuals. It is therefore necessary for nonprofits to articulate missions, build organizations, and design jobs that not only provide direction and the ability to execute the pursuit of that direction, but also serve as sources of motivation that transcend and substitute for pecuniary incentives.

The other key characteristic of the nonprofit sector is that most nonprofits engage in fund-raising, raising money from outside contributors or donors to subsidize the work that the organization does for its clients, whether those clients are less able to pay for themselves, or whether its work is done for the general societal good, as with environmental organizations. So the challenge for the nonprofit leader is motivating external stakeholders and supporters, as well as people within the organization. Here, the organization's mission becomes central. Although the mission is part of what energizes and inspires people, it also includes the organization's reason for being, or its purpose, and, hence, contributes to the definition of organizational direction.

Design

Design, in Barnard's words, is the "system of communication" within an organization. But this encompasses more than just the organization's telephone system or its bulletin board; it is the human system by which the parts of the organization interact with one another to produce coordinated action. This view is also reflected in contemporary management perspectives that characterize the leader as an organizational architect.[16]

The notions of organizational architecture and the related concepts of *fit* and *congruence* represent important advances in theories of organizational design. At the root of these terms is a more sophisticated view of organizational design, one that has expanded to encompass not just the boxes on an organization chart, but also a host of other formal and informal mechanisms that allow people in large, complex organizations to work together in an integrated fashion. For example, Tushman and colleagues focus on elements of design that extend far beyond the system of communication described by Barnard, yet the basic leadership function remains intact.[17] Similarly, Danny Miller and colleagues emphasize configurations—the clustering of "structural, environmental, and strategic variables"—as well as "trajectories," the evolution of configurations over time.[18] Whether it is cross-functional teams, information technology, intranets, voice mail, or communication technology, these are the technical, physical, and social mechanisms that enable coordination across the individuals in a large, formal organization.

Leaders on Leadership

Although we have talked at length about the ways academics have defined and advised managers to think about leadership, I believe it is just as instructive to spend some time looking at the way leaders themselves understand and experience their unique role.

One context that has afforded me an opportunity to explore this phenomenon is the Executive Program for Nonprofit Leaders, a two-week executive education program at the Stanford Business School, which I have directed for the last three years. Virtually all of the participants in this program are executive directors or CEOs of nonprofit organizations primarily in the United States but, in a few instances, from around the world. At the beginning of this program, I lead a discussion among the participants about of the nature of leadership. In particular, we talk about the role, the concerns, and the essence of leadership. We debate the utility of drawing a distinction between leadership and management, and we reflect on the issues that keep them awake at night and how these are related to their role as leaders.

Many of the comments that the participants make during this discussion support the centrality of the three key leadership functions I have described, but, more important, they also highlight the solitary nature of the responsibility that leaders experience for fulfilling these functions. For example, a number of participants talked about feeling that the organization was ultimately dependent on them to be successful. One observed:

> I came to the realization that, even though I don't have time to lead, my organization is not going to move forward until I make that time. And there's going to have to be some of the tree stuff that I have to reprioritize because I spend so much time getting—I have a very small agency. Three and a half full-time staff people. My tendency is to jump in and bail water and do all those things that we all do, but at some point that's just going to keep us staying in one place.[19]

Others reinforced the importance of setting and monitoring direction, whether vision, strategy, or mission, as part of facilitating that progress: "In observing in my own organization and the organizations I've been a part of, if left to their own devices, people tend to focus on the details in their own areas; and oftentimes end up going lots of different directions unless there's some sort of organizing vision."[20] Another participant agreed: "If you can develop a clear vision, everyone's all on the same page and everyone knows, 'Okay, sometimes it's chaotic, but we're all facing the same direction. We're all moving in the same direction.'"[21]

Still others, acutely aware that they had "abandoned" their organization for two full weeks to attend the Executive Program for Nonprofit Leaders, focused on the design function, particularly the degree to which they had been effective in building the organization's capacity in the form of systems and process: "Last night I realized we had a payroll snafu, so I was on the phone fixing that this morning. And then I thought, 'Well, did I leave enough information for our associate director so that she can handle everything while I [am] gone? Well, have I put enough systems in place that she'll be cool for two weeks?'"[22]

Another said the following:

> I used to try to do it all like any of us who have started with a
> small organization that grew into a large organization. I couldn't
> let go, because I thought the quality would suffer. And I've finally
> learned really to trust a lot of my managers to do it . . . and it feels
> very, very good. I can't say it honestly gives me a lot more time for
> leadership. Some, but as the organization grows—a lot of us know
> that, too—that as an organization grows, it becomes more and
> more demanding.[23]

Finally, perhaps the most striking feature of these leaders' reflections about leadership was that the challenge is actually even more daunting than just fulfilling the functions. It is that they must do this on an ongoing basis in a world that continues to change at an increasing pace. So the notion of leadership as managing change in order to ensure the continued vibrancy and effectiveness of the organization was a recurring one. And yet, especially given the perennially scarce resources and hand-to-mouth existence of many nonprofits, stability dominated the day-to-day agenda of most leaders, despite their commitment to change, learning, and growth: "The concept of stability is very enticing. My own problem is that I look for ways to manage for stability where I really ought to be looking for ways of leading for change because we like to embrace change and we're an organization that does, but, boy, there is something wonderful about the thought of stability."[24]

During an interview, Ford Foundation president Susan Berresford articulated the challenge of change in a particularly compelling fashion as she reflected on the skills and knowledge required of nonprofit leaders:

> I think we will all have to live with change constantly. The pace
> and scope and depth of change that occurs around us demands
> that the organizations we work in also be extremely flexible,
> extremely supple and quick, and, while holding to core values, be
> very adept. I think that's very difficult. A lot of people are un-
> comfortable when things are ambiguous or constantly moving and
> evolving. It requires a kind of confidence and willingness to adapt
> and hear things differently and try things out, and I think leaders
> are going to be challenged to both create the structures in which
> that's possible and inspire people to see this as an exciting and
> positive part of their lives, not something that's making them
> uneasy and threatening them all the time.[25]

Given its importance, we will return to the challenge of change as a topic worthy of exploration in its own right in chapter 7. But now we turn to the practical question of what, once leaders recognize the three functions of direction, motivation, and design, they need to know in order to fulfill them effectively.

Frameworks and Fulfilling the Functions

The key functions of leadership are shaping the direction of the organization, providing a foundation for motivation, and designing the organization in order to enable execution. For the organization to be effective, the leader needs either to do these functions, or to see that these three functions get done. Still, simply knowing the three functions is not enough to provide practical guidance to leaders, which requires a normative understanding of how to fulfill the functions effectively.

To do this, leaders need a theory or model of how to *analyze* an organization and its particular situation, and then *generate, evaluate, monitor,* and *modify* the choices that are being made with respect to each function. Is the direction a good one? Is the basis for motivation adequate and sustainable? Is it eliciting behavior consistent with the direction? Is the design supportive of the direction and motivation? Are all of the elements of the design consistent with one another? In an increasingly complex and dynamic world, all of these questions must be evaluated on an ongoing basis to ensure continued effectiveness.

Hence, to be useful in the sense of informing the fundamental decisions associated with the task of fulfilling these functions, knowledge must help leaders to understand and evaluate direction, to create conditions that will produce high levels of motivation, and to build the architecture of an effective organizational design. Moreover, such knowledge must also be sufficiently robust and flexible to be applicable to a wide variety of settings—as implied by the contingency perspective. The tools and ideas related to strategy, mission, and execution provide the specific knowledge by which a leader can actually fulfill the function of deciding what the direction of the organization is and then make sure it is a good direction. This means providing a motivation that is going to be compelling for the various stakeholders, and designing the organization in such a way that it is going to (at least eventually) lead to effective execution of the organization's mission and strategy.

Like the original frameworks themselves, this view of the role of leadership in mission, strategy, and execution can be conveyed in a way that lends itself to practical application only through the examination of real-world examples. We turn now to look at examples of how leaders fulfill the basic functions of direction, motivation, and design, drawn from both the nonprofit and for-profit world.

Putting the Leadership Functions into Practice: Case Examples

Innermotion: Setting and Monitoring Direction through Strategy

At a gut level, every leader knows that direction is important. In the nonprofit world, legendary Girl Scouts leader Frances Hesselbein's assertion resonates: "Everything begins with mission, everything flows from mission."[26] And, even though confusion abounds about the meaning of strategy, every executive director recognizes that she better have one. Funders, board members, and staff alike expect both mission and strategy to be clear, as well as compelling. The problem is that, even when they pass these tests, the direction is not necessarily an *effective* one. Moreover, the question whether a given direction is appropriately focused (neither too broad nor too narrow) is almost always debatable.

Consider the example of Innermotion, a young, entrepreneurial nonprofit focused on the problem of childhood sexual abuse.[27] Founder and executive director Sharon Daugherty, herself a survivor of childhood sexual abuse, created Innermotion with an ambitious mission: to eradicate child sexual abuse through the expressive arts, especially dance, while helping survivors access this creative outlet for themselves for healing. From a small part-time troupe of amateur dancers doing a couple of performances a year, Innermotion grew into a real organization with official, nonprofit 501(c)(3) status and grants from local and state governments, contributions from individuals, and fees from performances. In addition to public performances, Innermotion also provided a variety of therapeutic workshops for survivors of abuse. But, as the organization grew, questions arose about whether its fundamental direction was too broad. From the point of view of mission, it was unclear that the dual aspirations of educating and raising awareness of abuse and healing survivors could, or should, be pursued simultaneously. From the perspective of strategy, Innermotion's investment in its performances was in constant tension with government funders' prioritization of direct service (i.e., therapeutic workshops), a difficulty that was exacerbated by the organization's reliance on government grants.

Furthermore, competition in the nonprofit space for these limited government dollars was fierce, and traditional full-service rape crisis centers had a distinct advantage in obtaining them. Indeed, in June 2001, Daugherty was notified that a crucial annual grant of $60,000 provided under the Violence Against Women Act would be discontinued, primarily because Innermotion's activities did not fit definitions of the types of activities that should be funded. Innermotion's programs were not purely arts, nor were they purely social service. They were something in between. Loss of this large grant was potentially devastating to Innermotion, and it threatened the organization's very existence.

The rationale for the discontinuation put considerable pressure on Sharon Daugherty to consider focusing Innermotion's basic direction, particularly the economic logic of strategy. The organization could emphasize healing and hence its workshops (the kind of traditional direct services that government agencies would support), or it could emphasize performances and try to enhance Innermotion's general artistic appeal, perhaps attracting more arts funding and ticket revenue. These were particularly difficult decisions for Daugherty, because she was reluctant to give up on any of her organization's programs or constituencies.

Indeed, during a training program on strategy for nonprofit managers, Daugherty's peers suggested that she had to focus, eliminating or dramatically reducing some programs in the process. Daugherty described her reaction at the time:

> My fellow participants at the executive education program for nonprofit managers insisted that I needed to make a choice and let go of my aspirations [to heal sexual abuse survivors and eradicate sexual abuse through education and awareness]. When I heard their recommendations, I felt myself tighten up and choke up. I was about to cry but I wasn't sure why. Then as I reflected on my reaction, I realized that if I were to let go of the healing workshops, I'd be turning my back on survivors.[28]

This incident highlights the difficulty of the choices about organizational direction that confront leaders. Despite a passionate and reasonable belief that Innermotion's unique combination of education and healing (workshops and performances) supported one another and, in fact, were inextricably linked, Daugherty found herself in a situation in which the economic logic underlying Innermotion's current direction did not seem to be working. As a result, she faced agonizing choices about changing the strategy and possible mission of the entity she had founded. Although the frameworks can help leaders to evaluate and predict the impact of such choices, the courage, as well as responsibility, for making them lies at the core of the role and function of leadership.

Apple Computer: Cultivating Mission as the Basis for Motivation

While an analysis of Apple Computer's economic performance is a very interesting exercise, which we only scratched the surface of in chapters 2 and 4, one of the most fascinating things about the company and its continued survival is its psychological logic. Despite being a business, Apple is a classic example of the power of mission as a source of motivation for employees, customers, and even investors.

Since its inception, the values, purpose, goals, and vision have attracted people around the world to Apple. From its iconoclastic mockery of IBM—and later Microsoft—to its shameless promotion of the personal computer as a recreational plaything for the masses (witness the iLife suite of software, advertised as "Microsoft Office for the rest of your life," featuring a program for making music for fun—Garage Band), Apple appeals to its stakeholders' passions.[29] Although reason factors into the company's strategy, history suggests that the mission drove the strategy, just as it would for a nonprofit. Cofounder and current CEO Steve Jobs's vision of creating a computer that would not simply carry out its assigned tasks, but would also be fun and easy to use, led to the creation of the innovative Macintosh computer in 1984 and more recently to successes like the iMac, the iPod digital music player, and the iTunes music store.

The fanaticism and loyalty of Apple's customers are almost legendary and can be witnessed at the annual MacWorld event, nominally a conference but, in practice, a lovefest between Apple, its customers, and manufacturers of complementary products. This passion stems not from the products themselves, or from their features or performance, but instead from what the company and its products represent. Perhaps, even more than his technical or design savvy, what Steve Jobs's 1997 return to Apple brought (he was forced out of the company in 1986 by former CEO John Sculley) was a direct link to the motivational foundations of the firm's early success. Although Jobs's significance can easily be overestimated because of his mythic stature and celebrity as one of the business world's most prominent visionary leaders, this example illustrates the symbolic and rhetorical role of a leader in developing, articulating, and institutionalizing the meaning and significance that energize organizations and their stakeholders.[30]

People Express: Designing the Architecture of Execution

For many readers of the younger generation (I am thinking of my current crop of MBA students), People Express is more likely to be known as a quaint, if dated, business school case about an airline that has been defunct for close to twenty years. But for those of us who are old enough to have traveled to visit friends and family in the early 1980s, the name is likely to evoke fond memories of trips that were fast, cheap, and fun.

People Express was born in 1980 as a result of deregulation of the commercial aviation industry in the United States. Before passage of the Airline Deregulation Act in 1978, the Civil Aeronautics Board tightly controlled the routes that airlines flew and the prices they were allowed to charge for tickets. The primary goal of this heavy regulation of the commercial aviation industry was to ensure that airlines operated for the overall good of the American public. As a result of deregulation, the price controls and restrictions put in place by the federal government evaporated, and in their place emerged a new business landscape, ripe for aviation entrepreneurs. One person who saw the opportunities that this new landscape afforded was an aviation industry analyst named Donald Burr, who had risen to become president and COO at Texas International Airlines during the 1970s. A charismatic and inspiring leader, Burr envisioned not only a very different kind of airline, but also a fundamentally different kind of company and approach to managing people. Soon after resigning from Texas International in January 1980, he founded People Express Airlines.

People Express quickly attracted a passionate core group of employees, or, as they were called, "associates," and experienced dramatic growth from its inception. By 1985, only four short years after the company began flight operations, its annual revenues had rocketed to just shy of $1 billion.[31] The company achieved this growth by offering ticket prices that were as much as 50 to 80 percent lower than those offered by its major competitors (many of which appeared to be shell-shocked by the dramatic effects of deregulation on the industry), and by employing a workforce that provided customer service that was consistently pleasant, cheerful, and, often, even funny and entertaining. In addition, this same workforce was fast and efficient, providing customers with frequent, convenient flights, and providing the company with industry-leading productivity in terms of asset utilization.

This strategy seems to be a good, though not necessarily profoundly innovative or unique, one (there were many other low-cost, no-frills airlines started during the same period). However, what was distinctive about People Express was the way in which the airline designed its tasks, processes, and structures. Indeed, the company attracted more attention for its management practices than for its growth and success in the market, which was prodigious.[32]

Just as the federal government had deregulated the airline industry, Burr deregulated the people who came to work for People Express. Burr gave employees the freedom to make decisions at the lowest level possible (so long as they adhered to the company's precepts when they were making their decisions), and he trusted them to make the right decisions most of the time. This combination of freedom and trust was a heady experience for those who came to work for the airline, and it encouraged them to give their very best on the job while saving the company the expense (and the bureaucracy) that comes along with hiring a large cadre of middle managers to make decisions for line employees. Burr explained: "You have two parameters at People Express: take care of people; take care of customers. How could you be more free? I tell everyone, 'Make all the mistakes you want. No problem. But just remember, we're always guided by those precepts. We take care of each other, and we take care of our customers. Within those bounds, you can do just about anything.'"[33]

Other key aspects of the design of People Express included the following:

- *Management structure*: The company had only three levels of employees in its hierarchy
- *Infrastructure*: Minimal administrative support existed (even senior executives did not have secretaries), and the Spartan headquarters facility had no frills
- *Compensation*: Employees were compensated primarily through profit-sharing and stock ownership
- *Titles*: The company had "customer service managers" rather than "flight attendants"—everyone was a "manager"
- *Recruiting*: Selection of employees was based on sociability, team orientation, and preference for lack of structure

- *Jobs*: Tasks were designed to draw on multiple skills, be meaningful, and be performed by self-managing work teams
- *Culture*: Deeply rooted values of autonomy, equality, freedom, and taking care of others reigned

But, though Burr was able to run People Express with what might be viewed as a minimum of managerial interference, as growth continued unabated, the organization eventually seemed to falter beneath its own weight. Recruiting suffered, talented new hires were slow in coming, and employees began to burn out. As employee morale suffered, so did the company's legendary customer service: flights were delayed, service suffered, and customers began to look for other flight options.

These persistent structural problems, combined with a dramatic increase in competition by the major airlines, major investments in capital equipment (aircraft) and facilities, and declining ridership, began to impact People Express's bottom line. Although the company had shown its first profit in 1982, in the fourth quarter of 1984 People Express experienced a $9 million loss. Although Burr was able to return the company to profitability in 1985 by raising ticket prices, the company plunged back into a loss position by the fourth quarter, a position from which it would never recover.

The "final nail in the coffin" came when Burr decided that the acquisition of a western regional airline—thus giving the Newark-based airline a national presence—was the answer to People Express's financial woes. Burr entered into a bidding war with United and Continental Airlines over Denver-based Frontier Airlines. People Express ultimately won the war, but the price was dear. Frontier immediately began losing money, and its employees, who were of the "old school" style of management, had a completely different culture than the one that Burr had fostered at People Express. In 1986 People Express added Midwest-based Britt Airways and the Northeast-based Provincetown-Boston Airlines to its roster. In late 1986 the company collapsed, and People Express was acquired by Continental Airlines.

Business school students and faculty regularly analyze the demise of People Express and often contrast its failure with the success of Southwest Airlines, which uses a very similar business model. Although analysts debate the most important causes of this tragedy, was it a failure of strategy—competing head to head with the major air carriers in large cities and airports? Was it the company's excessive rate of growth? Was it hubris on the part of Don Burr? Was it the overpriced acquisition of Frontier Airlines?

A singular answer depends on one's perspective, but to an extent they all contributed. Yet, for the purposes of this chapter, estimating the relative importance of the various factors that led to the failure of People Express does not matter so much; the real significance of this cautionary tale is twofold: First, we need to recognize the central role that the design of the organization played in its early success—in particular, the way in which the strategy and mission became reality only through the pattern of choices that we have identified with the challenge of *execution*. Second, we see the degree of attention and careful planning that People's leader, Don Burr, invested in creating and managing this design, and ultimately the consequences of his decision to stray from it.

Conclusion

Despite the problems with the research and theory about the topic of leadership, leaders remain a key locus of attention and, arguably, a critical point of leverage in influencing the performance of organization. This influence may sometimes be direct (i.e., raising money, doing work of the organization, or making decisions that lead to performance outcomes). But more often it is indirect: it occurs through the impact that leaders have on a host of other factors that are well established determinants of performance, mission, strategy, and execution, which we have emphasized in this text, but also through impact on other factors, such as culture, innovation, and decision making.

Ultimately, even economically oriented strategy writers have acknowledged and even focused on the relationship between leadership and organizational performance. For example, in concluding his article "What Is Strategy?" Michael Porter observes,

> The challenge of developing or reestablishing a clear strategy is often primarily an organizational one and depends on leadership. . . . In many companies, leadership has degenerated into orchestrating operational improvements and making deals. But the leader's role is broader and far more important. General management is more than the stewardship of individual functions. Its core is strategy: defining and communicating the company's unique

position, making trade-offs, and forging fit among activities. The leader must provide the discipline to decide which industry changes and customer needs the company will respond to, while avoiding organizational distractions and maintaining the company's distinctiveness.[34]

In addition to reinforcing Barnard's view of the direction function, Porter also highlights the fact that leaders need to have clear models for thinking about and evaluating direction: "With so many forces at work against making choices and trade-offs in organizations, a clear intellectual framework to guide strategy is a necessary counterweight. . . . One of the leader's jobs is to teach others in the organization about strategy."[35]

To the extent that their impact is positive and determined not by chance but by expertise, then leaders matter because of their skills and knowledge. This is the link between leadership and the frameworks that are at the center of this text.

7

Strategic Change

Intelligent Adaptation

The Nature of Strategic Change

Many of the organizations used as examples in previous chapters faced dramatic shifts in their competitive environments or internal changes stemming from natural processes of growth or evolution. As a result, many were contemplating or undertaking significant changes in their fundamental direction. In a number of instances, these changes were "strategic" in the sense that that were explicitly designed to improve the organization's performance.[1] More specifically, these changes were intended to make the organization more prosperous, more effective at achieving its aspirations, or simply more likely to survive.

I want to stress that this chapter is concerned with change that is *purposeful* and *adaptive*. There are certainly other forms of organizational change that are legitimate topics of concern. However, given the agenda of this book, the focus here is on the more bounded phenomenon of strategic change, and especially on the role played by leaders. Again, as I noted in chapter 6, the basic assumption underlying this focus is that the quality of leaders' thought and action can influence organizational performance outcomes. Strategic change is one of the most critical and difficult forms of purposeful organizational adaptation. It is critical because it is fundamentally connected to a firm's long-term competitiveness and survival. It is difficult because of the complexity of the economic issues involved and the psychological and organizational barriers that must be overcome.

Given its importance and complexity, it is not surprising then that, as with the topics of strategy and leadership, much has been written about strategic change. And, as with strategy and leadership, the terrain is littered with a host of variegated definitions.[2] For example, the term *strategic change* has been used to refer to changes that are large-scale, are very important, involve major commitment of resources, or are based on a long time horizon. Because of the inconsistency in the literature, I want to make explicit the conception used in this chapter. Based on the notion of strategy developed in chapters 2, 3, and 4, I define strategic change as (1) change in the basis of the organization's competitive advantage or scope, or (2) change in policies, resource allocation, or activities, designed to enhance or sustain existing competitive advantage within the desired scope. Thus, we are concerned only with changes in strategy or changes explicitly designed to support the execution of strategy in a dynamic environment.[3]

By definition, then, we are not dealing with forms of organizational change that are not strategic. In fact, I would go so far as to assert that, for senior executives or leaders, if a change is not strategic in the sense of either (1) or (2) above, then they should not waste their time managing it.

Just as the need for a framework to inform our thinking about how to establish and evaluate direction led us to strategy and mission frameworks, the question of how to understand and control strategic change implies the need for its own framework. However, as I did with leadership in chapter 6, rather than highlighting a specific theory of change, I find it more useful to focus on how to *think* about strategic change at a much higher level—that of an overarching perspective. Specifically, this chapter addresses the following question: what are the basic types of skills and knowledge that leaders need if they are to be effective agents of strategic change?[4] As a way of beginning to answer this question, I will illustrate three generic categories of skill and knowledge by using a short, but classic, case study called the Dashman Company.[5]

Knowledge and Skills Required for Managing Strategic Change

Dashman Company

Set in 1940, the case focuses on a manufacturing company that supplies a range of equipment to the U.S. Army. The protagonist in the case is Mr. Post, a newly hired purchasing executive, who has been charged by Dashman's president, Mr. Manson, with helping the company address the problem of shortages in the availability of key raw materials. To deal with this problem, Mr. Post has decided to centralize purchasing through his

office at the corporate headquarters. Although the firm's twenty manufacturing plants had historically been encouraged to operate autonomously,
Post has sent out a memo directing the plants to notify him at least one
week before signing any contracts to purchase these raw materials. This
decision is approved by Manson and the board of directors.

However, contrary to the advice of his deputy, Mr. Larson, Post decides
not to visit the plants in person to discuss the change. In the weeks following distribution of the memo, most of the plants send replies assuring Post
of their cooperation. Yet, six weeks later, Post's office has not received a
single notification of raw materials purchases by the plants. Despite this,
reports from the field indicate that the plants are operating as usual.

This vignette raises a number of interesting questions: Is this an example
of strategic change? If so, is it effective? If not, why not and what should
have been done differently? The nature of the knowledge and skill necessary to answer these questions is the subject of this chapter.

Theory of Organizational Performance

The first step in understanding what knowledge is needed is to try to define
exactly what it is that Post and Manson are concerned about. The most concrete and obvious answer is that they want to ensure adequate supplies of
raw materials. But further probing of why they are worried about supplies
leads to the realization that the ultimate concern is Dashman's future performance. They believe that they need to do something—create change—in
order to ensure an acceptable level of performance (given that Dashman is a
business, we can assume this is defined in terms of long-term profitability).

This belief is based on facts and inferences about the company and its
environment. Hence, the knowledge involved is in effect a theory of performance and, particularly, a theory about organizational performance. This
is the first domain of knowledge necessary for managing strategic change.

A *theory of organizational performance* (TOP) provides the basis for explaining, predicting, and controlling performance. Such theories draw on
mental models of strategy (either formal frameworks or intuitive understandings) and of organizations (the entity—specifically processes, structures,
actions inside the black box of the firm) that produce the performance. In
our case, competitive advantage, logic, policies, and activities would be
elements of the specific framework. But, again, for the purposes of the
present chapter, we are interested in emphasizing the type of knowledge
in general and not specific frameworks.

Ultimately, in the Dashman case, Post has concluded, and Manson has concurred, that, according to their theory of performance, purchasing needs to be centralized. Although the theory itself is not particularly transparent, the implication is that this change will result in improved availability and distribution of raw materials and, therefore, to continued sales, profitability, and so on.

A Digression on the Meaning of "Theory"

I have argued that the first body of knowledge necessary for managing strategic change is a theory of organizational performance. But theories are things that we typically associate with scientists and researchers, so it is important to note that when I refer to a theory of organizational performance, I am not using the term *theory* in the academic sense. Rather, I am referring to a model in a leader's head that leads to choices about how to make her organization successful. These are often referred to as *lay* or *implicit* theories, or theories of action.[6]

Key about these everyday theories is that, even though they guide action, they tend to be tacit or outside of immediate awareness.[7] They are also universal; every manager has a TOP. He or she may not be explicitly aware of it, nor able to articulate it, but it is real, and it can be inferred from actions or elicited through reflection. The important point from the perspective of strategic change is that, to the extent that the TOP is rigorous, robust, or accurate, all else being equal, the choices and actions resulting from that theory are likely to lead to performance that is better than average—particularly in times of change.

A Theory of Performance, Continued

A theory of performance is the first kind of knowledge that is needed to manage strategic change. It is the basis for understanding the phenomenon or "thing" being managed and provides the basis for explaining, predicting, and controlling it. The theory of performance defines what performance is and how it is to be measured. It identifies factors that determine the level of performance, including both those that can and those that cannot be controlled. These factors include features of the environment (industry structure), features of the organization (strategy and design), and some sense of how these interact with one another to produce performance.

Thus, the theory of performance draws on the fields of strategy and organizational theory. I make this explicit because, historically, the field of strategy has focused primarily on the "firm" level of analysis, which is to say that it has been less concerned with the internal characteristics in dynamics of organizations (the entity producing for the performance) than it has with the aggregate choices and outcomes of the firm. In part, this is a function of strategy's roots in the field of economics, which tends to focus more on firms (and consumers) as primary actors in markets.[8]

From the perspective of leaders, a more complete understanding of the organization is necessary. Although semantically equivalent to the term *firm*, the word *organization* connotes a complex system that merits investigation in its own right. Thus, a complete TOP must concern itself with what goes on inside the black box and, hence, draw on the field of organizational theory, which deals with such fundamental questions as the following: What are the key elements in features of an organization? How do these features relate to one another? How do these features interact in order to generate performance outcomes, as well as other outcomes of interest?

Theory of Organizational Change

At some point in their lives, most organizations experience actual performance declines. The theory of performance provides a basis for understanding (explaining) that decline and identifying actions that might be taken to reverse it. Similarly, vigilant scanning, forecasting, or planning may lead to predictions that performance will or could decline in the future. Again, the theory of performance provides the basis for identifying what actions might be taken to reduce the risk of such declines. Of course, the cup is not always half empty, so the theory of performance can also lead to the identification of opportunities to improve performance.

When such situations arise, the next step involves how to go about implementing the changes (i.e., actions) implied by the theory of performance. In reality, the process of deciding to change and implementing change overlap. However, for analytical purposes, we will discuss them separately. To produce (rather than simply conceive) actual changes in strategy or execution, a leader must draw on a set of assumptions and an understanding of how change occurs in an organization.[9] This is the *theory of organizational change* (TOC). It is the second type of knowledge needed to manage strategic change. A TOC must deal with a variety of questions: What are the stages of a change process? What are the tasks and dynamics associated with each stage? What are the most important factors that drive and inhibit change? What are the different types or categories of change, and how does the type of change affect the answers to the previous questions?

Again, though I want to avoid a focus on specific theories of change, it is useful to illustrate what their key features look like. So, for example, the stages of change apparent in the formal theory of organizational change range from three-stage models adapted from the classic work of Kurt Lewin (e.g., Beckhard and Harris's *present state, transition,* and *future state*), to more elaborate models composed of ten or more steps.[10] In virtually all of these models, individual stages are associated with specific tasks that the leader or change agent needs to perform. For example, in the initial stages of change, critical tasks include creating a sense of dissatisfaction or readiness for change. Tasks in subsequent stages include developing and articulating a vision and generating political support. In later stages, tasks tend to revolve around changing the architecture and design of the organization and its systems in order to facilitate and support the implementation of change.[11] The main point here is that, however the primary tasks and activities are defined, they vary according to the stage of the change process. My own formulation of the key stages is illustrated in table 7.1

Using this model to elaborate a bit on the nature of the tasks, the first stage, identifying strategic threats and opportunities, is the seminal event. Recognition and comprehension of the existence of a threat or opportunity is the basis for establishing the need for change. But, from the leader's perspective, this begins as an individual insight. Many observers have pointed to the costs of change and made the simple point that, for change to occur, the motivation to change has to exceed the motivation not to change.[12] Whether described in terms of readiness or dissatisfaction, there has to be a critical mass of people willing to invest the energy necessary to implement change. In the case of strategic change, the impetus is an identifiable threat to (or opportunity to enhance) the organization's performance.

Formulating and evaluating alternative directions for change is the second stage. The tasks here correspond to the fundamental activities of problem solving: generating or searching for acceptable solutions and choosing among them according to a set of criteria. In the case of strategic solutions, change agents draw on their TOP to assess such things as the performance consequences of a particular change, the cost of undertaking that change, the likelihood of being able to successfully implement the change,

Table 7.1.   Stages of Strategic Change

Stage	Task
Stage 1: Identifying strategic threats and opportunities	Establishing the need for change
Stage 2: Formulating and evaluating alternative directions for change	Building a vision and analyzing strategic options
Stage 3: Identifying and managing barriers to change	Analyzing the organizational, individual factors that can inhibit change (e.g., concerns, interests, capabilities, resources etc.)
Stage 4: Implementing change	Initiate and oversee key elements of the change, shifts in individual activities, resource allocation decisions, and policies that support and instantiate the overall change. Involves reconfiguring architecture, incentive skills, assets, etc.
Stage 5: Monitoring and institutionalizing change	Ensuring that metrics and information necessary to track the progress of change at the operational level are available and are reviewed at appropriate intervals Creating enduring symbolic and structural shifts that embed new behaviors and choices at an institutional level

and the long-term sustainability of the strategy embodied by the change. Many of these dimensions parallel the dimension used to evaluate strategies in general, but they also include practical concerns related to the organization's ability to execute the desired strategy.

Identifying and managing barriers to change is the third stage. The tasks here include analyzing the individual, organizational, and environmental constraints that could inhibit the specific changes implied by the chosen solution. A host of specific "barriers" appear in the literature. I find it useful to group them into three broad classes (see table 7.2) to help protect against overlooking specific barriers.

Implementing change is the fourth stage, and it is perhaps the most complex, consisting of the largest number of discrete actions and initiatives and taking the most time. Implementation of many significant strategic changes can take place over a period of one to five years. It is here that the elements of a strategic change—shifts in activities, allocation of resources, and policies—take place. Because organizations are actually complex systems, these individual changes affect one another and engender

Table 7.2. Generic Barriers to Strategic Change

Level	Barriers	Description
Individual	Cognitive	Sources of biases or of error in recognizing the need for change related to information processing
	Emotional	Sources of active resistance to change related to affective responses to change or threat (e.g., defensiveness, self-efficacy)
	Behavioral	Limitations related to inability to enact new behaviors (e.g., skill or competence)
Organizational	Social	Sources of resistance stemming from existing social ties and relationships
	Cultural	Sources of resistance due to conflict between change and existing culture (e.g., shared values assumptions, identity)
	Structural	Sources of inertia due to limitations of existing structure formal features of organizational design (e.g., functional or product line responsibility)
	Economic	Sources of inertia due to economic feature of the organization (resources, capital, asset configuration, contracts, prior commitments, etc.)
	Informational	Sources of uncertainty or ambiguity about the need for change or effect of alternative directions for change stemming from incomplete or imperfect data
	Political	Sources of resistance due to the divergence of individual or subgroup interests from those of the organization (e.g., parochialism)
Environmental	Industry	Features of the industry structure that make strategic shifts or mobility more difficult
	Nonmarket	Features of the political economic environment, such as legal or regulatory provisions that prevent or impede strategic shifts—typically, these involve the interests of other institutional actors (e.g., government)

reactions in the organization that must also be accommodated by the implementation plan.[13]

Monitoring and institutionalizing change is the final stage (although the process is somewhat recursive, as new threats and opportunities are likely to emerge as existing change becomes stabilized). The key tasks here are tracking the progress of the change, and creating the formal and informal mechanisms that will keep the new behaviors, new structures, and new attitudes and routines in place. This is particularly important, given the observation that the progress of change is rarely linear or constant: many change agents and experts have noted the tendency of organizations under-going change to backslide or revert.

Types of Change

Another component of a theory of change is a typology of change. Like the basic assumption underlying the contingency approach to leadership introduced in chapter 6, the expectation seems reasonable that not all changes are the same with respect to the challenges or dynamics. Indeed, the basic contribution of a number of academic or formal theories of change lies in the distinctions that they make between various forms of change and the implications for how each should be managed. For example, various typologies identify types of change based on dimensions such as the following: *magnitude*, which is to say, incremental or evolutionary change versus discontinuous or revolutionary change; *urgency* of change (time available to make change); *impetus* for change (external versus internal); and *timing* and *locus* of initiatives (reactive versus proactive).[14]

These dimensions are often related to one another (and are, of course, only a subset of the categorizations in the literature). Any effort to integrate or elaborate on them is beyond the scope and purpose of this chapter. The importance of these dimensions in the context of this metatheory of strategic change is simply to stress their implications for the generalizability of any particular TOC.

TOC and Dashman Company

To return to the Dashman example, in stage 1 Manson and Post identified the shortage of supplies or raw materials as a strategic threat. The concern was that, in the face of uncoordinated purchasing, this shortage could lead to delayed production (idle plants) or suboptimal allocation of supplies (i.e., in ways that did not maximize profitability). Although there was no explicit process of identifying alternative solutions or directions for change, Post settled on centralizing purchasing.

In addition, though the case alludes to barriers to change (it was a busy time of year and there was a long tradition of allowing plants to operate autonomously), no consideration was given to how to overcome them. With respect to implementation, Post sent the memo out but then took no additional steps to facilitate implementation of the change. Finally, he did attempt to monitor the implementation. The case notes that Post received messages assuring headquarters of cooperation. Informal tracking of plant activity indicated that they were busy, and formal tracking of notices of contracts for raw materials indicated that no purchases were being negotiated. Finally, because these indicators suggest that the desired change may not have occurred, the next step of institutionalizing change is moot.

There are several possible interpretations of the events. Perhaps plants ignored the directive, despite the assurances of cooperation they provided. Perhaps they found a way to circumvent the request (e.g., smaller order sizes below $10,000), or maybe they had stockpiles and have not yet had to place orders.

Assuming we judge the change effort as unsuccessful, we turn to the TOC to understand why. Despite the sketchy nature of the case, many explanations come to mind. Some of the key tasks at a number of stages in the change process were not performed adequately. For example, there was no effort to persuade plants of the need for change. There appears to have been no assessment of the barriers to change (e.g., Dashman's culture of autonomy, and the limited authority of Mr. Post and his newly created position). In addition, the implementation seems to have been limited to sending out the memo. Both formal TOCs and intuition would suggest that considerably more effort and additional tactics might have been necessary to actually change the plant managers' patterns of behavior.

The purpose of this analysis is to illustrate the way in which a TOC is central to understanding and managing the change process. It was not that Mr. Post or Mr. Manson did not have a theory (or theories) of organizational change; they did. It is just that these theories appear to have been incomplete or flawed in ways that led actions based on them to be ineffective. Recognition of this fact should lead them to reflect on the gaps and limitations of their theories. But, in order to do so, they need to make the gaps and limitations explicit. The value of a metaframework of strategic change is that it would have led them to be explicit about their theories and critical of them from the outset.

Theory of Organizational Intervention

The last body of knowledge, or skill, that is necessary to manage strategic change is the most neglected yet often the most important. This is a *theory of organizational intervention* (TOI). In contrast to the TOC, intervention focuses on micro-level rules, principles, and actions used to implement the theory of change. By *micro-level*, I mean it deals with concrete actions and behaviors in face-to-face interactions that lead to changes in the beliefs, attitudes, and behavior of organizational members.

These individual-level changes aggregate to changes in the pattern of organizational activities, policies, and resource allocation decisions, which in turn produce strategic change. The timeframe of actions informed by the TOI is measured in seconds, minutes, and hours. The timeframe of actions informed by the TOC, by contrast, is weeks, months, and years. It is in this sense that the TOI is a more detailed guide to implementing the TOC.

For example, most theories of change include some principles about building political support for the change, which may be framed as establishing a coalition, getting buy-in, or getting key stakeholders on board. But, in order to actually do this, the change agent has to engage in conversations and interactions in which he or she persuades others that the envisioned change is a "good" idea. The TOI provides the interpersonal program that addresses the question, how to actually do this?

Given the complexity and variability of such situations, TOI is more like a skill than a formal theory. Much like putting in golf or executing a free throw in basketball, the knowledge is *tacit*. It is a kinesthetic, not a verbal, understanding. The knowledge exists only in the doing and cannot normally be decomposed or articulated.[15]

If one were to ask managers about their TOC, probing, for example, their view of the key stages or barriers, most experienced change agents would be able to describe the principles that guide their actions. But if one were to ask them about their TOI, one would likely receive vague and abstract descriptions: "Well I try to be persuasive," or "I try to be very open-minded and listen to people's concerns." One problem is that these espoused theories often depart dramatically from what people actually do.[16] Another is that they are also much more abstract. As a result, they are not as useful or transferable as explicit guides to action.

Nevertheless, they are central to effective change: without them, there would be no political support, no deep understanding of a vision, and no coordinated action on the part of the myriad of organizational actors that must exist to generate strategic change. Hence, the challenge is to map and elicit theories and knowledge that are highly skilled (in the sense of being outside of awareness, not necessarily in the sense of being effective) and make them accessible to reflection, evaluation, and modification. One way to do this is to observe carefully what change agents actually do as they try to implement their TOC. So, if, for example, building support were part of an individual's TOC, we could observe him in a meeting in which he attempted to build such support. By carefully analyzing the actual behavior, we could infer the rules or principles that the person was following. For instance, we might see him offering a subordinate some perk or favor in exchange for her support. From that we could infer that part of his TOI involves exchanges, or horse trading, to negotiate political support. This tactic might be contrasted with that of another leader, who, faced with the same situation, might tend to shout or belittle subordinates into agreeing to support a particular change. This individual's TOI involves intimidation or coercion to gain political support.

Depending on the circumstances, either, neither, or both of these approaches might work, but it is impossible to reflect on or evaluate either element of the two TOIs unless we can make them explicit. Because such behaviors, and the theories that produce them, are automatic and outside conscious awareness, it can be difficult to subject them to the same critical evaluation as we do TOPs or TOCs. For any given individual or TOI, it is possible to identify general principles that guide behavior in critical face-to-face interactions—how the individuals deal with conflict, how they deal with culture, how they communicate, and so on. These are all important elements of the TOI.

Again, my goal here is not to present or promote a particular TOI, but only to highlight its role in the process of strategic change. There are numerous writers and texts that offer advice that transcend the higher-level TOC and offer very concrete and useful advice about types of face-to-face interaction (e.g., communication, negotiation, persuasion, influence, and learning) that are key elements of any TOI.[17]

Theory of Organizational Intervention and Dashman

Revisiting the Dashman case from the perspective of the TOI, we might wonder what led Mr. Post to dismiss the advice of his deputy, Mr. Larson, about visiting with the plant managers. How does he see and deal with subordinates such that it did not occur to him to ask Larson why he thought it necessary to discuss the matter in person. Or, what led him to send out a memo without asking the recipients if the plan raised any concerns for them?

Although there is relatively little data on Post's TOI, without our being able to ask these types of questions, we can speculate that his theory contains some assumptions that, in a corporation, subordinates do what they are told. He presumably also has some beliefs about the relative efficiency and effectiveness of written versus face-to-face methods of communication.

Basing our conclusions on the subsequent events in the case, we might easily surmise that Mr. Post's assumptions were wrong. Still, without reflecting on the worldview that produced his actions or interventions, Post is unlikely to develop alternative models. As a result, he may not behave any differently in future change efforts. And, even in the present one, his next steps are likely to be informed by the same basic model. So, if he suspects that plants ordered in smaller batches or did not understand his instructions (rather than interpreting their lack of response as active resistance), he may simply try to send another memo, being more clear or more forceful. In accordance with our own TOI, we can speculate about the likely efficacy of such actions.

Criteria for Evaluating Theory

Embedded in the last comment are some of the key criteria that we use to judge how good a theory is: How accurate is it in predicting outcomes of choices prescribed by the theory? How effective is it in informing the design of actions that lead to the desired consequences? How wide a range of situations is the theory useful for dealing with? In academic circles, we talk of validity, reliability, and generalizability. These are simply more precise ways of talking about these basic questions.

Girl Scouts of the United States of America

To illustrate the way in which the TOP, the TOC, and the TOI can and should inform efforts to lead strategic change, let us take an in-depth look at a real-world example of a change effort under way at the Girl Scouts of the United States of America.

Despite its being recognized as one of the most successful and enduring nonprofit organizations and lauded as a shining example for businesses as well as for other nonprofits to follow, the Girl Scouts found itself facing significant challenges as it approached the twenty-first century. The organization's market share had been declining for some time; between 1989 and 2002, the number of girl members dropped from 3.1 million to 2.8 million even as the U.S. population grew. Though the organization's survival was certainly not in question, its leadership saw its economic prosperity declining. Interim CEO Jackie Barnes observed in a 2003 speech before the organization's national leadership summit, "In 2001, Boys and Girls Clubs raised $29.24 for every child served. Girls, Inc. raised $11.07 and Camp Fire Girls raised $2.45 for every girl served. Our data shows [sic] we raised $2.11 for every girl served."[18]

But more important than the economic trends was the threat to the Girl Scouts' psychological success as reflected in its ability to live up to the mission, "Every girl everywhere." The organization's own data indicated that the ethnic and socioeconomic composition of its membership was gradually becoming less and less reflective of the American population. Moreover, Girl Scouts who did come from poor, urban, and minority communities tended to be served through program structures and formats that were far more economically fragile than the traditional volunteer troop model.[19]

Although Girl Scouts had introduced a variety of initiatives and programs in an effort to modernize and adapt the organization (in many cases, successfully), in 2003 the fundamental questions about the organization's diversity and appeal remained burning concerns. In her address, Barnes went on to highlight the discrepancy between traditional models of girl scouting (troops led by full-time volunteers) and nontraditional models (after school, in school, facility based, and led by paid staff) and pose the rhetorical question, "Are we out of alignment—does the business model still fit our delivery systems?"[20] The implied answer was *yes*, but the challenge of realigning the organization and its systems, procedures, policies, and activities to address the needs of a new and changing target audience seemed daunting. From our point of view, the question is, how might the metaframework help the leadership of the Girl Scouts to think through and manage the ongoing process of strategic change?

First and foremost, it tells us that we need to have a robust model of organizational performance that will allow us to assess the need for change (strategic threats and opportunities) but later to make this case to the many stakeholders who will need to be persuaded that the need for change exists. Second, we know that, all else being equal, we are more likely to be effective in designing and leading the change process if we have a TOC that can think through and manipulate (in the best sense of the word) the levers that will facilitate change and deal with the barriers—and do this in a way that guides our choices about the timing and sequencing of key steps. Third, we will, it is to be hoped, recognize the importance of the face-to-face interactions and at least be able to identify and reflect on the TOI that guides our efforts to communicate, negotiate, debate and learn.

So what did the leadership of Girl Scouts actually do? By this point in its history, the organization had been exposed to formal models of strategy (via businesspeople on its boards, consultants, and the professional management training of many of its senior staff members). This base of knowledge led the organization's leadership to draw on notions such as market share to think about how well they were doing and why. Similarly, they looked at their prosperity in ways that compared it with a group of peers or competitors (for example, we find references to their fundraising success and penetration). They also looked at the changing nature of the environment, particularly demographic shifts and how they affected both what they were and what they wanted to be doing.

In evaluating alternative directions for change, the organization analyzed various aspects of its structure (centralization, decentralization, size, and governance) with respect to both the economic implications (costs) and the efficacy in terms of meeting the needs of its customers (girls of various ages in various segments). Indeed, the analysis reflected a level of strategic sophistication that exceeds what I have observed in many large corporations. Although there was some ambiguity around the precise impact of various options, the criteria by which alternatives should be evaluated were relatively well understood.

In this example, the major challenges involve barriers to change and the features of the Girl Scouts' culture, structure, and governance that make the implementation and institutionalization of change particularly difficult. Though the full story is too complex to detail here, one specific example is the organization's norms around decision making. These are heavily skewed toward very broad participation and the expectation of consensus—understandable given the roots and ethos of the Girl Scouts. However, the difficulty, as in many large organizations, was (and is) how to build the necessary degree of consensus in order to make and implement decisions that reflect a dramatic shift in the activities, policies, and resource allocation decisions (execution) among what are in effect over three hundred independent institutions (local councils) with their own unique contexts, interests, constraints, and concerns. It goes without saying that a real, meaningful, and actionable answer could fill an entire book. But, even on the sketchiest of levels, we can see in the following preparation for and design of the 2003 leadership conference elements of the leaders' TOP, TOC, and TOI.

TOP

The analysis of the need for change, as well as alternative directions, included explicit consideration of factors such as buyer/market segmentation and competitive advantage, cost, and economies of scale. In addition, evaluation of the options for change included considerations of the efficiency of the Girl Scouts organizational structure, the division of responsibilities between corporate level and the local chapters, and the impact those structures have on the ability to execute all new strategic initiatives.

TOC

A number of barriers to change received explicit attention. On reflection, the organization's leaders noted structural barriers, political barriers, and volunteers and their preferences with respect to various models. Economic barriers, such as the limited availability of resources for supporting alternative delivery systems, and behavioral barriers, such as the skills and knowledge of the existing staff to implement new models of delivery, were taken into consideration. Implementation steps included articulating and sharing a vision and using conferences as vehicles for bringing people together to communicate the need for change, as well as to explore solutions. The Girl Scouts also made use of consultants and outside experts, as well as investing in education and information systems to support the change, ultimately changing people in ways that would make the changes easier. At this point, institutionalizing and monitoring the change were not yet relevant, because the organization was in the midst of change.

TOI

The interaction designed to engage council presidents in discussion and exploration of the change included the following: extensive use of market data to establish need for change, appeals to values of social justice and equality, and active debate and use of small groups.

Conclusion

As in previous chapters, the lesson to be taken away from our illustration lies not in the specific practices or techniques used by the Girl Scouts.

Rather, it lies in a deeper understanding of, and appreciation for, the role of frameworks for dealing with a managerial challenge. There are a variety of resources for learning and applying specific frameworks (i.e., a particular TOP, TOC, or TOI), but recognizing the need for such tools and knowledge stems from having a metaframework that guides one's basic approach toward strategic change.

Finally, any metaframework, or theory of theories, should say something not just about what kinds of frameworks are necessary and their basic structure and properties, but also about how to evaluate and choose from among the many available frameworks, or, in the case of lay or intuitive theories, about how to develop and improve these models of the world.

In the world of science or professional theorizing, there are entire subfields devoted to methods and criteria for evaluating and testing theories. Suffice it to say most of this apparatus is far beyond the needs or interests of the average manager, so I offer only a simple and basic set of tests that the lay theorist or practitioner can apply to his or her own process of theory selection and development. Basically, what we want to know is, can we use the framework in real time to generate action, and will it produce the results that we intend? Specifically, we ask the following: How accurate is it in predicting outcomes of choices prescribed by the theory? How effective is it in informing the design of actions that lead to the desired consequences? And how wide a range of situations is the theory useful for dealing with?[21]

Of course, the entire book has to this point been primarily concerned with developing, explicating, and promoting a set of frameworks, or metaframeworks, for integrating mission and strategy. Though I have offered many examples of organizations and leaders, following or not following the prescriptions derived from these formal approaches, there remain many challenges and questions faced by the reader who is ready to draw on the ideas in this book to enhance the performance of his or her own nonprofit. Hence, we turn now to the final chapter, which offers some concrete guidelines about how to (and just as often how *not* to) do so in your own organization.

8

Avoiding the Pitfalls of Mission, Strategy, and Execution in the Real World

The objective of working through mission is to articulate a set of aspirations that inspire and focus the activities of an organization. The function of working through strategy is to provide the organization with a coherent and internally consistent plan that guides its operational choices and resource allocation decisions, and helps it to navigate through the competitive forces of its industry and nonmarket environments. The practical challenge is how to go from the dispassionate academic analysis of the classroom to the urgent and consequential decisions of the boardroom, executive suite, and the front lines of the organization.

As much as the frameworks and examples presented in the preceding chapters may seem clear and compelling, my experience working with real nonprofit leaders has led me to a deep appreciation of the difficulty involved in applying them to one's own organization. More specifically, over the last eight years, I have been engaged with a number of colleagues in teaching these ideas about mission, strategy, and execution to nonprofit leaders around the country.[1]

During the course of these executive programs, we do an exercise— admittedly, an academic one—in which participants analyze their own organization, typically in a team consisting of top managers and board members. Over the course of about eight hours, we work with them to simultaneously refine their analysis and deepen their understanding of the concepts and frameworks. In doing so, we have seen what people struggle with and what trips them up. In addition, in a number of organizations, we have seen the leadership embrace these ideas and actively use them to reshape their organizations' strategy, mission, and operations. These observations have been a rich source of insights about the challenges and pitfalls of putting these ideas into practice. This chapter explores the nature of these difficulties and tries to provide some advice about how to deal with them.

Rather than being grounded in empirical research and academic theories, these prescriptions emerge from the experience of real nonprofit leaders, as well as my own as codirector of the Center for Social Innovation at Stanford University, a well-endowed nonprofit, but a nonprofit nonetheless.[2] Although there are many reasons why analyzing one's own strategy and mission is more difficult than analyzing the strategy and mission of other organizations, I have noted two broad classes of difficulty: (1) psychological factors related to how we process information and make sense of our experience (including emotional reactions and biases), and (2) analytical factors related to the complexity of applying the core concepts of mission and strategy. I discuss each of these next.

Psychological Difficulties

One of the most basic challenges in application is information overload. Because we live in them on a day-to-day basis, we know much more about our own organizations. We are acutely aware of the subtleties of our tasks, intentions, and obstacles. Thus, the sheer magnitude of seemingly relevant data or information can be overwhelming. And, because every detail is not only salient, but also potentially significant, we encounter the proverbial problem of separating the forest from the trees.

Another key source of difficulty is the fact that, viewed from the inside, every organization consists of multiple perspectives and stakeholders, each of whom can have divergent perceptions or understandings of the organization's mission and strategy—especially if these have not been laid out explicitly in a formal mission statement or strategic plan. When we look at other organizations from the outside, we tend to see them as a single entity—a kind of black box—and identify their strategies in a pattern of corporate decisions and actions. In contrast, when we consider our own organizations, we become acutely aware of the subtle, and not-so-subtle, deviations in the preferences, priorities, and interpretations among individual staff or board members. Moreover, as part of a sector in which we value consensus and collaboration, we can find ourselves succumbing to the tendency to circumvent conflict by understating or ignoring these differences, which can lead to analyses that fail to make the hard choices necessary for effective integration of mission, strategy, and execution.

The challenge arises because we are passionate about and committed to our own causes. This passion can bias our perceptions in the direction of seeing what we *want* to be true, rather than what might *actually* be true. Passion and commitment to an organization's cause are central to the motivation of nonprofit staff, trustees, and donors, and are critical to the faith and perseverance that characterize a new class of nonprofit innovators who have been lauded as "social entrepreneurs."[3] At the same time, "wishful thinking" can and does contaminate the judgments that we make about the world around us, and about our own strengths and weaknesses.

A final source of difficulty is *vanity*. Over time, we become invested in the mission and strategy that we have developed or stewarded for our organizations, as well as the choices that we have made to execute them. Even for the most thick-skinned among us, identifying flaws or limitations in what we have built can easily be experienced as a negative reflection on our competence or judgment. Hence, discovering that the attribute that we have carefully honed over the last five years is in fact *not* a source of competitive advantage (when we were certain that is was, and promoted this erroneous belief widely) can be potentially threatening on a personal level.

Analytical Complexities

As if these psychological factors were not enough, the analytical aspects of developing and executing mission and strategy present their own unique challenges. These changes stem from the complexity and ambiguity inherent in applying a conceptual framework to a concrete situation. Complexity and ambiguity arise because of the limitations of the frameworks for dealing with the messy world of real organizations and industries.

For example, independent of sector, there are predictable strategic errors that managers make. Some of the most common examples are associated with the pursuit of growth, such as the failure to consider competitors' responses, and underestimating the differences between existing and new markets in decisions to expand an organization's scope. These errors lead to problems of overcapacity, hypercompetition, and failed mergers and acquisitions. The flip side of this error is a common tendency to overemphasize competitive dynamics and underestimate the potential for cooperation and the value of complements.[4]

Second, there are the complexities associated with extending for-profit frameworks to a nonprofit context. These stem not from sector per se, but rather from the primacy of social (rather than economic) value, and from the inherent difficulty of measuring this value.[5] It also stems from the relative inefficiency of the social capital market (grants, etc.) when compared to the capital market for the business world.[6] Although we discussed some of these issues from a theoretical perspective earlier in this book, this chapter will focus on the practical significance of these complexities and their implications for nonprofit organizations—and for those who lead them. Consistent with this basic objective, the next section of this chapter focuses on the key pitfalls associated with the processes of integrating mission, strategy, and execution in real organizations.

The Process of Developing Mission and Strategy

I noted very early in this text that strategic planning often bears little, if any, relationship to strategy and, in fact, may actually impede the development and articulation of a clear strategy and a compelling mission. At the foundation of this critique is the distinction between *process* and *outcome*. Whether it is developed deliberately and intentionally, or intuitively and emergently, a strategy is, ultimately, still an *outcome*. Thus my personal view is that robust strategy and compelling mission are more important than elaborate strategic planning or vision/mission exercises—in large part because the latter so often fail to generate anything resembling a real strategy or a truly inspiring mission statement. Nevertheless, the fact is that there still has to be some process by which both mission and strategy are produced and articulated.

One way to think about this subject is in terms of the following metaphor. If you are in Paris and you want to end up in Rome, there are many different ways to get there. Arriving at an effective strategy—like arriving at a destination—is an outcome. Strategic planning, like the journey, is unavoidable but, in the end, it does not much matter where the journey takes you, so long as you arrive at your destination. Of course, some routes are longer, more tiring, and riskier than others. So, though I do not have strong preferences or opinions about what the process should look like, I have noted a few key decisions and questions that arise in designing it (whether it be strategic planning or some other mechanism): Who gets to decide? What if we cannot agree? What comes first, mission or strategy? How much structure do we need?

Who Gets to Decide: Designing the Strategic Planning Process

So who is really in charge of designing the process of mission and strategy development, and who is in charge of making sure that the pitfalls that can (and often will) interfere with this process are dealt with effectively and efficiently, and that the quality of the resulting mission and strategy is good? Ultimately, the responsibility for accomplishing all this lies with those charged with leading the organization. Despite our fascination with charismatic individual leaders (like Jack Welch or Frances Hesselbein), this does not mean that we should focus solely on the organization's CEO or executive director. In fact, the responsibility actually lies at the nexus between an organization's chief executive, its board, and the senior management team. Why? Because, increasingly, we see the emergence of views emphasizing the distributed nature of leadership and responsibility.[7]

There is a tremendous amount of research demonstrating the value of employee participation in improving the quality of implementation and execution of strategy.[8] However, if the responsibility for fulfilling key leadership functions is distributed, then this distribution needs to be designed and monitored by the person or persons who have fiduciary responsibility for the organization, whether that be the executive director, senior staff, or the board of directors. No matter who is involved, to do the job effectively, those setting an organization's mission and strategy need—at a minimum—knowledge and frameworks that allow them to set an effective direction and to inspire key stakeholders. The answer to the more practical question, who actually gets to decide? depends on the political, cultural, and legal landscape that defines the governance structure for the organization.

What If We Cannot Agree?

The problem of intractable disagreement typically arises when there is a diverse group of decision-makers and stakeholders. This diversity (with respect to values, interests, and priorities) is in turn a function of ambiguity and fuzziness in mission and strategy. However, in some cases, it may result because an organization is simply unable to adequately describe and communicate its mission and strategy to the outside world and attracts people with widely differing understandings. The end result is tension between these different stakeholders. These tensions can paralyze the organization and may not be resolved until some people leave. Consider the example of Mountain View, California–based nonprofit Interplast. Tension within that organization, arising from the clarification and refinement of its mission, eventually caused the founder to leave. Although painful, this result was instrumental in Interplast's ability to evolve and adapt.

What Comes First?

Another question is, where does one begin, especially since most organizations are not starting from scratch and have an existing mission and strategy statement? I have argued that, for a nonprofit, mission must clearly come first. In most successful nonprofits, the mission will be clear and inspiring, as well as broadly understood and accepted. If it is not, then when choices about strategy and execution come to the forefront, there are likely to be conflicts and differences, which will be more difficult to resolve if they cannot be tested against a clear mission. In such cases, it is necessary to go back and work through the mission, testing it against the criteria outlined in chapter 1 and building a consensus among key groups.

Once the mission is in place, then strategy becomes the vehicle for determining how to secure the resources necessary to pursue the mission and to ensure the economic viability of the organization. There are many strategies that would be consistent with a given mission: recall the KQED public television case, in which many stations with fundamentally similar missions pursued very different strategies. Not all strategies are equally "good," however. Hence, the process also needs to include identifying, evaluating, and refining the existing strategy.

How Much Structure Is the Right Amount?

Although I am more inclined toward a process of deliberate development, good strategies can be generated through processes that are not as systematic or structured. I do think, however, that unstructured processes are less conducive to change and adaptation. Moreover, they are less likely to engender the understanding and acceptance that are critical to coherent and consistent execution. "Structured," however, does not necessarily mean strategic planning, though some of the more useful templates for how to structure the process of developing strategy and mission do come from the strategic planning literature.[9] Despite the difficulty and potential limitations of any process, the quality and robustness of a strategy can be judged independent of the process that was used to generate it, and the criteria and logic for doing this is the focus of this book.

I offer some final pieces of advice about process:

- Be clear that the output of the process is a strategy, with the elements of competitive advantage, scope, and logic.
- Do not overspecify the concrete choices of execution in the strategic plan. Often, the knowledge, expertise, and judgment necessary for making these choices—in light of the strategy—reside among those who do the day-to-day work of the organization.
- Understand that goals are important, as well as metrics by which progress toward these goals can be evaluated. But planning goals needs to be directly connected to the mission (primary goal) and the objectives implied by the strategy. These are the basis for knowing whether the strategy is being executed and, if so, whether it is working and when it might need to change.
- Do not mistake process for outcomes: careful and deliberate strategic planning does not necessarily produce a good strategy (or mission).

Understanding and Navigating the Pitfalls of Mission

Developing or evaluating core values and purpose is especially tricky because, in principle, these two elements of mission should be enduring. In the case of most existing organizations, the leaders are not likely to have the opportunity to revise the formal mission statement unless there is a major environmental or organization dislocation. Still, the static quality of core value and purpose is less of a problem than it might seem, since what we are really concerned with is the psychological and emotional logic that lives in people's hearts and minds.

Because of this orientation, the task of articulating mission is more about framing and making sense of "who we are" and "why we do what we do." The answers to these questions do not have to be written into the organization's formal mission statement or posted on its Web site, but they should be understood and accepted by those leading the organization.

Core Values

The most common problem in establishing or articulating an organization's core values is the laundry list phenomenon. On a first pass, we will often see organizations list seven to ten core values. As we noted in chapter 1, core values should be limited in number and represent values that the organization is willing to close its doors over rather than violate. Laundry lists arise because of two factors: (1) the failure to make the hard choices or deal with conflict, and (2) a pervasive tendency to believe that everything we care about should be reflected in an organization's core values, so that if we do not put something basic, like integrity, into our organization's core values, the implication is that we do not care about it or, worse yet, that we are dishonest. The problem with a laundry list of core values is twofold. First, simply listing a set of core values on a plaque or official company statement does not mean people will live by those values. Consider the assertions made in Enron's 1999 annual report: "We treat others as we would like to be treated ourselves. We do not tolerate abusive or disrespectful treatment. Ruthlessness, callousness and arrogance do not belong here."[10] Testimony from a host of senior and mid-level executives after the collapse of Enron made it clear that these values were empty rhetoric.

Second, the laundry list dilutes and diffuses the power and clarity of a limited and meaningful set of organizational precepts. When an organization ends up with a list of ten or more core values, that list becomes not only meaningless, but also unmanageable. As the number of core values increases, so does the likelihood that they will conflict with one another, leaving managers to ignore them and do whatever seems to be expedient at the moment.

One way of dealing with the proliferation of core values is to draw a distinction between *personal, societal,* or *professional* values, and values that are fundamentally *organizational.* For example, general societal values like honesty or freedom of speech, or personal values such as fidelity or piety, are different from organizational core values. The organizational core values should be distinctive. They should make a statement that helps to define "who we are" as an organization, not just as individuals or as a society. These values should have "bite," meaning they should define things that we would never do, but that other organizations might. They should raise our people's hackles and evoke a resounding chorus of "Hell yes, we will fight for that," or "Hell no, we will never, ever, under any conditions do that." For example, intellectual freedom for a university, or innovation for a high-tech firm, or meritocracy for a professional service firm, or aggressiveness for a professional hockey team could all be core (i.e., defining) values at the organizational level.

Purpose

As with the lack of focus or choice reflected in the laundry list of core values, some organizations have a purpose so broad you could sail a cruise ship through it; for example, "to make the world a better place," "to ensure opportunity for all," or "to promote social justice." As admirable as these aspirations may be, they do not provide the organization, the people within it, with sufficient clarity or focus to excel at their jobs. Not only is "making the world a better place" too broad, but thoughtful people can have very different ideas about how best to make the world a better place, or even about which outcomes are "better" and which are "worse."

So what leads to such broad statements of purpose? In many cases, it is simply the fear that, if the organization really engages the hard questions and choices, then important stakeholders will leave—be they board members, funders, staff, or others who seem indispensable to the organization's success. And, indeed, this fear is often well founded. There are plenty of potential funders who might agree that it is a good idea to make the world a better place and who would be happy to invest their money in the pursuit of such an outcome. But, when the organization has to decide whether to support educational reform or urban economic development, tensions will naturally arise, separating those with different perspectives and priorities. The pressures of securing adequate funding will tend to push the organization toward finessing such differences and preserving the broader statements of purpose.

A second problem with purpose is that many real-world examples are drab and boring. Indeed, I never cease to be amazed at how hard it is for nonprofit leaders to give voice or pen to the passion and deep sense of the importance of what they do. Largely, I suspect that this happens because the sense of purpose is a deep, tacit, and almost private thing that we are not used to talking about. Indeed, trying to produce it on demand in the context of the dreaded strategic planning exercise is somewhat like being directed to demonstrate affection in a public place or to "be creative" under the glare of the spotlight. At the same time, my colleagues and I have consistently found that a few probing questions and expressions of skepticism about the blasé rendition of the purpose that emerges on the first draft, can transform the humdrum into the magnificent in five minutes. By the time the third draft is articulated, I often find myself literally ready to write a check to the organization being discussed.

One of the factors underlying the initial tendency toward uninspiring statements of purpose is that they are often simply statements of strategy. Many mission statements simply summarize what an organization does and for whom, in effect offering descriptions of scope (products and services, and buyers). Remember that purpose is the element of the framework that is most often labeled as *mission*. By asking *why*—why the organization does what it does—it is fairly easy to get to the heart of the organization's true aspirations. These aspirations—or *purpose*—are always more inspiring and meaningful than a simple statement of what the organization does and for whom.

Primary Goals

Just as not everything we care about should be a core value, not every objective that we pursue should be a mission-level, or primary, goal. Primary goals are big, hairy, and audacious, and they "apply to the entire organization and take significant time and effort to accomplish."[11] One of the most common errors is including secondary goals in the mission.

Primary goal means just that: an objective that is superordinate and that informs and guides a host of subordinate goals. Because the primary goal is the one that goes in the mission, it should apply to the entire organization, and its importance and value should be self-evident. It is an end, not a means to an end. So again, as with core values, not everything you are trying to accomplish needs to be listed as a primary goal. This does not mean that the secondary goal will not be taken seriously or that we do not expect those responsible for it to hold themselves accountable. It just means that it is a goal or objective that is pursued in the service of a larger and more basic goal.

Consider the following example of a faith-based nonprofit—a church. The purpose is absolutely compelling and clear: "to know God and make Him known." But, then, there were a host of goals listed:

- Establish a college and seminary
- Build new facilities
- Engage every member of the church in some form of active service or ministry

- Engage every member in a discipleship relationship
- Establish growing neighborhood fellowship groups

All of these goals seem important enough, but most are instrumental: they are means to achieve a larger goal. The one that strikes me as the most basic is, "Engage every member of the church in some form of active service or ministry." This "gets the juices flowing"; moreover, in order to achieve it, we may need to build new facilities and establish fellowship groups.

The goal of establishing a seminary could also be a basic end, but we would need to link it more explicitly to the purpose. Why do we need to create a seminary? What if we built it and nobody came? It would probably not advance the purpose. So it becomes clearer that the seminary is a means to achieving some other goal, like training and developing new leaders who can advance the ministry. Keeping the mission free of *means* is important, because once they get on the list, they become ends in and of themselves, leading the organization to lose sight of the primary goal or goals, whose function is to guide and inspire action. Primary goals are ends that *have value in and of themselves* because they are milestones on the never-ending journey that is purpose.

When instrumental goals find their way into the mission, they create confusion because they take on a life of their own. This is why financial goals do not belong in an organization's mission: they can end up being pursued independent of the organization's true goal, whatever that may be. If having a balanced budget or an operating surplus were really ends in and of themselves, you would not be a nonprofit—you would become a pharmaceutical company. Although this declaration seems silly, the subtle and not so subtle ways in which commercial pressures can lead social-purpose organizations away from their true mission has become increasingly apparent.[12]

Consider a capital campaign or endowment, which might initially be established to ensure the continuity of an institution. But what happens when the institution ignores the need to divert financial resources from the endowment to support its primary goal? What happens is that it will likely find itself in a situation where its key talent leaves—and its reputation goes along with the talent. The organization may be left with an impressive endowment, but with little else that seems worth preserving.

Universities are sometimes the worst examples of such behavior when the endowment becomes sacrosanct. So, rather than tapping into it, the administration will close down the English department. The argument may not even be that it is too costly or unprofitable to run the English department, but that the quality of scholarship is just not up to standards. Of course, this argument ignores the fact that the department's quality may well have been eroded by years of neglect and underinvestment—all while the university's fund-raising apparatus was plowing major gifts into the endowment or named buildings rather than into general operating support. Although we all "know" that capital campaigns are not supposed to cannibalize annual giving, this belief flies in the face of the basic principles of competition and resource scarcity that have been central to the frameworks in this book.

Another problem with the primary goals of many organizations is that they are either too difficult or too easy. Primary goals are supposed to provide motivation and focus. We know that to do this they have to be challenging but attainable. Sometimes, when organizations do not give a lot of thought to appropriate goals, they can articulate goals that have already been achieved. This is like a local cable television provider, which has been granted a service monopoly by the city in which it operates, declaring a goal to be the best cable television provider in town. Because the organization actually has no other competitors, this goal is useless as a source of direction and inspiration.

In another case, a regional symphony decided it wanted to be a world-class orchestra but, as we probed what this really meant, it became clear that, though the organization could aspire to be an excellent and well-respected regional performer, it was not going to reach the heights of the top ten or even twenty orchestras in the world. Because this goal, in any reasonable scenario, was unattainable, it, too, had relatively little practical value, because no one took it seriously.

A final flaw that can plague primary goals that are too abstract is that that they do not pass the "Veuve Clicquot" test, meaning that you cannot really tell when you have accomplished them, so you do not know when to open the champagne. Often, primary goals will be extrapolated from purpose, as they should, but leaders do not go far enough in making them concrete. Though it is all right for purpose to be lofty and unattainable, a primary goal has to be something you can hold yourself accountable for.

For example, an organization working to help underprivileged youth in urban public schools defined its purpose as "to empower high-achieving youth to break the cycle of poverty." This is pretty good in terms of purpose, but then the organization framed its mission-level goal as, "We will provide all our students with the building blocks for a successful experience." This goal may advance the organization toward its purpose, but it is not concrete or specific enough for the organization to know when it has accomplished it.

Going a step further, "We will ensure that 100 percent of our students have reading skills at mean of their grade and can pass the mathematic skills test and demonstrate the three essential study skills within the next five years," holds their feet to the fire. It may be that 100 percent is too high, or that five years is too short, but the basic principle applies, which is that the primary goal needs to be defined in a way such that you know when you have accomplished it.

Vision

With respect to vision, unlike core values or goals, the most common problem is not that it typically contains too many elements or too much information, but rather that it contains too few or too little. Often, the vision is simply a restatement of organizational goals rather than the evocative and visual representation of a future in which the primary goal has been attained.

Making visions more *visual* is important, not just because it makes for more inspiring statements, but also because it serves to build greater convergence within the organization. To the extent that the details and nuances of the desired future can be rendered with greater fidelity, it creates an opportunity for leaders of an organization to identify features of a primary goal where there may be disagreement. Similarly, the richer the vision, the easier it will be to link the choices that will bring about its realization, and the easier it will be to assess or measure progress toward the vision as people work to bring it to reality.

The bottom line is this: Do not skimp on language in articulating the vision. Economy is good for core values, purpose, and goals, but vision has to be evocative and rich. It is not the place to be miserly.

Understanding and Navigating the Pitfalls of Strategy

Identifying and evaluating the strategy of your own organization is a task fraught with perils of both process and substance. We will start here by exploring some of the latter—the challenges of substance.

Scope

Perhaps the most common error that occurs in defining scope is overlooking a key element. Remember that scope specifies where we compete; it defines the arena or competitive space in which the organization operates. As I outlined in chapter 2, this consists of four primary dimensions: target buyers (including clients and donors), range of products and services offered, geography (e.g., cities, states, regions, or countries), and vertical integration of parts of the value chain in which the organization participates.

Overcoming this error is relatively simple: it involves looking at the scope to see if it addresses the choices along all of these dimensions. In some cases, geography and vertical scope may be less prominent if these are defined in part by (i.e., are universal across) the industry. For example, if we have defined the industry as environmental preservation in California, and all incumbents truly operate statewide, then geographic scope will not differ across these organizations and hence becomes less central to scope, from an analytical perspective. Similarly, if the industry is higher education and there is little variation in, or few choices about, vertical integration (i.e., most universities do not make their own faculty, students, or buildings), then vertical scope becomes less salient as a dimension of scope.

A second, more difficult error involves defining who the buyers are. Sometimes, organizations define buyers as those who use their services. The problem is that such a definition is tautological and provides no insight into how or why these customers chose the organization, which is to say that it does not help to illuminate competitive advantage. In addition, if the organization starts to lose customers to a competitor, the explanation is that they are just no longer in its scope. Clearly, this is a problem because it does not imply any corrective action. So who the buyer is needs to be defined in terms of attributes that are independent of their purchase or patronage decisions.

Closely related is a third error: defining buyers in ways that are abstract and unobservable. For example, "we serve disadvantaged children." The question is, how does anyone in the organization know whether a particular individual falls within that scope? Until this statement is specified in terms of observable characteristics (Latino, African-American, living below the poverty line, in urban setting, from single-parent families, reading below grade-level, etc.), then it is difficult to know who is part of and who is not part of the organization's scope. When this happens, disagreement and inconsistency can arise about how to structure programs and allocate resources, because staff members may be focusing on two or more different populations or sets of clients.

This is exactly what happened at the nonprofit Harlem Community Children's Zone, which moved from a broad scope that consisted of "disadvantaged children," to "families with children 0–18 [with a primary focus on younger children 0–5] living in the Harlem Children's Zone Project, a residential and commercial area between 116th and 123rd streets and between Fifth and Eighth Avenue, six blocks north of Central Park."[13]

A final error involves defining the scope of donors as anyone who might contribute to the organization. The problem with this is that it bears no relationship to competitive advantage, meaning that it does not differentiate between donors who are very likely to write you a check and those for whom doing so is a real long shot. Although it may be tricky to discern the underlying dimensions or characteristics of the donor who is likely to write you a check, doing so is a worthwhile endeavor. Sometimes, it may be as simple as naming traditional classifications (individuals, foundations, government, and corporations). But, in other instances, there may be more subtle characteristics, like a conservative ideology or a commitment to children's issues. Though these stray a bit from the admonition to be concrete, they can readily be made more concrete by identifying indicators such as patterns of giving, ties to specific causes through board members, or explicitly stated program areas in annual reports or publicly available documents.

The point here is to try to understand and target a subset of potential donors for whom our competitive advantage is likely to matter—and then to distinguish them from those for whom it is not—so that we can focus our time and energy on prospects that are more likely to pay off. A secondary benefit of a clearly identified and more homogenous set of donors is that it reduces the likelihood of receiving a grant that we do not want. Is there such a thing, you might ask? As I argued earlier, the answer is "absolutely." It would be any grant that is not consistent with your mission or that will require investments of resources and time in activities that do not contribute to or that could actually undermine your real basis of competitive advantage.

Competitive Advantage

Figuring out your organization's competitive advantage is usually much harder than identifying its scope. Competitive advantage is difficult to pin down because we tend to focus on the intentions and antecedents of true competitive advantage. What do I mean by *true competitive advantage*? The true competitive advantage lies in the features of the product or service—and sometimes the organization itself—that lead buyers to choose them over the available alternatives. In addition, buyers must be willing to pay a price that exceeds the cost of creating the product or services.[14]

Many executives fall prey to the error of listing every activity, resource, and skill that their organization possesses—or that they wish it did—as a competitive advantage. The problem is, not every strength is a competitive advantage. For example, often I will see something like "strong leadership," "talented and committed staff," "the best facilities," or "long-range planning" listed as an organization's competitive advantage. Although, in theory, any of these could be a competitive advantage, identifying them as such requires that we be able to identify a buyer (funder or client) who is willing to support or choose this organization over others because it does long-range planning, has strong leadership, or has the best facilities.

In most cases, it is more likely that these attributes allow the organization to do or to deliver something that is of direct value to buyers, such as reliability, flexibility, responsiveness, or efficiency. Hence, the first question to ask about any proposed competitive advantage is, who is the customer that cares about these attributes (assuming the organization really is better than its competitors on that dimension)? The second is, why do they care?

Invariably, it turns out that the committed staff or excellent leadership are merely imprecise explanations for the organization's ability to perform activities in ways that create unique sources of value for the buyers. For example, when probed, one organization that initially identified leadership as a competitive advantage eventually realized that the actual competitive advantage was the organization's reliability (minimal errors), timeliness, and responsiveness to special requests made by their clients. Not only are these qualities much more compelling than leadership as an explanation for the organization's success, but also they are far more specific, allowing choices about resource allocation, policies, and activities to be evaluated according to whether they contribute to enhancing this source of competitive advantage.

A second way in which specifications of competitive advantage can be problematic is that they can be defined at a level that is too abstract or general. The most common examples are "quality," "excellence," and "reputation." The difficulty is not that these are not real or legitimate bases of competitive advantages, it is that they are not specific enough. They do not provide guidelines for the choices of execution, nor do they provide a basis for evaluating particular decisions.

Let us consider, for a moment, my own institution, Stanford Business School. If we were to say, "Our competitive advantage is excellence" or "high quality," we could just as easily justify spending money on expensive rugs and artwork in the faculty lounge as we could justify competitive salaries for faculty or making investments in classroom technology to support student learning. What this illustrates is that, in order for quality or excellence to have any "bite" as bases of competitive advantage, they need to be defined in terms of specific product or service attributes.

Here is a good example of increasing the specificity with which competitive advantage is defined. A museum in one of our programs talked about the quality of its collections as a competitive advantage, but when asked to be more concrete the museum's leaders went on to define quality in terms of the "most authentic and comprehensive collection of historical documents and artifacts of our region anywhere in the world." This is much more informative, especially to those with the expertise and professional knowledge to understand exactly what authenticity and comprehensiveness would look like in a collection of historical documents and artifacts.

Closely related to the problem of abstract and vague specifications of competitive advantage is the failure to distinguish between *sources of competitive advantage* and *true competitive advantage* itself. Although both are inextricably linked in the causal chain—the competitive advantage would not exist without its source—it is important to separate them analytically for several reasons.

First, the link between a competitive advantage and its source can change over time. For example, a company might have a competitive advantage based on the quality and reliability of its products. Assume that, initially, the source of this quality was the skilled labor and handcrafted process. During the early period, investment in recruiting, training, and compensating its workforce would be consistent with, and the best means of, sustaining its competitive advantage. But then imagine that the company develops a proprietary material that contributes more to the quality and durability of the product than the labor-intensive process. Under this new scenario, though the competitive advantage remains the same, the source has changed and so should the nature or the firm's allocation of resources going forward. Second, there are typically multiple drivers or sources of a specific competitive advantage, and it is helpful to understand the contribution of each so that investments of additional resources can be targeted to the source that is most likely to strengthen or enhance the competitive advantage. Finally, different sources of competitive advantage may be more or less easily imitated by competitors. So, investments in, and attention to, sources that are relatively sustainable (i.e., not easily imitated) will pay off in better performance over the long haul.

In addition to these major pitfalls, there are others, which I summarize in the rest of this section.

Ignoring the Constraints Imposed by Industry Structure and Competitive Response

This is an error, discussed in chapters 2 and 4, which is often just as apparent in the business world as it is in the nonprofit sector. It is remarkably common to see organizations analyze the structure of their industry and conclude that just about every force is worsening and overall competition is increasing. Indeed, this may be accurate, given the trends affecting the sector. But the conclusion is often followed by growth projections, fund-raising goals, or capital campaigns that seem jarringly out of sync with the gloomy assessment of the environment. In helping nonprofit managers to understand this problem, I like to invoke the "Oliver Twist principle" by asking, "In a world teeming with hungry children (other nonprofits) why do you think you are the one entitled to have 'more'?" Although there are some circumstances in which an organization can legitimately expect to grow—even in a competitive environment—the competitive advantage had better be *really* compelling.

Confusing Industry Features with Competitive Advantage

I often hear organizations saying their competitive advantage is that "we are the only opera in town" or that "we are the only food kitchen." Although this monopoly status may be good for the organization's prosperity, it is a statement about the level of competition in the industry. To be more precise, if the industry is defined as operas or food kitchens and you are the only one in town, then there actually are no other competitors (and thus no competitive advantage), only substitutes. When there are no local competitors, the market has to be defined in terms of advantage relative to *substitutes* (e.g., local performing-arts organizations or nonlocal operas), not competitors. This process involves defining in a more precise way the nature of the aesthetic experience. In the case of one opera that we worked with, the organization's leaders described the "rich, sumptuous, and complex aesthetic experience for all of the senses that has a real impact on the audience." The description continued: "Opera speaks to the human experience, and they see, hear, and feel their lives in art."

Confusing Scope with Competitive Advantage

Sometimes, organizations list elements of their scope as competitive advantage, for example, "focus on at-risk children" or "statewide facilities." Although elements such as these can be related to competitive advantage, it is important to be clear about how and why. So, when an organization uses the phrase, "a clear focus on a particular client group," it often means that the organization is more efficient or more effective at serving that particular group, in part because the focus allows them to invest their resources and configure their activities to meet the needs of that target population. But the specific features of effectiveness or efficiency are the basis for the competitive advantage, not the choice of scope that enables the organization to create that advantage. Similarly, "statewide facilities" may mean that the organization can offer broad coverage of services, perhaps making it easier and more efficient for large buyers to contract for services with a single entity. This is akin to the "one-stop shopping" as a basis of competitive advantage, so it is important to make sure that the one-stop feature really is something that buyers care about, rather than a post hoc rationalization for the failure to focus the organization's efforts.

In other cases, considering the scope as competitive advantage is really a way of saying that "we are the only one that does X." Although this may be true, it is a statement about the level of competition in the industry or segment occupied by the organization. So, in certain smaller secondary metropolitan areas, some nonprofit arts organizations will say, "Our competitive advantage is that we are the only symphony, ballet, etc." Although being the only player is good news, it is *not* competitive advantage. In fact, it is a clue that perhaps a broader definition of the industry would be more useful, such as "performing arts." Even if the industry definition remains "symphony," the competitive advantage has to be defined relative to the "substitutes" of ballet, opera, theater, and so forth.

Mistaking Subsidized Prices (Low or Free) for Cost Advantage

The problem with identifying subsidized prices as cost advantage is that doing so implies that the organization has a cost advantage that probably does not really exist. In reality, the organization is just passing along a subsidy, which any organization can do. It also begs the question: why does the funder provide the resources to this particular organization to subsidize the fee? If in fact there is no subsidy (or no subsidy greater than in the average organization), then there must be a cost advantage, which implies that the organization must not do, or must do more cheaply, the same activities as its competitors or peers. Thus, in the case of cost advantage, we need to understand where the cost advantages actually come from.

Understanding and Navigating the Pitfalls of Industry Analysis

We have already talked at length about the most vexing of problems in the practical application of industry analysis, that of defining the industry to be analyzed. Recall the Goldilocks principle: keep trying alternative definitions of an industry until you find one that is neither too broad nor too narrow, but just right. But how does one know when a particular definition is just right?

Often, unfortunately, one does not. But, because of the importance of this analysis to an organization, it is a good practice to work through multiple iterations of the industry analysis with different definitions to see which one is most helpful for understanding and evaluating the key strategic choices facing the organization. It is also helpful to be on guard for some common mistakes.

One error is to define the industry in terms of the scope of one's own organization. This can be a problem if it blinds managers to attractive strategic possibilities. For example, imagine if Toyota in the 1970s had defined its industry as small, fuel-efficient, low-cost automobiles. If this had occurred, the company would never have seen or considered the possibilities of building trucks, sport utility vehicles, or luxury sedans (the Lexus brand), missing out on key market opportunities and millions of dollars of profit in the process. Even though these are more accurately described as segments rather than industries, the line between the two is often blurred, and the example illustrates the basic point rather dramatically.

Another error is an overly broad industry definition that results when an organization fails to recognize that it has become a multibusiness enterprise. Because expansion occurs gradually, a social service agency that finds itself running substance abuse programs, job training, and day care programs may not recognize that these should be viewed as distinct industries. Although there may be, and hopefully are, ties between these services that confer advantages based on a sound corporate strategy, this is a separate analysis as illustrated in chapter 5.

In some cases, it is possible that the nature of competition is such that all or most providers across a range of social services are integrated and that they are seen as such by funders and clients. In this instance, it would be appropriate to analyze the various services at the higher, more generic level of social services rather than in a particular area. However, just as many larger general retailers, like Sears, discovered in the 1980s and 1990s, such structures can change dramatically with the entry of new specialized competitors, such as appliance, housewares, and electronics retailers.[15] The lesson is that industry definitions should be based on the dynamics and basis of competition. Even though substitutes are captured in the industry analysis, substitutes are typically listed as a generic class of organization. The "lumping" can obscure managers' understanding of the specific strategies and tactics of individual players who may eventually become more direct "competitors" as the industry structures change. An especially powerful example of this is the convergence of industries, such as telephone, cable, and data in recent years.

Having identified the industry, you may still encounter a variety of other errors that arise as you conduct the actual analysis. Two are next discussed separately.

Misidentifying as Suppliers Actors Who Influence Clients' Choices

The logic seems reasonable, that those who direct clients to the organization in a sense "supply" the customer. One might put courts, hospitals, or guidance counselors into this group for at-risk youth programs. But the term *supplier* refers only to those who sell to the industry products or services necessary to produce the product or service. So, for a nonprofit that offers computer training programs, suppliers would be computer hardware (Dell, Apple, Hewlett-Packard, etc.) and software (Microsoft, Intuit, etc.) manufacturers, as well as staff. Indeed, in most nonprofits, the primary supplier is the staff that runs the organization and provides its products and services. A good way to think about this is to look at the expenses in the organization's budget and ask who are the primary vendors that receive checks at the end of the month. Usually, the bulk of the money will go to staff, and maybe rent and utilities.

So where do those who influence the buyer's decision to buy fit in the analysis? Unless they are really buyers themselves, as in the case of parents of young children who have decisions to make about whether to watch Sesame Street or Mickey Mouse, they should be noted as decision influencers and included as part of the analysis of the needs or decision criteria of the real client or buyer. So, though the courts may require an at-risk youth to perform community service, and though this requirement does indeed shape the decision, ultimately the client is the youth himself or herself. The only exception would be if the court both contracts with a nonprofit to provide such services on a regular basis, and directs youth to the program, in which case the court would be an institutional buyer.

Identifying Difficulties of Operating in the Industry as Barriers to Entry

Frequently, I have seen nonprofit leaders list "difficulty raising money," or "low salaries," or "intense competition" as barriers to entry. Although these factors may indeed deter potential entrants, they are also bad for the incumbents—those already in the industry. By definition, barriers to entry are good for incumbents and bad for potential entrants. For example, existing long-term contracts or regulation in the form of licensing is good if you already have contracts or a license, but bad if you do not—the situation faced by new entrants. "Difficulty raising money" is a statement about the level of prosperity and hence competition in the industry itself, not a barrier to entry. If raising money ever became easy, one can imagine that a host of new organizations would crop up to compete for the abundant funds, thereby increasing the level of competition and returning the difficulty of raising money back to its original level.

Evaluating Your Strategy

Having studied the pitfalls of strategy and industry analysis, and having assiduously tried to avoid them, you will end up with a strategy. Below are two final sets of criteria that may be helpful in evaluating that strategy. The first relates to general properties of good versus bad strategies. The second relates to specific tests that your strategy should pass.

Good versus Bad Strategies

Conceptually, there are a number of different characteristics that distinguish good strategies from bad ones. Good strategies

- Possess internal consistency, or *integration* of goals and policies of functional activities
- Provide a clear guide to *resource allocation* decisions
- Match an organization's *capabilities* with appropriate *opportunities* in its environment
- Specify clearly the type of *competitive advantage* desired, how to achieve it, and over what scope
- Make clear and consistent *choices* and *trade-offs*
- Are *sustainable*—cannot be imitated by competitors

Tests of a Good Strategy

Operationally, a good strategy should also pass six practical tests.

- *The GE test*: Using no visual aids whatsoever, you should be able to describe the strategy in one paragraph or less.
- *The bus test*: If a knowledgeable observer of your industry found your strategy on a bus, he or she should be able to tell that it belongs to your organization and not to one of your competitors.
- *The vanity test*: Role play from the perspective of a competitor and ask yourself, "What would my competitor list as our competitive advantages?"
- *The sustainability test*: Ask yourself, "Why can't competitors do the same thing that we are doing?"
- *The twenty-dollars-on-the-table test*: What "funding," "grants," or "contract" would you refuse because they are inconsistent with your strategy?
- *The industry test*: Does your strategy deal with problems posed by the industry?

Understanding and Navigating the Pitfalls of Integration

Ultimately, mission and strategy have to be integrated. Primary goals are the key link between the two. Strategy provides a plan for how the organization will secure and allocate the resources necessary to achieve its primary goals. To the extent that the strategy is robust and deals with the challenges posed by the industry analysis, we can be reasonably confident that the organization will not fail to achieve its objectives because of economic factors.[16]

For two things to be integrated, they first have to be recognized as distinct entities. Herein lies the most pernicious and common pitfall of integration: the conflation of economic and psychological logics. When decision-makers do not have a clear conception of what mission is, what it is supposed to do for an organization, what criteria should be used to evaluate it, and how these are distinct from strategy, they are prone to evaluate elements of mission primarily from an economic perspective. Instead, they should be evaluating them from a psychological perspective: are they motivating, have they inspired us, do we want to do this?

By the same token, managers who conflate strategy with mission will argue that because something is "the right thing to do," or "is consistent with our values," therefore it *has* to work. But, just because something is the right (in the moral sense) thing to do and something you desperately want to do, that does not mean it will necessarily be viable in the marketplace.

Questions and judgment of strategy must be subjected to a different logic and different tests. Unfortunately, the literature on nonprofits often fails to make a clear distinction between mission and strategy. And, even to the extent that it does, the models used to evaluate strategy and mission are not particularly robust. The reason that the distinction between strategy and mission is so important is that a psychological logic alone, no matter how compelling, is not going to lead to an economically sustainable organization. And, similarly, an economic logic, no matter how powerful or sustainable, is not going to motivate staff, donors, and the public over the long haul if it does not engender the kind of passion that comes from a compelling psychological logic. Both economic and psychological logics are essential to long-term success in the nonprofit sector.

One example of conflating mission and strategy that we have already noted is the appearance of financial goals in the mission statement. They simply do not belong there. If you are really serious about the financial goals as an *end* as opposed to a *means*, then you probably should not be a nonprofit. You should be an investment bank or a pharmaceutical firm. What people forget is that the money is drawn to the organization as a function of something else compelling that it be so drawn—most typically, the organization's mission. The appearance of financial goals in the mission is a classic confusion of ends and means. It is not that nonprofits should not have goals that are financial in nature (e.g., build an endowment, or achieve a balanced budget). It is just that these goals do not belong in the mission. They are secondary or instrumental goals, not the primary goal that is central to the psychological logic.

Finally, be careful to distinguish mission-related issues from strategic issues. The former are about the organization's identity, its values, purpose, and goals. Do not defend choices related to these types of issues on the basis of an economic logic. Similarly, do not invoke the organization's mission to justify a choice that is primarily intended to improve the organization's funding or financial viability.

In situations where a given choice has implications both for strategy and for mission and there is a tension between the two—meaning that economics push the choice one way, and core values or purpose push the choice another way—then there is a need to balance the economic and psychological logics. Over time, mission should triumph, but not necessarily in every situation. If an organization never compromises when tensions arise, its viability is threatened unless it has an endowment large enough to sustain continuous neglect of strategic imperatives. But note that even Harvard University, one of the oldest and richest nonprofits in this country, with a $19 billion endowment, makes compromises, from raising tuition to limiting expenditures even for its core educational activities.

So, though there is no hard and fast rule, it is important to watch for patterns in the way tensions are managed over time. On one hand, we need to ask whether the organization is losing its soul (i.e., the problem of commercialism and social enterprise as earned income). On the other hand, we also need to ask whether it is making choices that reflect an unrealistic or unsustainable view of its economic viability and that will ultimately destine it for oblivion.

Constraints on the Execution of Mission and Strategy

Finally, perhaps one of the most pervasive challenges in executing mission and strategy in the nonprofit setting is the tyranny of intractable contexts and inflexible resource constraints. By context, I am referring here to the fact that, for many nonprofits, the external world is working just as hard to create or exacerbate social or environmental problems as the organization is working to address them. As fast as job training or welfare-to-work programs try to get the disenfranchised back into the workforce, for example, new clients are being created by recession, outsourcing, and foreign competition.

Resource constraints are the sine qua non of nonprofits, whether explained in terms of the poor functioning of the social capital market, or the low priority of the social needs and problems themselves. Consider the mismatch between the need for, and the availability of, resources in areas like health care, education, and the environment. To dramatize these difficulties, I want to close with a parable that builds off of a story about the troubles of Apple Computer in 1997, while it was under the leadership of CEO Gil Amelio. The story was recounted by a fellow Silicon Valley CEO, recalling a conversation he had with Amelio at a 1996 cocktail party:

> Amelio told us: "Apple is a boat. There's a hole in the boat, and it's taking on water. But there's also a treasure on board. And the problem is, everyone on board is rowing in different directions, so the boat is just standing still. My job is to get everyone rowing in the same direction so we can save the treasure." After he turned away, I looked at the person next to me and asked, "But what about the hole?"[17]

In the nonprofit world, life is a little more difficult, and the metaphor would have other elements. Imagine being on a boat with a hole in it that is taking on water. Now, add to the picture the fact that there are others out there—say, some pirates, on a much bigger ship—who are shooting at you with cannons and trying to blow new holes into your boat. Then imagine that 25 percent of your crew are engaged in an active mutiny because they think the boat should either stay where it is or go back to where it came from. While you are trying to evade the pirates, these "mutineers" are busy drilling their own new tiny little holes in the hull of your organizational ship. And, by the way, consider the fact that there's not enough food or fuel on your boat because when you went to get supplies at the port, you had to go to the back of the line because your boat is a third-class citizen. Why? Because your cargo is not a conventional "treasure" of gold, silver, exotic spices, or rare tea, but rather it is a boatload of poor people—call them refugees—whom you rescued when their island home was destroyed by a volcanic eruption. Moreover, these refugees look different from the people who make up the power structure in your own civilization, and most of the population sees your cause as a dubious endeavor.

So facing such odds and travails, why do you do it?

You do it because it is the right thing to do, because it is virtuous and noble, and because compassion is part of your character. You see the value in your cargo, not just because of your compassion, but because you know that helping others makes for a world that is not only safer and more stable, but also more just.

In addition to being overly dramatic, I suppose that this parable and its point may also be unnecessary—somewhat like preaching to the choir—because, having reached the end of this book, you are probably the kind of person who already understands just how difficult and important the task of leading and managing our nonprofit organizations really is. But, if this parable rings more than a little bit true, does not that make understanding and embracing the power of mission, strategy, and execution even more important for nonprofits?

I believe that it does.

Notes

INTRODUCTION

1. M. Sinclair and J. Jones, "Special Report: Nation's Largest Charities Weathered Skittish 2003," *The Nonprofit Times*, 2004, <http://www.nptimes.com/Nov04/sr1.html> (accessed 25 January 2005).

2. E. T. Boris and C. E. Steuerle, "Scope and Dimensions of the Nonprofit Sector," in *The Nonprofit Sector: A Research Handbook*, 2nd ed., edited by W. W. Powell and R. Steinberg (New Haven, Conn.: Yale University Press, in press).

3. U.S. Bureau of Economic Analysis, *National Income and Product Account Table* (Washington, D.C.: 2001), table 1.7, cited in Boris and Steuerle, "Scope and Dimensions."

4. Boris and Steuerle, "Scope and Dimensions."

5. P. Brest, "Smart Money: Making Foundation Support of Nonprofits Strategic for Both Parties," *Stanford Social Innovation Review* 1, no. 3 (2003): 44–53; C. Letts, W. P. Ryan, and A. Grossman, *High Performance Nonprofit Organizations: Managing Upstream for Greater Impact* (New York: Wiley, 1999).

6. *Grantmakers for Effective Organizations*, 2003, <http://www.geofunders.org> (accessed 22 December 2003).

7. N. Wish and R. Mirabella, *University and College-Based Programs in Nonprofit Management in the Year 2000* (South Orange, N.J.: Center for Public Service at Seton Hall University, 2001).

8. B. Tucker, 2000, <http://www.smarterorg.com> (accessed October 2003).

9. S. Oster, "Nonprofit Management: Is Managing Save the Children Any Different from Managing General Motors?" *Yale Management* 4 (1992): 16–21.

10. H. Hansmann, "Economic Theories of the Nonprofit Sector," in *The Nonprofit Sector: A Research Handbook*, edited by W. W. Powell (New Haven, Conn.: Yale University Press, 1987), 27–42.

11. S. M. Oster, *Strategic Management for Nonprofit Organizations* (New York: Oxford University Press, 1995), 17–22.

12. See, for example, M. W. Meyer and L. G. Zucker, *Permanently Failing Organizations* (Newbury Park, Calif.: Sage, 1989); ibid.

13. For example, there is a tradition in organizational sociology of de-emphasizing sectoral distinctions. See C. Perrow, *Complex Organizations: A Critical Essay* (New York: Random House, 1986); W. R. Scott, *Organizations: Rational, Natural and Open Systems*, 3rd ed. (Englewood Cliffs, N.J.: Prentice Hall, 1992).

14. M. C. Jensen, "Value Maximization, Stakeholder Theory, and the Corporate Objective Function," *Journal of Applied Corporate Finance* 14, no. 3 (2001): 8–21.

15. I. C. MacMillan, "Competitive Strategies for Not-for-Profit Agencies," *Advances in Strategic Management* 1 (1983): 61–82; F. W. McFarlan, "Working on Nonprofit Boards: Don't Assume the Shoe Fits," *Harvard Business Review* (1999): 64–76; Oster, *Strategic Management*; M. E. Porter and M. R. Kramer, "Philanthropy's New Agenda: Creating Value," *Harvard Business Review* (1999): 121–30.

16. C. I. Barnard, *The Functions of the Executive* (Cambridge, Mass.: Harvard University Press, 1968 [originally published 1938]).

17. J. C. Collins and J. I. Porras, *Built to Last: Successful Habits of Visionary Companies* (New York: Harper Business, 1997); J. P. Kotter, *A Force for Change: How Leadership Differs from Management* (New York: Free Press, 1990); D. Nadler, M. Tushman, and M. Nadler, *Competing by Design: The Power of Organizational Architecture* (New York: Oxford University Press, 1997); J. Pfeffer, *The Human Equation: Building Profits by Putting People First* (Boston: Harvard Business School Press, 1998).

18. Even nonpecuniary rewards like recognition and approval are related to long-term mobility and advancement, and hence compensation, in an efficient labor market.

19. Collins and Porras, *Built to Last*; Nadler, Tushman, and Nadler, *Competing by Design*; M. Tushman and C. A. O'Reilly, *Winning through Innovation: A Practical Guide to Leading Organizational Change and Renewal* (Boston: Harvard Business School Press, 1997).

20. For example, some organizations or companies may have social goals or objectives. These can encompass multiple dimensions beyond just financial returns. See, for example, R. S. Kaplan and D. P. Norton, *The Balanced Scorecard: Translating Strategy into Action* (Boston: Harvard Business School Press, 1996).

21. I owe the term *prosperity* to my colleague, Joel Podolny.

22. P. Ghemawat, *Commitment: The Dynamic of Strategy* (New York: Free Press, 1991); M. E. Porter, "What Is Strategy?" *Harvard Business Review* 74, no. 6 (1996): 61–78.

23. J. R. Galbraith and R. K. Kazanjian, *Strategy Implementation: Structure, Systems, and Process* (St. Paul, Minn.: West, 1986); L. G. Hrebiniak and W. F. Joyce, *Implementing Strategy* (New York: Macmillan, 1984); B. Woolridge and S. W. Floyd, "Strategic Process Effects on Consensus," *Strategic Management Journal* 10 (1989): 295–302.

24. K. R. Andrews, *The Concept of Corporate Strategy*, 3rd ed. (Homewood, Ill.: Irwin, 1987); M. E. Porter, *Competitive Advantage: Creating and Sustaining Superior Performance* (New York: Free Press, 1985); G. Saloner, A. Shepard, and J. Podolny, *Strategic Management* (New York: Wiley, 2000).

25. P. F. Drucker, M. De Pree, and F. Hesselbein, *Module III: Leading through Mission with Frances Hesselbein*, VHS video (San Francisco: Jossey-Bass, 1998).

CHAPTER 1

1. The organization must be "organized and operated exclusively" to provide specific public benefits or perform socially valuable functions. These "exempt" purposes can be educational, charitable, religious, or artistic ones, among others. Consistent with this requirement, the organization is also prohibited from distributing any portion of the net earnings to "any private shareholder or individual." Similarly, distinguishing it from public sector, the law also prohibits nonprofits from engaging in political activities, specifically from "attempting, to influence legislation . . . or intervene[ing] in any . . . political campaign." 26 U.S.C. § 501.

2. P. Ghemawat, *Strategy and the Business Landscape* (New York: Addison-Wesley, 1999); D. C. Hambrick and J. W. Fredrickson, "Are You Sure You Have a Strategy?" *Academy of Management Executive* 15, no. 4 (2001): 48–59; G. Saloner, A. Shepard, and J. Podolny, *Strategic Management* (New York: Wiley, 2000).

3. For one of the few examples of the discussion of the distinction between strategy and mission in the nonprofit context, see V. K. Rangan, "Lofty Missions, Down-to-Earth Plans," *Harvard Business Review* 82, no. 3 (2004): 112–19.

4. For example, one hundred shares of a mutual fund have a price that is determined by the market. This price and expected return can be compared with shares of other funds. The shares can be distributed among multiple individuals, and they can be traded between investors who, given the same expectations of future value, should be indifferent between having the shares or having the cash equivalent to their present value.

5. Although there are intriguing efforts to monetize or integrate social value with economic value, these have yet to be operationalized. J. Emerson, "Where Money Meets Mission," *Stanford Social Innovation Review* 1, no. 2 (2003): 38–47; J. Gertner, "A New World Order: Jed Emerson's Capitalist Utopia. Can Social Value Reward Investors, Companies?" *Money* 31, no. 12 (29 October 2002): 118–23.

6. This assumes competitive markets and the absence of anomalies called *externalities*. See, for example, classic and contemporary arguments of Friedman and Jensen, respectively. M. Friedman, "The Social Responsibility of Business Is to Increase Its Profits," *New York Times Magazine* (13 September 1970): 32–33, 122, 124, 126; M. C. Jensen, "Value Maximization, Stakeholder Theory, and the Corporate Objective Function," *Journal of Applied Corporate Finance* 14, no. 3 (2001): 8–21.

7. H. Hansmann, "Economic Theories of the Nonprofit Sector," in *The Nonprofit Sector: A Research Handbook*, edited by W. W. Powell (New Haven, Conn.: Yale University Press, 1987), 27–42.

8. R. H. Frank, "Can Socially Responsible Firms Survive in a Competitive Environment?" in *Codes of Conduct: Behavioral Research into Business Ethics*, edited by D. Messick and A. Tenbrunsel (New York: Russell Sage Foundation, 1996), 86–103.

9. A. E. Preston, "The Nonprofit Worker in a For-Profit World," *Journal of Labor Economics* 7, no. 4 (1989): 438–63.

10. J. C. Collins and J. I. Porras, *Built to Last: Successful Habits of Visionary Companies* (New York: Harper Business, 1997).

11. R. W. Johnson, *People Must Live and Work Together, or Forfeit Freedom* (Garden City, N.Y.: Doubleday, 1947), quoted in F. J. Aguillar, and A. Bhambri, "Johnson & Johnson (a): Philosophy and Culture," Harvard Business School Case no. 9-384-053, Boston, 1983.

12. D. Packard, speech given to HP's Training Group 8 March 1960, courtesy Hewlett-Packard Company Archives, 1960, quoted in Collins and Porras, *Built to Last*, 58.

13. Collins and Porras, *Built to Last*.

14. Ibid.; Saloner, Shepard and Podolny, *Strategic Management*, 24–28.

15. T. J. Peters and R. H. Waterman, *In Search of Excellence: Lessons from America's Best-Run Companies* (New York: Harper & Row, 1982); P. M. Senge, *The Fifth Discipline: The Art and Practice of the Learning Organization* (New York: Doubleday, 1990); P. M. Senge, "Learning Organizations," research talk at Harvard Business School, Boston, 1989.

16. Although Collins and Porras use the term *vision* as the overarching concept, eschewing *mission* as too fraught with ambiguity and misuse, I have opted to use *mission* as the umbrella term because it is so deeply entrenched in the lexicon of the nonprofit sector. Nonprofit leaders who have drawn on

the framework also seem to make this translation. See, for example, K. N. Stauber, "Mission-Driven Philanthropy: What Do We Want to Accomplish and How Do We Do It?" *Nonprofit & Voluntary Sector Quarterly* 30, no. 2 (2001): 393–401. For consistency, I have also adapted the terms used to describe the key elements.

17. As a result of the lack of research on mission and performance in both the nonprofit and for-profit settings, we are much more reliant on this one study than we will be when we examine the economic logic of strategy in chapter 2.

18. Collins and Porras, *Built to Last*, 222.

19. H. Seifter and P. Economy, *Leadership Ensemble: Lessons in Collaborative Management from the World's Only Conductorless Orchestra* (New York: Times Books, 2001), 26.

20. American Red Cross, Community-Services, <http://www.redcross.org/more/commserv> (accessed 28 August 2003).

21. Harvard University, Office of the President, updated 22 February 2000, <http://www.founders.howard.edu/presidentReports/Mission.htm> (accessed 28 August 2003).

22. Of course, for a newly founded organization, core values are established as the organization is built, but usually tacitly; J. I. Porras, "The Leader as Vision Builder," lecture, Executive Program for Nonprofit Leaders, Stanford, Calif., 3 March 2004.

23. P. F. Drucker, M. De Pree, and F. Hesselbein, *Module III: Leading through Mission with Frances Hesselbein*, VHS video (San Francisco: Jossey-Bass, 1998); Collins and Porras, *Built to Last*, 224–25.

24. Collins and Porras, *Built to Last*, 235.

25. Ibid., 232.

26. E. A. Locke and G. P. Latham, *A Theory of Goal Setting and Task Performance* (Englewood Cliffs, N.J.: Prentice Hall, 1990); R. H. Schaffer and H. A. Thomson, "Successful Change Programs Begin with Results," *Harvard Business Review* 70, no. 1 (1992): 80–89.

27. Collins and Porras, *Built to Last*, 233.

28. Apple Computer, *Apple Computer Inc., Annual Shareholders Meeting January 24, 1984*, VHS video (Cupertino, Calif., 1984).

29. Ibid.

30. Ibid.; C. Booth, and D. S. Jackson, "Steve's Job: Restart Apple," cover story, *Time* (18 August 1997): 28–34. Available online at <http://search.epnet.com/direct.asp?an=9708260271&db=buh> (accessed 30 January 2005).

31. City Year, 2003, "Who We Are," <http://www.cityyear.org/about/whoweare.cfm> (accessed 1 September 2003).

32. City Year, 2003, "About City Year: Overview," <http://www.cityyear.org/about/index.cfm> (accessed 1 September 2003).

33. Ibid.

34. Ibid.

35. J. L. Bradach and N. Sackley, "City Year: National Expansion Strategy (A)," Harvard Business School Case no. 9-496-001, Boston, 1995.

36. City Year, "Who We Are."

37. Bradach and Sackley, "City Year: National Expansion Strategy (A)."

38. *Time* (2 June 2003): 66–69.

39. This example draws heavily on J. A. Phills, E. Martenson, and G. Scott, "American Repertory Theatre in the 1990s (A)," Stanford University Graduate School of Business Case no. SI-16A, Stanford, Calif., 2002.

40. Collins and Porras, *Built to Last*, 222.

41. A. Holmberg, ed., *The Lively ART* (Chicago: Dee, 1999), 261.

42. J. I. Ayala, J. K. Falstad, and C. L. Hart, "American Repertory Theatre: 1988," Harvard Business School Case no. 9-688-120, Boston, 1.

43. R. Brustein, *Who Needs Theatre?* (New York: The Atlantic Monthly Press, 1986), xiv.

44. Ayala, Falstad, and Hart, "American Repertory Theatre: 1988," 1.

45. Phills, Martenson, and Scott, "American Repertory Theatre in the 1990s (A)," 2002.

46. Ibid.

47. Brustein, *Who Needs Theatre?* xiv.

48. Phills, Martenson, and Scott, "American Repertory Theatre in the 1990s (A)," 116.

49. R. K. Greenleaf, 1978, "The Leadership Crisis: A Message for College and University Faculty," Robert K. Greenleaf Center, <http://www.greenleaf.org/catalog/item.php?itemID=28> (accessed 25 January 2005).

50. Dean & Deluca, 2004, "How May We Help You?" <http://www.deandeluca.com/cgi-bin/ncommerce3/ExecMacro/store/customer_assistance.d2w/report> (accessed 2 May 2004); J. A. Phills, M. Roda, S. Sciascia, N. Shah, and R. Wilson, "Dean & Deluca: Developing a Mission Statement," Yale School of Management, New Haven, Conn., 1998, 10 (case study).

CHAPTER 2

1. For discussion of the distinctions between creating and capturing, see G. Saloner, A. Shepard, and J. Podolny, *Strategic Management* (New York: Wiley, 2000). Also, although there has been more debate in recent years about the extent to which businesses *should* include social responsibility as one of their purposes, most classic and contemporary thinking in financial economics posits the creation of value as the primary and sole purpose of business. See, for example, M. Friedman, "The Social Responsibility of Business Is to Increase Its Profits," *New York Times Magazine* (13 September 1970): 32–33, 122, 124, 126; M. C. Jensen, "Value Maximization, Stake-

holder Theory, and the Corporate Objective Function," *Journal of Applied Corporate Finance* 14, no. 3 (2001): 8–21. And, with the notable exception of some advocates who frame corporate social responsibility as a moral imperative, multidimensional conceptions of performance are generally invoked in the service of maximizing long-term profitability. See, for example, R. S. Kaplan and D. P. Norton, *The Balanced Scorecard: Translating Strategy into Action* (Boston: Harvard Business School Press, 1996).

2. See especially Porter's distinction between strategy and operational effectiveness. M. E. Porter, "What Is Strategy?" *Harvard Business Review* 74, no. 6 (1996): 61–78.

3. R. A. Burgelman and A. S. Grove, *Strategy Is Destiny: How Strategy-Making Shapes a Company's Future* (New York: Free Press, 2002).

4. I owe the term *prosperity* to Joel Podolny, and the notion of "control over one's destiny" to Robert Burgelman.

5. M. Beene, *Autopsy of an Orchestra: An Analysis of Factors Contributing to the Bankruptcy of the Oakland Symphony Orchestra Association* (San Francisco: Beene, 1988).

6. Ibid.

7. Ibid.

8. J. A. Phills, "The Sound of No Music: The Perils of Conflating Mission and Strategy," *Stanford Social Innovation Review* 2, no. 2 (2004): 44–53.

9. Sun Tzu, *The Art of War* (New York: Oxford University Press, 1963); C. von Clausewitz and A. Rapoport, *On War* (Baltimore, Md.: Penguin Books, 1968).

10. *Oxford English Dictionary*, 2nd ed., 1989, OED Online, Oxford University Press, <http://dictionary.oed.com/cgi/entry/00238990/00238990se1> (accessed 22 July 2003).

11. K. R. Andrews, *The Concept of Corporate Strategy*, 3rd ed. (Homewood, Ill.: Irwin, 1987).

12. H. I. Ansoff, *The New Corporate Strategy* (New York: Wiley, 1988).

13. P. Ghemawat, *Strategy and the Business Landscape* (New York: Addison-Wesley, 1999).

14. D. C. Hambrick and J. W. Fredrickson, "Are You Sure You Have a Strategy?" *The Academy of Management Executives* 15, no. 4 (2001): 48–59; Porter, "What Is Strategy?"

15. A. Bhide, "Hustle as Strategy," *Harvard Business Review* 64, no. 5 (1986): 59–66; K. M. Eisenhardt, "Strategy as Strategic Decision Making," *Sloan Management Review* 40, no. 3 (1999): 65–73; G. Hamel, "Strategy as Revolution," *Harvard Business Review* 74, no. 4 (1996): 69–81; G. Hamel and C. K. Prahalad, "Strategy as Stretch and Leverage," *Harvard Business Review* 71, no. 2 (1993): 75–85.

16. Porter, "What Is Strategy?"

17. A. M. McGahan and M. E. Porter, "How Much Does Industry Matter,

Really?" *Strategic Management Journal* 18, no. 6 (1997): 15–31; R. P. Rumelt, "How Much Does Industry Matter?" *Strategic Management Journal* 12, no. 3 (1991): 167–85; R. Schmalensee, "Do Markets Differ Much?" *American Economic Review* 75, no. 3 (1985): 341–51.

18. See, for example, Ghemawat, *Strategy and the Business Landscape;* S. Oster, *Modern Competitive Analysis,* 2nd ed. (New York: Oxford University Press, 1994); M. E. Porter, *Competitive Advantage: Creating and Sustaining Superior Performance* (New York: Free Press, 1985); Saloner, Shepard, and Podolny, *Strategic Management.*

19. Porter, *Competitive Advantage.*

20. These elements are drawn from Saloner, Shepard, and Podolny, *Strategic Management.* These authors actually identify a fourth element of strategy: *goals.* "Goals" is not included here because I do not find their arguments for including goals particularly compelling. The fact is that, even with a goal such as "dominate the market," or "be the cost leader in such and such," the ultimate goal is really to maximize profits. And, in the case of nonprofits, achieving the mission is analogous to maximizing profit. For-profit organizations, if they are behaving the way economists say that they should, are trying to maximize their profitability—that is their ultimate goal, and it is the same for every organization. So to include it as part of strategy seems redundant.

21. See for example, Hambrick and Fredrickson, "Are You Sure You Have a Strategy?" Oster, *Modern Competitive Analysis;* M. E. Porter, *Competitive Strategy: Techniques for Analyzing Industries and Competitors* (New York: Free Press, 1980); Porter, *Competitive Advantage;* Saloner, Shepard, and Podolny, *Strategic Management.*

22. Porter, *Competitive Strategy.*

23. S. P. Bradley, P. Ghemawat, and S. Foley, "Wal-Mart Stores, Inc.," Harvard Business School Case no. 9-794-024, Boston, 1994; P. Ghemawat, S. P. Bradley, and K. Mark, "Wal-Mart Stores in 2003," Harvard Business School Case no. 9-704-430, Boston, 2003.

24. Associated Press, "Shopper Is Knocked Unconscious as Sale Begins," *New York Times,* 30 November 2003, 30.

25. J. Schwartz, "Ideas and Trends; How Low Can DVD Players Go?" *New York Times,* 7 December 2003, 5.

26. J. Useem, "One Nation under Wal-Mart: How Retailing's Super-power—and Our Biggest Most Admired Company—Is Changing the Rules for Corporate America," *Fortune* (18 February 2003): 64–72.

27. C. Power and R. R. Melcher, "From 'Bloody Awful' to 'Bloody Awesome'—British Airways' Grand Alliances Could Turn It into an Empire," *Business Week* (9 October 1989): 97–98.

28. *Mergent Online,* 2003, <http://www.mergentonline.com/compdetail. asp?company_mer=14036&company=1000148> (accessed 28 August 2003).

29. J. P. Kotter and J. K. Leahey, "Changing the Culture at British Airways," Harvard Business School Case no. 9-491-009, Boston, 1990.

30. S. E. Prokesch, "Competing on Customer Service: An Interview with British Airways' Sir Colin Marshall," *Harvard Business Review* 73, no. 6 (1995): 100–12.

31. M. E. Porter, "Towards a Dynamic Theory of Strategy," *Strategic Management Journal* 12, special issue (1991): 95–117.

32. Specifically, it must describe how the policies, resource allocation, and configuration of activities support the organization's competitive advantage and scope. This latter task is the execution of strategy, which will be explored in greater detail in chapter 4.

33. In the context of strategy, the state of the world is typically thought of in terms of the competitive environment as represented by industry structure. I will introduce an analytical framework for evaluating industry structure in chapter 3.

34. City Year, 2003, "About City Year," <http://www.cityyear.org/about/index.cfm> (accessed 1 September 2003).

35. J. L. Bradach, and N. Sackley, "City Year: National Expansion Strategy (A)," Harvard Business School Case no. 9-496-001, Boston, 1995.

36. Ibid., 7.

CHAPTER 3

1. Although I use the term *organization*, the focus is really the business-unit level. However, for simplicity we will combine business and corporate effects, since evidence suggests that even in multibusiness organizations the key factor that influences performance at the firm level is the segment or business unit. A. M. McGahan and M. E. Porter, "How Much Does Industry Matter, Really?" *Strategic Management Journal* 18, no. 6 (1997): 15–31.

2. Increasingly, however, more attention is being devoted to the role of so-called nonmarket factors, such as political, regulatory, and other influences. See, for example, D. P. Baron, *Business and Its Environment*, 3rd ed. (Englewood Cliffs, N.J.: Prentice Hall, 2000). Although these factors are also important for nonprofits, they are the province of the field of political economy and are beyond the scope of this text, which focuses on organizational and industrial economic perspectives on strategy.

3. J. S. Bain, *Barriers to New Competition: Their Character and Consequences in Manufacturing Industries* (Cambridge, Mass.: Harvard University Press, 1956); R. Schmalensee, "Do Markets Differ Much?" *American Economic Review* 75, no. 3 (1985): 341–51.

4. McGahan and Porter, "How Much Does Industry Matter, Really?"; R. P.

Rumelt, "How Much Does Industry Matter?" *Strategic Management Journal* 12, no. 3 (1991): 167–85; Schmalensee, "Do Markets Differ Much?"

5. P. Ghemawat, *Strategy and the Business Landscape* (New York: Addison-Wesley, 1999).

6. M. E. Porter, "How Competitive Forces Shape Strategy," *Harvard Business Review* 57, no. 2 (1979): 137–45.

7. R. E. Caves, "Industrial Organization, Corporate Strategy and Structure," *Journal of Economic Literature* 18, no. 1 (1980): 64–92.

8. K. R. Andrews, *The Concept of Corporate Strategy*, 3rd ed. (Homewood, Ill.: Irwin, 1987); Ghemawat, *Strategy and the Business Landscape*; P. Wack, "Scenarios: Uncharted Waters Ahead; How Royal Dutch-Shell Developed a Planning Technique That Teaches Managers to Think about an Uncertain Future," *Harvard Business Review* 63, no. 5 (1985): 72–90.

9. Identifying competitors requires first defining the industry, a task that is actually more difficult than one might think, because it involves a number of decisions about how broadly to draw the boundaries of the industry. For now we will set aside this source of complexity; however, I will deal with it in detail after laying out the basic elements of the framework.

10. G. Saloner, A. Shepard, and J. Podolny, *Strategic Management* (New York: Wiley, 2000).

11. Ibid.

12. M. H. Bazerman, J. Baron, and K. Shonk, *You Can't Enlarge the Pie: Six Barriers to Effective Government* (New York: Basic Books, 2001).

13. To be more precise, financial calculus would also have to take into account the potential profitability relative to the cost of capital associated with entering the industry. Ghemawat, *Strategy and the Business Landscape*.

14. P. Ghemawat and D. Dyer, "The U.S. Airline Industry—1978–88 (A) and (B)," Harvard Business School Case no. 9-897-021, Boston, 1996 (abridged).

15. This is also related to supplier power, which I will discuss in a few pages.

16. J. A. Phills and L. Koenig, "The Seattle Theatre Industry," Stanford Graduate School of Business Case no. SI-37, Stanford, Calif., 2003, 1.

17. H. Hansmann, "Economic Theories of the Nonprofit Sector," in *The Nonprofit Sector: A Research Handbook*, edited by W. W. Powell (New Haven, Conn.: Yale University Press, 1987), 27–42.

18. J. G. Dees, "Enterprising Nonprofits," *Harvard Business Review* 76 (1998): 54–65.

19. S. M. Oster, *Strategic Management for Nonprofit Organizations* (New York: Oxford University Press, 1995).

20. See detailed discussion of positioning based on buyer segmentation in M. E. Porter, "What Is Strategy?" *Harvard Business Review* 74, no. 6 (1996): 61–78.

21. J. L. Bradach, *Franchise Organizations* (Boston: Harvard Business School Press, 1998).

22. I owe this insight to Sharon Oster, who made this point in an extremely helpful review of an earlier draft of this book.

23. A final comment on applying industry analysis to nonprofits is that competition among nonprofits for funding can also be viewed as a "social capital market," which is analogous to the for-profit capital markets (stocks, bonds, and mutual funds) through which companies raise money from investors. In the capital market, all companies, regardless of industry, "compete" with one another for capital in a market that is highly efficient. The problem with extending the analogy to nonprofits is that, while investors are purchasing a standardized commodity (a combination of risk and expected financial return), donors in the nonprofit world are pursuing some form of "social value," or even personal benefit that is not only ill defined but also various across funders. Hence, it may be more useful to view competition for funding in terms of a product-market lens (i.e., with use of the industry analysis framework).

24. Hansmann, "Economic Theories of the Nonprofit Sector"; Oster, *Strategic Management for Nonprofit Organizations.*

25. M. E. Porter, *Strategy: Techniques for Analyzing Industries and Competitors* (New York: Free Press, 1980).

26. A. Brandenburger and B. Nalebuff, *Co-opetition* (New York: Doubleday, 1996), 12.

27. Ibid., 4.

28. I owe this expression to my colleague, Chip Heath.

29. R. R. Augsburger, I. J. Miliman, and J. Abbott, "KQED-TV San Francisco," Stanford Business School Case no. PM29, Stanford, Calif., 1990.

30. In addition to its television operations, KQED also operated a second public station, KQEC Channel 32, and a radio station, KQED Public Radio 88.5 and 89.3. For the purposes of this case, I focus primarily on the KQED Channel 9 television station.

31. "About KQED," 17 July 2003, <http://www.kqed.org/about/index.jsp> (accessed 18 January 2005); see also J. Silber, "KQED Tackles Money Woes," *Contra Costa Times*, 11 July 2003, 1.

32. The Cable Center, "Cable History Timeline," 20 July 2003, <http://www.cablecenter.org/history/timeline/decade.cfm?start=1940> (accessed 18 January 2005).

33. Augsburger, Miliman, and Abbott, "KQED-TV San Francisco."

34. Individual public television stations tend to highlight the affluence and education of their viewers (especially supporting "members"). See, for example, KQED Public Broadcasting, 2005, "TV Audience Demographics," <http://www.kqed.org/support/sponsorship/tv/audience-demographics.jsp>

(accessed 30 January 2005); and WGCU Public Media, 2005, "Audience Highlights," <http://www.wgcu.org/support/audience.html> (accessed 31 January 2005). However, reflecting its public service emphasis, PBS itself adopts a more populist stance, stressing the breadth of its audience and largely ignoring demographic differences. See PBS, 2005, "About PBS-Coporate Facts: The Public Television Audience," <http://www.pbs.org/aboutpbs/aboutpbs_/corp.html> (accessed 30 January 2005).

35. This refers to the 1972 FCC Cable Television Report and order, 36 F.C.C.2d 143 (1972), "requiring cable operators to carry signals from local television stations in the communities they served. . . . [T]he regulation was developed to ensure that 'viewers' choices would not diminish." The order was relaxed in 1987 and slated for elimination five years later. As quoted in Augsburger, Miliman, and Abbott, "KQED-TV San Francisco," 4.

CHAPTER 4

1. P. Ghemawat, *Commitment: The Dynamic of Strategy* (New York: Free Press, 1991); R. Martin, *Strategic Choice Structuring* (Cambridge, Mass.: Monitor, 1997); M. E. Porter, "What Is Strategy?" *Harvard Business Review* 74, no. 6 (1996): 61–78.

2. M. E. Porter, "Towards a Dynamic Theory of Strategy," *Strategic Management Journal* 12, special issue (1991): 95–117.

3. These distinctions are based on H. Mintzberg, "Patterns in Strategy Formulation," *Management Science* 24, no. 9 (1978): 934–48; and C. Argyris and D. A. Schön, *Theory in Practice* (San Francisco: Jossey-Bass, 1974), respectively.

4. *Merriam-Webster Online Dictionary*, 2002, <http://www.merriam-webster.com> (accessed 14 August 2003).

5. K. R. Andrews, *The Concept of Corporate Strategy*, 3rd ed. (Homewood, Ill.: Irwin, 1987), 13.

6. Policies are distinct from implicit rules, which would be considered *norms*.

7. The routinized nature of activities is one of their central features. Some writers actually use the notion of routines to define *activities*. See, for instance, G. Saloner, A. Shepard, and J. Podolny, *Strategic Management* (New York: Wiley, 2000). The basic idea, however, is the same.

8. M. E. Porter, *Competitive Advantage: Creating and Sustaining Superior Performance* (New York: Free Press, 1985); Porter, "What Is Strategy?"

9. Porter, "What Is Strategy?" 62.

10. Ibid.

11. C. A. O'Reilly, "Southwest Airlines," Stanford Business School Case no. HR1A, Stanford, Calif., 1995, 4.

12. Porter, "What Is Strategy?"

13. Ibid.

14. *Mergent Online*, 2003, <http://www.mergentonline.com/compdetail. asp?company_mer=14036&company=1000148> (accessed 28 August 2003).

15. Porter, *Competitive Advantage*.

16. Porter, "What Is Strategy?" 72.

17. O'Reilly, "Southwest Airlines," 9.

18. In principle, choices precede and result in actions. To illustrate, I may choose a diet and opt for a low-carbohydrate diet—Atkins. Choice is an important element of strategy—subsequent choices about foods and meals— but unless action corresponds to choices there will be no results in terms of weight loss and goals.

19. J. L. Bradach, "Going to Scale: The Challenge of Replicating Social Programs," *Stanford Social Innovation Review* 1, no. 1 (2003): 17–23; P. Brest, "What the Nonprofit Sector Can Learn from Home Improvements," unpublished manuscript (Menlo Park, Calif.: William and Flora Hewlett Foundation, 2003); H. Hatry, *Performance Measurement* (Washington, D.C.: Urban Institute Press, 1999).

20. Feed the Children, 2003, "About Feed the Children," <http://www. christianity.com/CC_Content_Page/0,,PTID3425|CHID101900|CIID,00. html#rfacts_missionstatement> (accessed 19 September 2003).

21. Bradach, "Going to Scale"; Brest, "What the Nonprofit Sector Can Learn"; Hatry, *Performance Measurement*.

22. B. A. Weisbrod, "The Nonprofit Mission and Its Financing," in *To Profit or Not to Profit: The Commercial Transformation of the Nonprofit Sector*, edited by B. A. Weisbrod (New York: Cambridge University Press, 1998), 1–22.

23. J. A. Phills, E. Martenson, and G. Scott, "American Repertory Theatre in the 1990s (A)," Stanford University Graduate School of Business Case no. SI-16A, Stanford, Calif., 2002.

24. J. A. Phills and E. Martenson, "American Repertory Theatre in the 1990s (B)," Stanford University Graduate School of Business Case no. SI16A, Stanford, Calif., 2003.

CHAPTER 5

1. A. Brandenburger and B. Nalebuff, *Co-opetition* (New York: Doubleday, 1996).

2. Recall that earlier in this book we noted that how narrowly or broadly an industry is defined is part of the challenge of industry analysis.

3. K. R. Andrews, *The Concept of Corporate Strategy* (Homewood, Ill.: Irwin, 1987); H. I. Ansoff, *Corporate Strategy; An Analytic Approach to Business Policy for Growth and Expansion* (New York: McGraw-Hill, 1965);

A. D. Chandler, *Strategy and Structure: Chapters in the History of the Industrial Enterprise* (Cambridge, Mass.: M.I.T. Press, 1962).

4. J. Lintner, "The Valuation of Risk Assets and the Selection of Risky Investments in Stock Portfolios and Capital Budgets," *Review of Economics and Statistics* 47 (1965): 13–37; W. Sharpe, "Capital Asset Prices: A Theory of Market Equilibrium under Conditions of Risk," *The Journal of Finance* 19 (1964): 425–42.

5. P. G. Berger and E. Ofek, "Diversification's Effect on Firm Value," *Journal of Financial Economics* 37, no. 1 (1995): 39–66; L. H. P. Lang and R. M. Stulz, "Tobin's *q*, Corporate Diversification, and Firm Performance," *Journal of Political Economy* 102, no. 6 (1994): 1248–80.

6. See reviews in P. Ghemawat, *Strategy and the Business Landscape* (New York: Addison-Wesley, 1999), and D. J. Collis, "Corporate Strategy: A Conceptual Framework," Havard Business School Note, Boston, 1991.

7. J. Hopkins et al., "AOL and Time Warner Announce Merger," CNN Street Sweep, Atlanta, Ga., 2000, transcript of television show. Available online from Lexis-Nexis database (accessed 12 January 2004).

8. A. Klein, *Stealing Time: Steve Case, Jerry Levin, and the Collapse of AOL Time Warner* (New York: Simon & Schuster, 2003); N. Munk, *Fools Rush In: Steve Case, Jerry Levin, and the Fall of AOL Time Warner* (New York: Harper Business, 2004); K. Swisher, *There Must Be a Pony in Here Somewhere: The AOL Time Warner Debacle and the Quest for a Digital Future* (New York: Crown Business, 2003).

9. M. E. Porter, *Competitive Advantage: Creating and Sustaining Superior Performance* (New York: Free Press, 1985), 318.

10. M. E. Porter, "From Competitive Advantage to Corporate Strategy," *Harvard Business Review* 65, no. 3 (1987): 43–59. Quote on 43.

11. D. Berger, "About Wine: Gallo, Bolla Seek to Upgrade Image," *Los Angeles Times*, 1 February 1990, 9.

12. Porter, "From Competitive Advantage to Corporate Strategy"; G. Saloner, A. Shepard, and J. Podolny, *Strategic Management* (New York: Wiley, 2000).

13. Although two less concrete mechanisms include portfolio management (allocating capital across units more effectively) and restructuring (taking unrelated businesses in trouble and turning them around), both are more suspect. In addition, given their primarily financial (versus operational or strategic) focus, they are less applicable to the nonprofit sector. See ibid.

14. A. M. McGahan and M. E. Porter, "How Much Does Industry Matter, Really?" *Strategic Management Journal* 18, no. 6 (1997): 15–31; R. P. Rumelt, "How Much Does Industry Matter?" *Strategic Management Journal* 12, no. 3 (1991): 167–85.

15. A. E. Pearson, *Johnson & Johnson Hospital Services: Question and*

Answer Session with James E. Burke, Chairman and CEO, VHS video, Harvard Business School, Boston, 1989.

16. Ibid.

17. Saloner, Shepard, and Podolny, *Strategic Management.*

18. Porter, *Competitive Advantage*, 331.

19. Saloner, Shepard, and Podolny, *Strategic Management.*

20. O. E. Williamson, *Markets and Hierarchies: Analysis and Antitrust Implications* (New York: Free Press, 1975).

21. Saloner, Shepard, and Podolny, *Strategic Management.*

22. For a systematic study of the success of corporate diversification efforts, see Porter, "From Competitive Advantage to Corporate Strategy."

23. H. K. Radice, "Control Type, Profitability and Growth in Large Firms: An Empirical Study," *Economic Journal* 81, no. 323 (1971): 547–62.

24. I. C. MacMillan, "Competitive Strategies for Not-for-Profit Agencies," *Advances in Strategic Management* 1 (1983): 61–82.

25. P. Sturner, "Changing Times Fell Career Action Center," *Palo Alto Weekly*, 26 June 2002, <http://www.paloaltoonline.com/weekly/morgue/2002/2002_06_26.cac26.html> (accessed 20 January 2005).

26. Porter, *Competitive Strategy*, 41.

27. D. J. Roberts, *The Modern Firm: Organizing for Performance and Growth* (New York: Oxford University Press, 2004).

28. J. Emerson and F. Twersky, *New Social Entrepreneurs* (San Francisco: The Roberts Foundation, 1996).

29. J. E. Austin, "From Almsgiving to Strategic Alliances," *Stanford Social Innovation Review* 1, no. 2 (2003): 49–55.

30. J. E. Austin, *The Collaboration Challenge: How Nonprofits and Businesses Succeed through Strategic Alliances* (San Francisco: Jossey-Bass, 2000), 20.

31. Ibid., xi.

32. These do not include industry-wide coalitions or associations with the goal of influencing industry structure, which I deal with in the following section.

33. The actual evidence of a relationship between social responsibility and financial performance is inconclusive; however, high-profile media coverage and the attention of consumers and policy-makers appear to have put concerns about this issue on managers' radar screens. J. D. Margolis and J. P. Walsh, *People and Profits? The Search for a Link between a Company's Social and Financial Performance* (Hillsdale, N.J.: Erlbaum, 2001).

34. D. P. Baron, *Business and Its Environment* (Englewood Cliffs, N.J.: Prentice Hall, 2000).

35. J. Browne, "Leading a Global Company: The Case of BP," speech at Yale School of Management, New Haven, Conn., 18 September 1998.

36. J. Browne, address at Stanford Business School, Stanford, Calif., 11 March 2002).

37. Pew Center on Global Climate Change, 2004, "Global Warming Basics: Glossary," <http://www.pewclimate.org/global-warming-basics/full_glossary/terms_d.cfm> (accessed 6 February 2004).

38. A. Cowell, "British Petroleum Planning 'Firm' Cuts in Emissions," *New York Times*, 19 September 1998, 2.

39. Pew Center on Global Climate Change, 2004, "History and Mission," <http://www.pewclimate.org/about/history_and_mission> (accessed 6 February 2004).

40. Ford Foundation, 1998, "Ford Foundation Grant of $50 Million Will Generate $2 Billion in Affordable Mortgages for 35,000 Low-Wealth Home Buyers: Press Release," <http://www.fordfound.org/news/view_news_detail.cfm?news_index=7> (accessed 11 December 2003).

41. Susan Berresford, interview with the author, Yale University, New Haven, Conn., February 1999.

42. M. E. Porter, "The Competitive Advantage of the Inner City," *Harvard Business Review* 73 (1995): 55–72.

43. R. M. Kanter, "From Spare Change to Real Change: The Social Sector as Beta Site for Business Innovation," *Harvard Business Review* 77 (May–June 1999): 122–32.

44. H. Hansmann, "Economic Theories of the Nonprofit Sector," in *The Nonprofit Sector: A Research Handbook*, edited by W. W. Powell (New Haven, Conn.: Yale University Press, 1987), 27–42; C. Letts, W. P. Ryan, and A. Grossman, *High Performance Nonprofit Organizations: Managing Upstream for Greater Impact* (New York: Wiley, 1999); M. E. Porter and M. R. Kramer, "Philanthropy's New Agenda: Creating Value," *Harvard Business Review* 77, no. 6 (1999): 121–30; I. Unterman and R. H. Davis, "The Strategy Gap in Not-for-Profits," *Harvard Business Review* 60, no. 3 (1982): 30–40.

45. These criteria come generally from Porter's body of work but are restated slightly. Porter, "From Competitive Advantage to Corporate Strategy."

46. As with corporate strategy, the calculus about the relative importance of a given alliance may be influenced by evaluation of the relationship among various alliances if there are multiple alliances. That is, assuming the existence of alliance A and B, alliance D may be more valuable (economically or socially) than C. But, absent A or B, then C may dominate D. This analysis is analogous to the evaluation of business units with respect to corporate strategy. However, it is beyond scope of this chapter.

47. Although this applies to the corporation or public-sector agency just as much as to the nonprofit, since the focus of this text is nonprofit I stress the implications of the alliance for the nonprofit organization.

48. K. Zernike and A. Walker, "City Year Slips as It Rushes to Grow," *Boston Globe*, 18 August 1996, A1.

49. M. Olson, *The Logic of Collective Action: Public Goods and the Theory of Groups* (Cambridge, Mass.: Harvard University Press, 1971).

50. Hansmann, "Economic Theories of the Nonprofit Sector"; S. M. Oster, *Strategic Management for Nonprofit Organizations* (New York: Oxford University Press, 1995).

51. "Drug Firms Spend Millions to Battle Importation Plan," *Wall Street Journal*, 13 October 2003, 15; and *Food & Drug Letter* No. 690 "Fresh Off 2003 Victories, PHARMA Lobbying Faces New Challenges," 19 December 2003; ibid.

52. The notion of new and old funder enthusiasms comes from W. Bowen, T. Nygren, and S. Turner, *The Charitable Nonprofits* (San Francisco: Jossey-Bass, 1994).

53. Barriers to exit include any factor that reduces the likelihood that underperforming or failing organizations will exit (close down or sell their assets) from an industry. In nonprofits this encompasses psychological (as well as traditional economic) barriers, such as concerns about abandoning clients in need, or it can stem from extraordinary commitment of a few funders to keep a particular organization from failing. For more on exit barriers, see K. R. Harrigan, *Strategic Flexibility: A Management Guide for Changing Times* (Lexington, Mass.: Lexington Books, 1985); M. E. Porter, "Please Note Location of Nearest Exit: Exit Barriers and Planning," *California Management Review* 19, no. 2 (1976): 21–34.

54. Much of the background for this example is based on personal communication between the author and Tom Fannela, President of KTEH Public Television in San Jose (6 February 2004).

55. These were Theater for New Audiences and the Resident Theater Initiative. For accounts of these programs see J. Breslauer, "The Nea's Real Offense; Agency Pigeonholes Artists by Ethnicity," *The Washington Post*, 16 March 1997, G01; A. Hersh, "$7m Grants Go to 15 Nonprofits to Develop Audiences," *Back Stage*, 21 August 1992; The Lila Wallace–Reader's Digest Fund, 1996, "Building Audiences: Stories from America's Theaters: What Theaters Are Learning About the Role of Programming in Attracting Audiences." <http://www.wallacefoundation.org/WF/KnowledgeCenter/KnowledgeTopics/ArtsParticipation/RoleofProgramming.htm> (accessed 8 April 2005).

56. The scope and rationale for differential treatment of nonprofits remains unclear and contested. See W. M. Landes and R. A. Posner, "Market Power in Antitrust Cases," *Harvard Law Review* 94 (1981): 937–96; and A. J. Vaughn, "The Use of the Nonprofit 'Defense' under Section 7 of the Clayton Act," *Vanderbilt Law Review* 52 (1999): 557–98.

57. For the purposes of this argument, I set aside the question whether the existing number of organizations actually produces an optimal level of efficiency and choice for the market as a whole.

58. Saloner, Shepard, and Podolny, *Strategic Management*.

59. Vaughn, "The Use of the Nonprofit 'Defense'"; O. S. Choe, "A Missed Opportunity: Nonprofit Antitrust Liability in Virginia Vermiculite, Ltd. v. Historic Green Springs, Inc.," *Yale Law Journal* 113, no. 2 (2003): 533–40.

60. Williamson, *Markets and Hierarchies*; O. E. Williamson, "The Economics of Organization: The Transaction Cost Approach," *American Journal of Sociology* 87, no. 3 (1981): 548–77.

61. Typically, if the other business were closely related, it would be folded in with the existing unit as in the case of an acquisition.

CHAPTER 6

1. For my own part, I am generally agnostic about the relative utility or importance of these different frames or lenses onto organizations. However, because leadership appears to be one of the most enduring and dominant in terms of our attention and scholarly and popular fascination, I rely on it in this chapter. This, however, is not meant to deny the particular appeal of other perspectives and lenses or frames.

2. M. M. Chemers, "Leadership Research and Theory: A Functional Integration," *Group Dynamics* 4, no. 1, special issue (2000): 27–43.

3. J. Pfeffer, "The Ambiguity of Leadership," *Academy of Management Review* 2, no. 1 (1971): 104–12.

4. Consider the following list of popular and influential management books that use these constructs as the basis for normative prescriptions about how to enhance organizational performance: C. Argyris and D. A. Schön, *Organizational Learning II: Theory Method, and Practice* (Reading, Mass.: Addison Wesley, 1996); T. E. Deal and A. A. Kennedy, *Corporate Cultures: The Rites and Rituals of Corporate Life* (Reading, Mass.: Addison-Wesley, 1982); I. L. Janis and L. Mann, *Decision Making: A Psychological Analysis of Conflict, Choice and Commitment* (New York: Free Press, 1977); R. M. Kanter, *The Change Masters: Innovation and Entrepreneurship in the American Corporation* (New York: Simon & Schuster, 1983); D. Nadler, M. Tushman, and M. Nadler, *Competing by Design: The Power of Organizational Architecture,* (New York: Oxford University Press, 1997); J. Pfeffer, *Competitive Advantage through People* (Boston: Harvard Business School Press, 1994); M. E. Porter, *Competitive Advantage: Creating and Sustaining Superior Performance* (New York: Free Press, 1985); P. M. Senge, *The Fifth Discipline: The Art and Practice of the Learning Organization* (New York: Doubleday, 1990); M. Tushman and C. A. O'Reilly, *Winning through Innovation: A Practical Guide to Leading Organizational Change and Renewal* (Boston: Harvard Business School Press, 1997).

5. J. Pfeffer, "The Ambiguity of Leadership."

6. For examples of work that links these concepts to strategy see J. B. Barney, "Organizational Culture: Can It Be a Source of Sustained Competitive Advantage?" *Academy of Management Review* 11, no. 3 (1986): 656–65; C. M. Christensen and M. Raynor, *The Innovator's Solution: Creating and Sustaining Successful Growth* (Boston: Harvard Business School, 2003); Nadler, Tushman, and Nadler, *Competing by Design.*

7. P. R. Lawrence and J. W. Lorsch, *Organization and Environment* (Boston: Harvard Business School Press, 1967); V. H. Vroom and P. W. Yetton, *Leadership and Decision Making* (Pittsburgh, Penn.: University of Pittsburgh Press, 1973).

8. C. I. Barnard, *The Functions of the Executive* (Cambridge, Mass.: Harvard University Press, 1968 [originally published 1938]).

9. J. E. McGrath, *Leadership Behavior: Some Requirements for Leadership Training* (Washington, D.C.: U.S. Civil Service Commission, 1962), as quoted in J. R. Hackman and R. Walton, "Leading Groups in Organizations," in *Designing Effective Work Groups*, edited by P. S. Goodman (San Francisco: Jossey-Bass, 1986), 72–119.

10. Hackman and Walton, "Leading Groups in Organizations."

11. Barnard, *The Functions of the Executive*, 215.

12. Ibid., 217–34.

13. J. C. Collins and J. I. Porras, *Built to Last: Successful Habits of Visionary Companies* (New York: Harper Business, 1994); Kanter, *The Change Masters*; T. J. Peters and R. H. Waterman, *In Search of Excellence: Lessons from America's Best-Run Companies* (New York: Harper & Row, 1982); Senge, *The Fifth Discipline*.

14. J. P. Kotter, "What Leaders Really Do," *Harvard Business Review* 68, no. 3 (1990): 103–11.

15. See, for example, J. R. Hackman, "The Design of Work Teams," in *Handbook of Organizational Behavior*, edited by J. W. Lorsch (Englewood Cliffs, N.J.: Prentice Hall, 1987), 315–42; Lawrence and Lorsch, *Organization and Environment*; D. Nadler and M. Tushman, *Strategic Organization Design: Concepts, Tools and Processes* (Glenview, Ill.: Scott Foresman, 1988); J. Pfeffer, *The Human Equation: Building Profits by Putting People First* (Boston: Business School Press, 1998). Barnard's ideas also influenced the work of Nobel Laureate Herbert Simon.

16. Collins and Porras, *Built to Last*.

17. Nadler, Tushman, and Nadler, *Competing by Design*; Tushman and O'Reilly, *Winning through Innovation*.

18. D. Miller and P. H. Friesen, *Organizations: A Quantum View* (Englewood Cliffs, N.J.: Prentice Hall, 1984); D. Miller, *The Icarus Paradox: How Exceptional Companies Bring about Their Own Downfall* (New York: Harper, 1990).

19. J. A. Phills, T. Orion, and J. T. Stowell, interviews with participants in the Executive Program for Nonprofit Leaders and Executive Program for Nonprofit Leaders–Arts, unpublished author interviews on videotape (Stanford, Calif.: Graduate School of Business, Stanford University, 2002–2003).

20. Ibid.

21. Ibid.

22. Ibid.

23. Ibid.

24. Ibid.

25. Susan Berresford, interview with author, Yale University, New Haven, Conn., February 1999.

26. P. F. Drucker, M. De Pree, and F. Hesselbein, *Module III: Leading through Mission with Frances Hesselbein*, VHS video (San Francisco: Jossey-Bass, 1998).

27. This example is based on J. A. Phills and P. Laub, "Innermotion (A)," Stanford Business School Case no. SI-25, Stanford, Calif., 2002; and J. A. Phills and T. Orion, *Innermotion on the Move*, directed by T. Orion, in J. A. Phills and T. Orion, CSI Videocase SI-25v, DVD (Stanford, Calif.: Stanford Business School, Center for Social Innovation, 2003).

28. Phills and Laub, "Innermotion (A)," 1.

29. Apple Computer, 2004, <http://www.apple.com/ilife> (accessed 6 February 2004).

30. The Apple CEO has been featured frequently on the covers of national magazines like *Business Week, Time,* and *Fortune.* See, for example, C. Booth and D. S. Jackson, "Steve's Job: Restart Apple," *Time* 150, no. 28 (18 August 1997): 150, 28–34; P. Burrows, R. Grover, and T. Lowry, "Show Time! Just as the Mac Revolutionized Computing, Apple Is Changing the World of Online Music," *Business Week* (2 February 2004): 56–63; A. Hesseldahl, "Selling Steve's Vision," *Forbes.com*, 16 December 2003, <http://www.forbes.com/2003/12/16/cx_ah_1216adapple_print.html> (accessed 18 January 2005).

31. M. Beer, "People Express Airlines: Rise and Decline," Harvard Business School Case no. 9-490-012, Boston, 1990), 1.

32. See for example, ABC News 20/20, "What a Way to Run an Airline" (New York: American Broadcasting Corporation), as cited in Beer, "People Express Airlines"; R. A. Dubin, "Growing Pains at People Express," *Business Week* (28 January 1985), 90–91.

33. Beer, "People Express Airlines."

34. M. E. Porter, "What Is Strategy?" *Harvard Business Review* 74, no. 6 (1996): 61–78, esp. 77. See also R. L. Martin, *The Responsibility Virus: How Control Freaks, Shrinking Violets—and the Rest of Us—Can Harness the Power of True Partnership* (New York: Basic Books, 2002).

35. Porter, "What Is Strategy?" 77.

CHAPTER 7

1. This chapter focuses on strategic change and not changes at the level of mission. This is because values and purpose should be enduring. Although goals and vision do evolve, they do so over very long periods of time.

2. This was a topic of considerable interest in the 1980s and early 1990s. A few of the many works on strategic change include C. J. Fombrun, *Turning*

Points: Creating Strategic Change in Corporations (New York: McGraw-Hill, 1992); C. R. Hinings and R. Greenwood, *The Dynamics of Strategic Change* (New York: Blackwell, 1988); A. M. Pettigrew, ed., *The Management of Strategic Change* (New York: Blackwell, 1988); J. B. Quinn, "Strategic Change: Logical Incrementalism," *Sloan Management Review* 20, no. 1 (1978): 7–21; N. M. Tichy, *Managing Strategic Change: Technical, Political, and Cultural Dynamics* (New York: Wiley, 1983).

3. This is a *prospective* view. It defines strategic change by its rationale and intent. *Retrospective* views identify change as strategic based on its consequences. Although of interest from a theoretical point of view, this perspective is not of interest here because it is less relevant to the prescriptive concern with what leaders should do, rather than academic analyses of what they did.

4. The basic notion of the three theories is adapted from unpublished work by noted family therapist David Kantor. D. Kantor, "Model Building," Cambridge, Mass., 1998.

5. R. S. Meriam, F. E. Folts, and G. F. F. Lombard, "Dashman Company," Harvard Business School Case no. 9-642-001, Boston, 1942.

6. C. Argyris and D. A. Schön, *Theory in Practice* (San Francisco: Jossey-Bass, 1974); C. S. Dweck and E. L. Leggett, "A Social-Cognitive Approach to Motivation and Personality," *Psychological Review* 95, no. 2 (1988): 256–73; R. E. Nisbett and L. Ross, *Human Inference: Strategies and Shortcomings of Social Judgment* (Englewood Cliffs, N.J.: Prentice Hall, 1980).

7. M. Polanyi, *The Tacit Dimension* (Garden City, N.Y.: Doubleday, 1967).

8. D. M. Kreps, *A Course in Microeconomic Theory* (Princeton, N.J.: Princeton University Press, 1990).

9. The qualifier "in an organization" is important, because one would expect a theory of organizational change to differ from theories of change in individuals, groups, or nations.

10. K. Lewin, "Group Decisions and Social Change," in *Readings in Social Psychology*, edited by E. E. Maccoby, T. M. Newcomb, and E. L. Hartley (New York: Holt, Reinhart, 1958); R. Beckhard and R. T. Harris, *Organizational Transitions: Managing Complex Change*, 2nd ed. (Reading, Mass.: Addison-Wesley, 1987); R. M. Kanter, B. A. Stein, and T. Jick, *The Challenge of Organizational Change: How Companies Experience It and Leaders Guide It* (New York: Free Press, 1992).

11. Although there are numerous formal frameworks that are, in effect, theories of organizational change, many share similar themes and structures. A. A. Armenakis, S. G. Harris, and K. Mossholder, "Creating Readiness for Organizational Change," *Human Relations* 46, no. 6 (1993): 681–703; R. M. Kanter, B. A. Stein, and T. Jick, "The Challenges of Execution: Roles and Tasks in the Change Process," in *The Challenge of Organizational Change,*

edited by Kanter, Stein, and Jick, 369–94; J. P. Kotter, "Leading Change: Why Transformation Efforts Fail," *Harvard Business Review* 73, no. 2 (1995): 59–68; D. A. Nadler and M. L. Tushman, "Beyond the Charismatic Leader: Leadership and Organizational Change," *California Management Review* 32, no. 2 (1990): 77–97.

12. M. Beer, "Leading Change," Harvard Business School Case no. 9-488-037, Boston, 1988; R. M. Kanter, "Managing the Human Side of Change," *Management Review* 74, no. 4 (1985): 52–56.

13. For classic accounts of the systems view of organizations see D. Katz and R. L. Kahn "Organizations and the Systems Concept," in *Perspectives on Behavior in Organizations*, edited by J. R. Hackman, E. E. Lawler, and L. W. Porter (New York: McGraw-Hill, 1983 [orig. pub. 1978]), 97–101; W. R. Scott, *Organizations: Rational, Natural and Open Systems*, 3rd ed. (Englewood Cliffs, N.J.: Prentice Hall, 1992).

14. Armenakis, Harris, and Mossholder, "Creating Readiness"; R. M. Kanter, B. A. Stein, and J. D. Jick, "The Big Three Model of Change," in *The Challenge of Organizational Change*, edited by Kanter, Stein, and Jick, 3–19; D. A. Nadler and M. L. Tushman, "Organizational Frame Bending: Principles for Managing Reorientation," in *Managing Change: Cases and Concepts*, edited by T. D. Jick (Boston: Irwin, 1993 [orig. pub. 1989]), 225–41; J. B. Quinn, *Strategies for Change: Logical Incrementalism* (Homewood, Ill.: Dorsey Press, 1980); M. L. Tushman and C. A. O'Reilly, "Ambidextrous Organizations: Managing Evolutionary and Revolutionary Change," *California Management Review* 38, no. 4 (1996): 8–30.

15. Polanyi, *The Tacit Dimension*.

16. Argyris and Schön, *Theory in Practice*.

17. For a few examples, see C. Argyris, *Overcoming Organizational Defenses* (Boston: Allyn & Bacon, 1991); R. B. Cialdini, *Influence: Science and Practice*, 4rd ed. (Boston: Allyn & Bacon, 2001); R. Fisher, W. Ury, and B. Patton, *Getting to Yes: Negotiating Agreement without Giving In*, 2nd ed. (Boston: Houghton Mifflin, 1992); D. A. Schön and M. Rein, *Frame Reflection: Toward the Resolution of Intractable Policy Controversies* (New York: Basic Books, 1994); R. Schwarz, *The Skilled Facilitator* (San Francisco: Jossey-Bass, 1994); P. M. Senge, C. Roberts, and A. Kleinér, *The Fifth Discipline Fieldbook: Strategies and Tools for Building a Learning Organization* (New York: Doubleday, 1994); D. Tannen, "The Power of Talk: Who Gets Heard and Why," in *Negotiation: Readings, Exercises, and Cases*, edited by R. J. Lewicki, D. M. Saunders, and J. W. Minton (Boston: Irwin/McGraw-Hill, 1999), 160–73.

18. J. Barnes, "Courageous and Strong," Girl Scouts of the United States of America 2003 Executive Leadership Summit, Cleveland, Ohio, 2003.

19. J. L. Heskett, "Girl Scouts of the U.S.A. (A)," Harvard Business School Case no. 9-690-044, 1989; Girl Scouts of the United States of America, 2002,

<http://www.girlscouts.org/news/factsheet/GSFactsheet_nov02.pdf>
(accessed 28 January 2004).

20. Barnes, "Courageous and Strong."

21. In academic circles, we talk of validity, reliability, and generalizability. For the interested reader, some classic sources include the following: D. T. Campbell, and J. C. Stanley, *Experimental and Quasi-Experimental Designs for Research* (Chicago: Rand McNally, 1966); T. D. Cook and D. T. Campbell, *Quasi-Experimentation: Design and Analysis Issues for Field Settings* (Boston: Houghton Mifflin, 1979); R. Dubin, *Theory Building* (New York: Free Press, 1969); T. Kuhn, *The Structure of Scientific Revolutions*, 2nd ed. (Chicago: University of Chicago Press, 1970); K. R. Popper, *The Logic of Scientific Discovery*, 2nd ed. (New York: Harper & Row, 1968).

CHAPTER 8

1. Through our collaboration in teaching this material to nonprofit executives, Joel Podolny, Edward Martenson, and Chip Heath have developed or contributed to many of the ideas and insights in this chapter. In particular, I would highlight their role in formulating the tests of a good strategy and the pitfalls of mission and strategy.

2. In this sense, I have written this chapter primarily for practitioners, such as executive directors, board members, or consultants who are actively engaging in the task of integrating mission and strategy.

3. D. Bornstein, *How to Change the World: Social Entrepreneurs and the Power of New Ideas* (New York: Oxford University Press, 2004); J. G. Dees, J. Emerson, and P. Economy, *Enterprising Nonprofits: A Toolkit for Social Entrepreneurs* (New York: Wiley, 2001).

4. Illustrations of many of these errors can be found in books on strategy e.g., A. Brandenburger and B. Nalebuff, *Co-opetition* (New York: Doubleday, 1996); R. A. D'Aveni and R. E. Gunther, *Hypercompetition: Managing the Dynamics of Strategic Maneuvering* (New York: Free Press, 1994); J. E. Russo and P. J. Schoemaker, *Decision Traps* (New York: Doubleday, 1989); R. A. Stringer and J. L. Uchenick, *Strategy Traps: And How to Avoid Them* (Lexington, Mass.: Lexington Books, 1986).

5. R. N. Anthony and D. W. Young, *Management Control in Nonprofit Organizations*, 6rd ed. (Burr Ridge, Ill.: Irwin/McGraw-Hill, 1999); H. Hansmann, "Economic Theories of the Nonprofit Sector," in *The Nonprofit Sector: A Research Handbook*, edited by W. W. Powell (New Haven, Conn.: Yale University Press, 1987), 27–42.

6. W. F. Meehan, D. Kilmer, and M. O'Flanagan, "Investing in Society: Why We Need a More Efficient Social Capital Market—and How We Can Get There," *Stanford Social Innovation Review* 1, no. 4 (2004): 35–43.

7. D. Barry, "Managing the Bossless Team: Lessons in Distributed Leadership," *Organizational Dynamics* 20, no. 1 (1991): 31–48; M. H. Brown and D. M. Hosking, "Distributed Leadership and Skilled Performance as Successful Organization in Social Movements," *Human Relations* 39, no. 1 (1986): 65–80.

8. R. E. Cole, *Work, Mobility, and Participation: A Comparative Study of American and Japanese Industry* (Berkeley: University of California Press, 1979); V. H. Vroom and A. G. Jago, *The New Leadership: Managing Participation in Organizations* (Englewood Cliffs, N.J.: Prentice Hall, 1988).

9. J. M. Bryson, *Strategic Planning for Public and Nonprofit Organizations* (San Francisco: Jossey-Bass, 1988); K. P. Kearns, *Private Sector Strategies for Social Sector Success: The Guide to Strategy and Planning for Public and Nonprofit Organizations* (San Francisco: Jossey-Bass, 2000); P. C. Nutt and R. W. Backoff, *Strategic Management of Public and Third Sector Organizations: A Handbook for Leaders* (San Francisco: Jossey-Bass, 1992).

10. Enron, 1997–2000, "Our Values," <http://www.enron.com/corp/investors/annuals/annual99/values.html> (accessed 21 January 2005).

11. J. C. Collins and J. I. Porras, *Built to Last: Successful Habits of Visionary Companies* (New York: Harper Business, 1997).

12. B. A. Weisbrod, ed., *To Profit or Not to Profit: The Commercial Transformation of the Nonprofit Sector* (New York: Cambridge University Press, 1998).

13. *Harlem Children's Zone*, 2001, <http://www.bridgespangroup.org> (accessed 16 April 2004).

14. See Porter's classic emphasis on this point. M. E. Porter, *Competitive Strategy: Techniques for Analyzing Industries and Competitors* (New York: Free Press, 1980).

15. See, for example, the analysis in P. Ghemawat, *Commitment: The Dynamic of Strategy* (New York: Free Press, 1991).

16. This view of goals and strategy differs from that of Saloner et al., who include goals as a part of strategy. My own view is that, though some of the goals they identify, such as dominating the market or being the low-cost producer, explicate the logic of strategy, the ultimate end is still maximizing profit or the creation of economic value for the firm's owners. Since this is shared by all for-profit firms, it seems to me that it goes without saying. The higher-order objectives, or purpose, properly belong in the mission, because they are about something greater than profit: they deal with the psychological logic of meaning and values. Given the centrality of this logic for nonprofit, it is especially important not to lump these goals into the strategy, or economic logic. G. Saloner, A. Shepard, And J. Podolny, *Strategic Management* (New York: Wiley, 2000).

17. B. Schlender and W. Woods, "Something's Rotten in Cupertino," *Fortune* (3 March 1997): 100–7. Available at <http://global.factiva.com> (accessed 30 January 2005).

Index

Apple Computer, 32–35
business example, Apple Computer,
    32–35
City Year, 35–38
discovering organization's mission,
    42–47
evaluating mission, 41–42
framework for understanding and
    analyzing mission, 26–32
nonprofit examples, 35–41
what it should not be expected to do,
    20–21
what mission is, 22–26
what mission is not, 20–21
what mission should be expected to
    do, 22–26
psychological difficulties, 190–191
Public Broadcasting Service (PBS), 98
purpose, 24, 28–30, 39–40, 44–45,
    197–198
purposeful and adaptive, change that
    is, 172

question marks, 121

raising money, difficulty, 210
raison d'être, 24
random access memory (RAM), 33
Readers Digest Audience
    Diversification Programs, 146
real versus imagined competitive
    advantage, 64
real world, execution in, 189–215
analytical complexities, 191–192
evaluating strategy, 210–211
execution of mission and strategy,
    213–215
navigating pitfalls of industry
    analysis, 208–210
navigating pitfalls of integration,
    211–213
navigating pitfalls of mission, 195–
    201
navigating pitfalls of strategy, 201–
    208
process of developing mission and
    strategy, 192–195
psychological difficulties, 190–191
recipients
    Medicaid, 83
    Medicare, 83
Red Cross, American, 27

relationships
    interorganizational, 118
    intraorganizational, 118
research and development (R&D), 105
resource allocation decisions, policies,
    and activities, 18
resource allocations, 104–106, 110–
    111
    policies, and activities, 101–106
resources, 110
responses, constraints imposed by
    competitive, 206
responsibility, fiscal, 42
retrospective lens, 99
robust, 56
Rubicon, 131–132
Rubicon Bakery, 129
Rubicon Landscape Services, 129–130
Rubicon Programs, corporate strategy,
    128–132
Rubicon Programs Incorporated, 129

salaries, low, 210
scale, economies of, 58
Schools
    Harvard Business, 158
    Stanford Business, 160, 205
    Yale (Drama), 38
scope, 56–57, 202–203
    geographic, 90–91
Sculley, John, 32–33, 166
sectoral differences, dealing with, 8–10
Self Help, 137
Senge, Peter, 26
services, substitute products or, 76
Sesame Street, 210
situational approach, 157
Smithsonian Museum, 84
social needs and problems, nonprofits
    in addressing, 3–4
social value, 22
societal values, 196
sources, competitive advantage and its,
    62
Southwest Airlines, 102, 110
spillovers
    interrelationships and, 123–124
    types of interrelationships and, 124–
    125
Stanford Business School, 160, 205
Stanford University, 190
stars, 121